Looking into Primary Headship

Looking into Primary Headship:
A Research Based Interpretation

Geoff Southworth

 The Falmer Press

(A member of the Taylor & Francis Group)
London • Washington, D.C.

UK   The Falmer Press, 4 John Street, London WC1N 2ET
USA   The Falmer Press, Taylor & Francis Inc., 1900 Frost Road, Suite 101,
      Bristol, PA 19007

First published in 1995

A catalogue record for this book is available from the British Library

Library of Congress Cataloging-in-Publication Data are available on request

ISBN 0 7507 0371 7 cased
ISBN 0 7507 0372 5 paper

Jacket design by Caroline Archer

Typeset in 9.5/11 pt Bembo by
Graphicraft Typesetters Ltd., Hong Kong.

Printed in Great Britain by Burgess Science Press, Basingstoke on paper which has a specified pH value on final paper manufacture of not less than 7.5 and is therefore 'acid free'.

Contents

Dedication

For Ben

Acknowledgments

In preparing this book and the thesis from which it has arisen I have been aided and encouraged by many other persons. Conversations with colleagues at the University of Cambridge Institute of Education and elsewhere have helped me to develop and clarify my thinking. I should especially like to acknowledge the support given to me by Jennifer Nias who always offered constructive and valuable responses to my ideas. I should also say thank you to Barry MacDonald, John Elliott and Louis Smith. Special thanks should go to Rita Harvey for preparing the manuscript of this book.

More than any other I am indebted to the person I call Ron Lacey. He is the subject of the case study and the focus of the enquiry upon which this book is based. This research could not have been undertaken without him. Nor would it have been completed and published without his continuing interest and commitment to the research. In every sense he is a key figure in this study.

Permissions

The author and publishers are indebted to HMSO for permission to include the material in Appendix 1.

Abbreviations Used

AERA	American Educational Research Association
CDO	Community Development Officer
DES	Department of Education and Science
DfE	Department for Education
ESRC	Economic and Social Research Council
ERA	Education Reform Act
EWO	Educational Welfare Officer
HE	Higher Education
HMI	Her Majesty's Inspectors
ILEA	Inner London Education Authority
INSET	In-service Education and Training
INT	Interview data
LEA	Local Education Authority
LMS	Local Management of Schools
MBWA	Management By Wandering About
NAPE	National Association for Primary Education
NCC	National Curriculum Council
NFER	National Foundation for Educational Research
OU	Open University
PTA	Parent Teachers' Association
RE	Religious Education
SEAC	Schools Examination and Assessment Council
SMTF	School Management Task Force
WSCDPS	Whole School Curriculum Development in Primary Schools Project

Introduction

This book is concerned with primary school headship. I embarked upon the research because my responsibilities at the University of Cambridge Institute of Education included providing school management courses for primary school headteachers. Over time, I became aware that the literature focusing upon primary school management and leadership did not fully reflect the accounts and concerns of the heads I worked with on management courses. Moreover, as I searched the literature dealing with primary heads and school management, I recognized that there had been little research conducted into primary headteachers. As I looked at the literature and listened to the many heads with whom I worked I realized that there was scope for a further exploration of headship.

The notion of exploration is apposite. I embarked on the journey which has led to this book without any clear sense of a destination. Originally my strongest concern was to look more closely into headship. Previous research with which I had been involved (Nias *et al.* 1989) had convinced me of the benefits of participant observation, detailed description and close-up studies. So, from an early stage, I determined to study a headteacher by observing him/her at work inside his/her school.

As the research progressed I began to travel over terrain which was sometimes familiar and sometimes new to me. What I observed and analysed stimulated my thinking on methodology. I investigated the idea of producing a portrait of the subject and saw parallels with biography. As the study developed, the data prompted me to explore three main issues: *leadership*, *power* and *identity*. That the study was concerned with leadership was hardly surprising. As for power, while I recognized it was a part of headship I did not expect it to feature to the extent it did. By contrast, the notion of identity was a discovery for me and my understanding of headship.

Separately, each of these three notions is a major field of study; together they form a considerable body of knowledge. Just as initially there was a temptation to keep collecting data on the head I observed at work, as the fieldwork ended this desire was replaced by my wishing to keep reading more about each of the three issues. Indeed, for a period, I was caught up in a cycle whereby the more I read, the more I felt I needed to read. This cycle was eventually broken when I recognized two things. First, the research is essentially speculative rather than conclusive. It is in every sense an exploration and not a colonization. I have undertaken only an initial mapping of the issues and recognize that more work is needed to test and develop the ideas I raise here. Second, the enquiry is concerned primarily with integrating the three issues in terms of how they relate to primary headship. While I need to demonstrate an understanding of the salient features of each issue, my aim has been less to develop an encyclopaedic knowledge of each and more to do with juxtaposing the three in order to discover the relationships between them and to attempt a synthesis of them.

By giving this book the title of *Looking Into Primary Headship: A Research Based Interpretation* I want to suggest three things. First, that the book is derived from research. This book is not simply a commentary on headship, nor is it merely a personal set of opinions about how I think primary heads should behave. Rather, the book is based upon a school-based enquiry which studied what one headteacher actually did. Second, by the words looking *into*, as against looking *at*, I want to convey that I have not been concerned just with the surface appearance of headship. Instead, I believe I have not only described one head's work, but also delved into what this meant to the individual himself. Third, by using the word interpretation I want to signal that both the research on which this book is based (i.e., the intentions, objectives, data and its analysis) and this report of the findings (i.e., the case study, the reflections and hypotheses derived from the study) represent my views about what I witnessed and noted. I do not believe that what I offer here is all there is to know about headship, far from it. Neither do I feel I am providing some objective and neutral account about this headteacher. Although I have tried to be self-conscious about my subjectivity, nevertheless, much of the material here has been mediated by me — so the book is a glossed account of headship.

In publishing this research I have one specific goal in mind. I hope to provide, in a public form, an account and analysis of what a headteacher did. I want to do this because it seems to me that we lack any such study. In a sense, we do not know what heads do. I hope this study casts a little light on the work of heads by looking closely at what one headteacher did and said about his work. The book is divided into three parts.

Part I deals with the study's origins and methods. In Chapter 1 I explain why I embarked on the research, review the literature concerned with primary school headteachers, note the issues which arise from the literature and set out the preliminary questions which guided the early phase of this study. Chapter 2 deals with methodology. I present what I mean by educational ethnography, critically describe how I conducted the research and highlight what I have learned from the process. I have included a chapter on methodology because all too often researchers do not tell their readers enough about their methodologies. I therefore include this chapter to avoid this omission rather than to advocate that my approach should be emulated by others.

Part II covers the case study and my reflections upon it. The subject of the case study is Ron Lacey, headteacher of Orchard Community Junior School. Chapter 3, the study, is subdivided into four parts. The first deals with Ron's background and context. The second examines what he did as headteacher. The third part focuses on how he controlled what happened in the school. The fourth offers a portrait of his headship and looks at the personal and professional dimensions of headship. Also within Part II of the thesis is Chapter 4. This chapter deals with Ron's response to the case study of himself, my reflections upon the study and sets out the main conclusions I draw from the study.

Part III consists of Chapters 5, 6 and 7 and my conclusions for the study as a whole. In Chapter 5 I provide a theoretical explanation for the conclusions set out in Chapter 4. The chapter deals with two issues: the morality of domination and the conditions which allow heads to dominate the schools they lead. The discussion throughout the chapter extends and develops the conclusions I draw from the case study; at the end of the chapter I offer a hypothesis as to why primary heads take it for granted that they will be dominant in their schools. Chapter 6 continues the discussion begun in Chapter 5. I examine whether there are other ways of conceptualizing headship than one where the head is the dominant person in the school. I review school management theorizing and find that critical theorists provide the most cogent challenge to the bureaucratic rationale which sustains the idea of dominating leaders. Following on from this finding I examine the notion of critical leadership.

Chapter 7 considers the implications of critical leadership for headteacher development. I am critical of existing trends in headteacher development because they are grounded in a wholly instrumental rationale. I next go on to argue that discussion groups offer an appropriate context for developing heads, alongside challenges to their assumptions about leadership. I also argue that headteacher development needs to be complemented by programmes of teacher development.

In Chapter 8 I present the main points of the study, highlight the major outcomes and offer some recommendations for the development of heads and some avenues for possible future research. The book can be read in a number of ways. Those readers who are strongly interested in the work of headteachers should especially focus on Chapter 1, Chapter 3 and Chapter 4. Those who are interested in qualitative research should read Chapter 2, as well as Chapters 3 and 4. Students and practitioners of school management and leadership should try to read the whole text!

There is one other point I should like to make. What I offer here is neither a definitive set of insights, nor a model of how to conduct research. Rather, I have only tried to set out how I embarked upon and completed a school-based enquiry and what my present understandings about headship are. For sure, there is more to learn and much left to study. This book is not the terminal point, only a way-station I have reached and at which I have paused for a while. I am convinced there is much more to explore and territory I need to revisit.

Part I

Origins and Methods

Chapter 1

Literature Review

There are three related reasons why I embarked upon this study. The first is my personal experience of headship. For three years, ten school terms (1980–3), I was headteacher of a junior school in Leyland, Lancashire, with approximately 300 children on roll. Second, my work as tutor in Primary Education and Management at the University of Cambridge Institute of Education has involved me in working with large numbers of primary school headteachers on a variety of courses and activities (50- and 20-day courses; LEA conferences; workshops on leadership; residential courses; consultant to a headteacher support group). Third, as a consequence of these two I have taken a strong interest in the literature concerned with primary school headship (research reports, articles and books — both generic educational management texts and accounts specific to the work of primary heads). However, the literature, though insightful in some ways, fails to portray the essence of the experience of headship as I remember it and as I believe many of the heads I have worked with appear to experience the job. Generally the literature concerned with headship either takes a monocular view of the work, by focusing upon one aspect of the job, or presents too simple and neat a picture. Although some writers have provided useful analyses, these have often been abstractions which only partially reflect the reality of headship (Hughes 1976:59). There is a general failure to come to grips with the 'street realities' of headship (Ball 1987:81). Headship is presented as a rational set of tasks and responsibilities. The interaction between categories is not considered, nor is the affective dimension of dealing with people given attention.

The more I read and studied the literature, the more I listened to other heads talk about their work and the more I matched these to my own recollections of headship, the greater my sense of dissatisfaction with the published and public picture became. Eventually this dissatisfaction motivated me to contemplate undertaking a study into headship which might attempt to remedy some of the deficiencies in the existing literature and test some of the assumptions and ideas therein.

This chapter provides a critical review of the literature which focuses upon primary school headteachers. The review will serve two purposes. First, it will identify weaknesses, shortcomings and inadequacies in the literature. Second, it will provide a preface to the research as a whole, since the study has been conceived, in part, as a response to these perceived deficiencies in the published accounts.

The chapter is divided into three sections. The first, and longest section reviews the literature concerned with primary headship. This section is subdivided into five parts. In the second section I note the issues arising from the literature.

In the third section I set out the questions I formulated in response to the deficiencies I perceived in the literature and which stimulated and guided this enquiry. These questions served as 'guiding questions' (Smith 1990:8) for this research and need to be made explicit in order to demonstrate the conceptual and methodological roots of this study.

Review of the Literature

Some General Observations

While throughout the 1980s and 1990s there was increasing interest in school management, little has changed since Baron (1980:5), reviewing education management research, noted, 'The neglect of the headteacher position in the infant and junior school is particularly marked.'

No major study into primary school headteachers has been undertaken in this country. Despite widespread recognition of the importance of the position, there has been no large-scale funded investigation of British primary headship (Coulson 1988a:3). Primary heads therefore lack a data base which would enable them to relate their work to a large sample of heads (Laws and Dennison 1991:279).

By contrast secondary school headteachers have been studied in greater detail. The Project on the Selection of Secondary Headteachers was a three-year investigation, funded by the DES, based explicitly upon the premise that headteachers are important figures in their schools and represent a large scale investment (Morgan *et al.* 1983:1). Hall *et al.* (1986), in a study funded by the Leverhulme Trust, focused on secondary headship in action. Using an ethnographic approach 15 heads were observed at work both within and outside their schools. Four of these 15 were observed in depth on a regular basis for a year (Hall *et al.* 1986:6). Weindling and Earley (1987) report upon a National Foundation for Educational Research (NFER) project undertaken in 1982–4 which, using a range of methods, such as questionnaire survey, interview and case study, examined the first years of secondary headship. This was a national project, since the researchers attempted to study all secondary heads who took up their first appointment in England and Wales during the school year 1982–3 (1987:9).

International comparisons also show that in this country our knowledge of primary heads is shallow. Australia, for example, has produced *A Descriptive Profile of Australian School Principals* (Chapman 1984) which presents detailed, factual information concerning school principals (personal backgrounds; formal education; work experience). No such comparable data base exists for heads in England and Wales. In the USA there is a National Centre for Educational Leadership based jointly at the Universities of Harvard and Chicago. Moreover, the wealth of research into school leadership in North America is also reflected in both the literature (see Wolcott 1973; Kemtz and Willower 1982; De Bevoise 1984; Sergiovanni and Corbally 1984; Blumberg and Greenfield 1986; Greenfield, W. 1987; Sheive and Schoenheit 1987; Burdin 1989) and research associations such as the American Educational Research Association.

Given the sparseness of material available on primary headship in England and Wales and the lack of large-scale research investigations into the work of these heads, 'writing and research on the topic remains the province of individuals, mainly heads themselves' (Coulson 1988a:3). Consequently such research as has been undertaken is limited in scope and timescale. Several of the studies are limited in scope because they are undertaken by individuals, for example, questionnaire surveys of small samples of heads, sometimes as part of higher degree courses (MA/MEd/MPhil assignments; see Coulson 1974; Lloyd 1981; Holtom 1988). They are limited in time because there is a tendency to adopt a short rather than long-term focus — time studies over single days. Methodologically such investigations favour personal experience reports and small quantitative studies. While some of this work has generated useful insights and understandings into matters such as power, the absence of any thorough synthesis and publication of the work means that it has little influence upon policymakers and practitioners alike.

The literature can be divided into four categories. These categories are of unequal size and are not discrete. They are:

- headship and leadership style;
- prescriptions;
- descriptions;
- headship and school effectiveness.

These will now be examined in turn.

Headship and Leadership Style

According to Coulson

> In the 1960s and 1970s much of the discussion of headship utilised Lewin's (1944) autocratic-democratic dimensions, the Ohio State leadership studies (e.g. Hemphill and Coons 1954; Halpin 1966), or role analysis (e.g. Getzels and Guba 1957).
>
> (Coulson 1988a:3)

Later work continued to explore heads' authority and their leadership styles. Coulson (1976) drew attention to the close identification between head and school and described the characteristic (male) headteacher style as 'paternalistic'.

> At the root of the primary head's paternalism lies the ego-identification which he normally has with the school. He tends to think of it as 'his' in a very special way and therefore to feel a deep sense of personal responsibility for everything and everyone in it.
>
> (Coulson 1976:286)

Coulson is critical of the paternalistic style (1976:287–90; 1978:80–1) and suggests 'collegiality' as an alternative. Waters also underlines the head's freedom to adopt a style 'which suits both his personality and the situation' (1979:56).

Nias (1980) interviewed 99 graduates who, after a specialized one-year PGCE course, had taken jobs in infant and junior schools. The questions that these teachers were asked in interview were designed to chart their views on teaching as a career. So strongly were these teachers' views affected by their present satisfaction with teaching, which, in turn, they associated with their headteachers' success as managers, that Nias elected to examine their views on school leadership and job satisfaction or dissatisfaction (1980:255). Her analysis employs a threefold typology of leadership styles developed from Halpin (1966) and Yukl (1975): Initiating Structure, Consideration and Decision-Centralization, each being an independent dimension along which leadership can be distributed (Yukl 1975:162). Nias' study confirms Yukl's typology. However, Nias also proposes three 'leadership types' since individual leaders can be differently positioned, in respect of different characteristics, along each of the three dimensions of leadership style. The resulting spread can be grouped into three leadership types which she names: passive, positive and Bourbon (Nias 1980:261). Positive-type heads were the most favoured by the teachers in her sample: they established a sense of cohesion in the school, gave support and encouragement to individuals and displayed high standards of personal commitment and professional competence.

Winkley (1983) introduces another variable to the discussion. While utilizing autocratic–democratic dimensions of leadership he suggests that these are not fixed styles but, rather, stages of development in school leadership. The idea is advanced as a firm hypothesis although in places Winkley seems to be engaged in a very speculative exercise. Nevertheless, the idea is not without merit. He suggests that there are three stages to headship (autocracy, democracy, the autonomy of the group), each of which is an advance on its predecessor, in terms of the head's tenure and maturity. It is an interesting idea which others have touched upon (Craig-Wilson 1978; Waters 1979; Lloyd 1985; Nias *et al.* 1989) although none has done so in a detailed way.

Lloyd (1985) examined the role perceptions of 50 primary heads. Starting with Yukl's three-dimensional theory of leader behaviour and drawing upon interview data Lloyd proposes six headship types: nominal, coercive, paternal, familiar, passive and extended professional. The last group he regarded as the most effective and, within his sample, the single largest group, prompting him to suggest that there was a trend away from the 'head-centred' approach to leadership.

> Although the primary school head clearly remains a potentially influential and powerful figure, with the capacity to impose a very personal and egotistical regime in the school, this is no longer perceived desirable by over half the heads in this sample. The evidence suggests that the paternal and coercive headship types, which may once have been the most common approaches to primary school leadership, are now in decline.
>
> (Lloyd 1985:304)

Lloyd suggests that the 'extended professional' approach, whereby teacher collaboration and development are actively encouraged and where the school moves forward in a jointly agreed way (p. 304), is replacing the head-centred, paternalistic style. However, such a claim was perhaps over-confident given his acknowledgment that over half the heads who comprised the 'extended professional's group found it difficult to combine high levels of initiating structure with high levels of decision decentralization. The difficulty of achieving such a combination led Lloyd to note that there was a strong likelihood of those heads who were enthusiastic for initiating structures to adopt a style in which the head played a more dominant role and which began to assume the characteristics of the paternal approach to leadership (p. 304). In other words 'extended professional' leaders also lean towards paternalistic leadership and the differences might not be sufficiently significant to warrant Lloyd's claim.

One feature of the above analyses is the predominance of a paternalistic male role conception. This has been noted and explored by Johnston (1986). He investigated, using a questionnaire approach and factor analysis, the gender differences in teachers' preferences for primary school leadership. The teachers were drawn from eight primary schools which comprised an opportunity sample for the study. Johnston's analysis shows five dimensions of headship: director, co-ordinator, controller, authoritative leader, facilitative leader. He argues that his analysis identifies a number of differences among the preferences of male and female teachers for male and female heads. In particular, different expectations for leadership were noted as arising from the gender preferences of teachers (Johnston 1986:224). These expectations align closely with conventional societal assumptions: male heads are expected to be more directive, authoritative and task-oriented and female heads more facilitative, considerate and example-setting. Moreover, his findings

> reflect the continuance of traditional societal assumptions about males as authority figures and of the paternalism which is traditionally associated with the male head in the primary school who is working with a preponderance of female staff.
>
> (Johnston 1986:224)

Together these articles and studies provide some valuable insights into primary headship. They suggest that although primary school heads may adopt a range of styles there is some evidence for saying that one particular style is relatively common if not pre-eminent. This style has been called *paternalistic*, a term which Coulson (1976) shows is a blend of personal control and moral authority and has much in common with the Victorian concept of 'pater familias' (p. 276). Moreover, 'although most heads now affect a benevolent image and have made some moves towards "democratizing" their schools, the traditional, centralized pattern persists.' (1976:285)

Centralized personal control also stems from the way some heads are high on initiating structure and low on decision decentralization. Moreover, such an approach appears to be acceptable to the followers and may in particular be a preference of teachers who are led by male headteachers. The lack of decision decentralization has caused some researchers to advocate greater delegation by heads, although not at the expense of them 'abrogating their responsibilities' (Boydell 1990:22) or reducing their power (see Hellawell 1991:335).

However, these studies tend to assume that style is an unproblematic notion. Also, the value connotations of terms such as *autocratic* and *democratic* are not explored. The applicability to educational settings of categories generated in other contexts, such as industry and commerce is not questioned, nor is their relevance to primary schools examined. Instead the studies are forms of category analysis, and since the categories are taken as given, headship may be tailored to fit the categories rather than the reverse. In short, there is a danger that these studies are Procrustean analyses.

There is one further difficulty to note. These studies are based upon data collected from interviews and questionnaires. Therefore, the interpretations are based upon what heads and teachers believe heads do (Coulson 1988a:5). Neither the data nor the conclusions drawn from them are based upon observation of heads in action.

Prescriptions

This section of the literature is broadly concerned with school management issues. Most of the material is published in book form thus being easily accessible to headteachers who wish to read about school management and leadership. The books are basically 'how to do headship' texts (Holtom 1988:55) and focus upon the issues heads need to be aware of and the skills they need to discharge their responsibilities. They offer ways of approaching or dealing with problems common to primary headteachers, such as internal communications, staff selection, financial management, and delegation. Many are written by practising heads or LEA advisers/inspectors with experience of primary headship (see Whitaker 1983; Craig 1987; Dean 1987; Kent 1989; Nightingale 1990). Others are produced by lecturers in Higher Education, usually those who organize management courses for headteachers (see Day *et al.* 1985; Paisey and Paisey 1987; Bell 1988; Hill 1989).

Across these books three issues can be identified. First, there tends to be an uncritical acceptance by the writers of management and organizational theories developed in other settings. Few raise to prominence issues of transfer and relevance when adopting these theories (Southworth 1987:1–4). Nor has any examination of the underlying values of these theories been undertaken. Second, they take a reasonably consistent view of a headteacher's work. All devote space to school organization; children; staff; governors; parents; leadership; curriculum; management of change. While the writers attach different emphases to these aspects of a head's work, cumulatively the texts provide a uniform view of a headteacher's responsibilities. Third, all the texts locate the head at the centre of the school. For example, Day *et al.* (1985:7) state that the 'head is regarded by all groups as the focal point of school life' and include a diagram (Day *et al.* 1985:7, Figure 1.1) which places the head at the centre of a network of communications involving governors, LEA, parents, pupils, staff and community. Likewise Hill says,

> The central importance of the headteacher is not only one of the most consistent findings of research, but it is also a finding that has been supported repeatedly by committees of enquiry and one with which parents, teachers, inspectors and children alike would also readily agree. . .To find that everyone regards *you* as the most important determinant of the quality of the whole school can be daunting for a new head; more established heads are merely having their suspicions confirmed. . .The headteacher of a British primary school does, after all, possess more legal authority to direct the labour of others, both staff and children, than almost any other holder of a public office.
>
> (Hill 1989:56–7)

The pre-eminence of the headteacher within his or her school is strongly emphasized.

As a counterbalance to the importance of the headteacher several writers argue for the involvement of other staff and counsel the devolution of leadership to others (see Dean 1987:1; Bell 1988:45; Hellawell 1991:336). Indeed, Wallace believes that

> Implicit within the plethora of policy statements, surveys, enquiries and inspection reports (emanating from central government, HMI, and other informed groups) lies a model of good management practice. Evidence of the 'official' model is contained in positive statements and may be inferred from criticisms expressed about schools. . .In essence, good curriculum management is seen as a process where all professional staff participate actively in negotiating an agreed curriculum and contribute jointly to planning, implementing and evaluating its delivery. . .
>
> (Wallace 1988:25)

Such calls for staff participation in the management of the school create for heads a dilemma between participation and control (Ball 1987:157–60). While on the one hand heads are being urged to involve staff, on the other, they are being told that they remain in control and are responsible for all that occurs in the school. Only Southworth (1987:61–73) appears to have drawn attention to this dilemma with reference to primary school heads, and no empirical work appears to have been undertaken to investigate how individual heads resolve the issue in their respective schools.

The overall impression to be gained from these prescriptive texts is that heads are *the* single most influential person in the school. It is clear that staff consultation, delegation and participation in decision-making are to be regarded by heads as

> concessions rather than professional necessities and Renshaw's assertion (1974:9) that most primary schools remain 'static, hierarchical and paternalistic' with little real collective involvement in decision-making and with staff at the mercy of heads' 'spontaneous and intuitive' whims probably still holds for many schools, if not so extensively as in the early 1970s.
>
> (Alexander 1984:163)

Furthermore, because much of this literature emanates from heads or those who work closely with them, the texts contain an explicit and implicit set of beliefs about how heads should perform the job. Yet the prescriptions lack empirical evidence. Moreover, they are exhortatory accounts based upon the predilections of individuals. In research terms, this section of the literature amounts to little more than commentaries from individuals drawing upon their acquaintance with or experience of headship. The significance of the texts is in the way they conceive a particular and, across the texts, consistent role model for heads. It should not escape attention, either, that this role model is derived from a group of predominantly male authors.

Descriptions

Descriptions of primary headteachers' work can be divided into five groups. First, there are those which list the duties and responsibilities of heads. Writers such as

Harling (1981) and Whitaker (1983) presented such lists which might have served to provide the foundations of a job specification. In recent years these lists have been superceded by the DES. 'School Teachers' Pay and Conditions Document' (DES 1989) sets out the conditions of employment of headteachers. These conditions are presented in three sections: overriding requirements; general functions; professional duties (see Appendix 1). The largest of these sections is the latter one which encompasses school aims, appointment of staff, management of staff, liaison with staff unions and associations, curriculum, review, standards of teaching and learning, appraisal, training and development of staff, management information, pupil progress, pastoral care, discipline, relations with parents, relations with other bodies, relations with governing body, relations with authority, relations with other educational establishments, resources, premises, appraisal of headteacher, absence, teaching, and daily break. Such a list of responsibilities may not suggest omnicompetence, but it does suggest that the head has a formidable range of duties and needs to exert considerable influence, if not control, over the school's operations and personnel.

Second, there are other official descriptions of what heads do which need to be taken into account. For example, HMI's (Wales) report on leadership in primary schools (DES [Welsh Office] 1985) acknowledges that within schools it is heads who have the highest authority to make decisions and that their effectiveness as leaders is a crucial influence upon the life and work of schools. The work of heads is described as being composed of two sets of factors: external and internal. External factors include working with the school's governors and responding to LEA guidance on the curriculum and administration. Internal factors were seen as the most influential in shaping heads' perceptions of role. Nevertheless, HMI recognized that heads retained considerable autonomy in determining curricular matters, pedagogic issues and general school policies (1985:2).

The internal factors which influenced heads' perceptions of their role include

the need to administer and maintain the school organisation, the need for clearly defined policies, the need to evaluate the curriculum and standards of work and the need to build a team of competent teachers.

(DES (Welsh Office) 1985:3)

HMI noted that the leadership of the head was a key factor in the design and implementation of the curriculum (p. 8). Indeed, their constant reference to the heads' responsibilities and obligations signals HMI's belief that heads are the linchpins of their schools.

Similarly, the ILEA report into primary education acknowledges that

The head is always, in law as well as in fact, responsible for the situations in his or her school. Successful heads have interpreted these considerable powers and duties wisely. They have not been authoritarian, consultative, or participative as a matter of principle; they have been all three at different times as the conditions seemed to warrant, though most often participative.

(ILEA 1985:66)

While this comment accepts that heads are powerful persons, it also suggests that their leadership is less about principle and more about pragmatism.

Indeed, there is a tendency in many of the descriptive accounts to disregard the ethics of leadership. For one thing, leadership is preoccupied with function; task accomplishment is what matters and the achievement of the task need not necessarily follow any moral principles but only meet the demands of the situation. For another, although heads are described as being responsible for others, such as teaching and non-teaching staff and children, little attention is devoted to the ethical aspects of personnel management. The moral and ethical issues of leadership are muted if not absent. Functions and tasks are presented as if value-free, and so too the management of people. This creates an over-simplified and disturbing view of leadership.

The third group consists of investigations which have studied actual head-teacher behaviour. Several studies have been conducted into how headteachers spend their time. Clerkin (1985) analysed the time diaries of three primary heads, supported by evidence from 40 heads who completed a questionnaire. His analysis shows that heads' most time-consuming activities were various kinds of face-to-face communications with staff and pupils and general administrative duties (p. 292). More significantly, his analysis

> indicates that headteacher activity is more often about tackling a high intensity of tasks with frequent interruptions rather than a systematic ordering of curricular or organizational programmes based upon agreed policies or clearly understood management structures. . .this can sometimes lead to situations where the majority of a head's energy is devoted to 'keeping the school ticking over' in the short run with only limited opportunity to consider important longer term issues.
>
> (Clerkin 1985:298)

Harvey (1986) investigated 32 heads' intended and actual use of time. Extra teaching to cover for absent colleagues and unanticipated or unexpectedly prolonged visits accounted for differences between the two. Harvey concluded that heads needed to develop coping strategies to deal with the unexpected (p. 66).

Another strand of this sub-group of enquiries has been what Coulson (1988a:5) calls *Mintzberg-type* studies. These are studies derived from Mintzberg's (1973) observational study of managerial work in commercial settings. Using structured observation Kemtz and Willower (1982) conducted a study into the work behaviour of five elementary school principals in the USA. They found that the principals were generally reactive to events. Moreover, the principals were often engulfed by a tide of everyday events so that deliberate and thoughtful decision-making was problematic (Kemtz and Willower 1982:77).

In England Davies (1987) adopted a similar approach (open-ended observation, diary methods) to study four primary heads. Davies noted that each head was at the centre of the school's information network and was in a unique position to have knowledge about what went on in the school (1987:45). However, the heads' days were also characterized by brevity, variety and fragmentation with nearly one-quarter of all activities undertaken being interrupted (p. 44).

The fourth group is made up of observational studies of headteachers at work. Coulson (1986) has provided an interpretative and impressionistic account of an undisclosed number of heads' managerial work, based largely upon participant observation (Coulson 1988a:6). However, the precise details of his methodology are not reported. What emerges is a form of category analysis, since he too relies upon Mintzberg's classification, albeit modified to incorporate Hughes' (1976) distinction between chief executive and leading professional roles in headship. Coulson argues that there is a close identification between heads and their schools and, as a result, the actions and attitudes of headteachers are expected by teachers to exemplify to a high degree the personal and organizational values which are expected of other members of staff, an observation supported by other studies (Nias *et al.* 1989; 1992). Moreover,

> It has been suggested that the head as Figurehead and Spokesman represents and symbolises the school. This symbolic aspect of leadership is also important for the head in his capacity as Leading Professional for, in Sergiovanni's (1984) words, 'The symbolic leader assumes the role of "chief" and by emphasising selective attention (the modelling of important goals and behaviours) signals to others what is of importance and value.'
>
> (Coulson 1986:78)

Here Coulson moves our understanding of headship onto a rather different plane. While the work of heads can be described as hectic and fragmented, Coulson suggests that the significance of heads' work lies in the meaning of their actions to themselves and their staff groups. Elsewhere, Coulson has said:

> An important issue raised by studies based upon the observed behaviours of heads or other managers is that activities vary little whether the individual is more or less effective (Manasse 1985:443). As Gronn has emphasised, the difference may be found more in the purposes behind the actions and the meanings ascribed to them than in the observed behaviours themselves.
>
> (Coulson 1988a:6)

The same point was made by Nias, Southworth and Yeomans (1989) in their ethnographic study of five primary schools' cultures. In some detail the authors describe the headteachers' part in developing and sustaining their schools' cultures. Heads were shown to be very important figures in their schools, so much so that they are described as the owners of them (1989:99) because of their close association with the school and the way in which they established a sense of mission for it (p. 98). These notions of ownership and mission led the researchers to claim that the heads were the founders of their schools' cultures. In that capacity the heads exemplified and promoted a set of educational, social and moral beliefs which, in three of the schools, became the foundational values which were shared by all or the great majority of the staff. While these heads, according to Southworth (1988a), behaved in ways similar to those depicted in the time study reports and in Coulson's (1976; 1986) work, the research also showed that each head worked steadily towards establishing and maintaining a set of shared beliefs amongst the staff. In other words, the significance of the heads' work lay not so much in their behaviour as in the meaning of their behaviour.

A similar picture of headship emerges from Nias, Southworth and Campbell's (1992) study of whole school curriculum development in five primary schools. The heads of these schools provided a vision for the staff and school. Moreover,

They all worked hard in a variety of ways to secure their staff's allegiance to their particular visions and to ensure that the educational beliefs and values on which these rested were put into practice in classrooms. Sometimes the heads relied upon their authority and were direct in their efforts to establish a common set of educational beliefs among their teachers. At other times they were indirect, relying upon influence rather than authority.

(Nias, Southworth and Campbell 1992:148–9)

These heads were 'powerful figures who exercised a controlling influence upon the school and its development' (p. 247).

Nias *et al.* are not the only researchers to have undertaken ethnographic research which casts lights upon the work of heads. Acker (1988) has also conducted such a study within a larger project producing an insightful picture of a (female) headteacher's work in an urban primary school. It too supports the picture of the head's work as varied, fragmented and people-centred (1988:5–6). Yet Acker goes on to say that this was a cause of some dissatisfaction to the head who often experienced a discrepancy between what she wanted to do and the situation which circumstances forced her into (p. 7). Acker shows that the events the head dealt with or was caught up in had emotional, dynamic and dramatic qualities (p. 7). Also,

Although Mrs Clarke [the head] was clearly the dominant figure in staff meetings, she was sometimes jokingly disparaging about her own tendencies to forget things. . .[the use of humour] served to soften the edge of the 'formidable concentration of power' (Alexander 1984:161) vested in the primary headteacher. . .fragmentation and constant changes in the head's work were counteracted. . .through the stability provided by the school's ethos. The head, the 'educational supercook' (Burgess 1983) or less respectfully 'the school's resident and sole philosopher' (Alexander 1984:180), has a key role in shaping the values of the school.

(Acker 1988:31–2)

Acker, in line with Nias *et al.* (1989), argues that headship is deeply concerned with values.

These four studies (Coulson 1986; Acker 1988; Nias *et al.* 1989; Nias *et al.* 1992) begin to build a reasonably consistent picture of primary heads. They show that heads are busy and energetic individuals, enduring an unpredictable flow of work. Yet they also present heads as central and powerful figures in their schools, striving to install and spread amongst the staff a set of commonly held educational beliefs. Heads operate at two levels: a high level of abstraction, for example, defining their beliefs about the social and moral purposes of education; and at a more mundane level in terms of their day-to-day actions (Nias *et al.* 1989:122). These two levels are not disconnected. The seemingly mundane actions (dealing with lost property, messages, petty disputes) of a head are opportunities for heads to behave in ways consistent with their beliefs about interpersonal relations (consideration, tolerance). As Duignan (1988:3) has said, and Acker's (1988) and Nias *et al.* (1989; 1992) studies support, leadership within an organization is filtered and transacted through the myriad, brief, fragmented, everyday routines and chores that are part of complex organizational life. It is the way in which such actions take place that determines whether the organization is vibrant and exciting, or dull and frustrating (Duignan 1988:3).

Two further points need to be made. First, such understanding of the work of heads were possible, perhaps, only because these researchers spent relatively long periods of time in the schools, becoming fully acquainted with the norms and mores of the schools as organizations and settings. Second, meanings were discovered because the researchers in all three projects made use of participant observation. They saw for themselves what the heads did, interviewed staff and the heads and then began to interpret, in the light of these data, what was the meaning of the heads' actions for the staff and the heads.

The fifth group of texts focus upon the changing nature of headship. As I embarked upon this investigation, as well as during the fieldwork and analysis phase of the research, the consequences of the 1988 Education Act began to be felt in schools, for example, Local Management of Schools (LMS); opting out; open enrolment; the introduction of the National Curriculum. Some of the anticipated impact upon the work of the primary headteacher began to be discussed and described in the literature. Nightingale (1990:77–85), for example, notes the tension between primary head as teacher and head as manager (see also Boydell 1990; Hellawell 1991). Edwards (1989) notes the widening role of the primary head. Mortimore and Mortimore present six heads' views on headship in England and Wales. The editors note that the headteachers who contributed to the book had been living through the transition from the old order to the new and did not know whether to welcome or regret the changes (1991:128). The heads referred to 'the aftermath of the recent legislative hurricane' (p. 15) and the effects of LMS (1991:29 and 46).

Alexander, Rose and Woodhead also draw attention to the changing nature of headship. There are four points to highlight from their discussion paper. First, they noted that there 'are two broad approaches to primary headship', the head as administrator and the head as educational leader (1992:46). Second, Alexander *et al.* suggest that the advent of LMS was creating the view that primary heads must be administrators. Third, Alexander *et al.* reject 'absolutely' (p. 46) this view. Fourth, they argue that primary heads should take a lead in ensuring the quality of curricular provision by maintaining an overview of the school, judging its strengths and weaknesses, monitoring the teaching and learning and providing a 'vision of what their schools should become' (1992:47). Two points can be made about Alexander *et al.*'s thinking. First, in rejecting so strongly the possible impact of LMS upon the head's role, they signal a deep concern about the potential effect of contemporary change. Their shrill note betrays both their anxiety about the direction of headship and the fact that these are forces at work which could change the work of heads. Second, in arguing for educational leadership they continue to regard heads as the singlemost important figures in their schools.

Webb's (1994) research suggests that headship has altered in some ways but not in others. In terms of the tasks heads perform there is in the 1990s a greater administrative load to bear because of LMS. Heads have also had to come to terms with teacher appraisal, competing in the market place for pupils because of open enrolment and dealing with the burgeoning responsibilities of school governors. Yet in other ways, heads continue to work much as they did in the 1980s (at least insofar as our limited knowledge base allows us to make such judgments). Webb's survey of fifty schools and the implementation of the National Curriculum at Key Stage Two shows that the heads in the surveyed schools worked in ways similar to those described by Nias *et al.* (1989; 1992). All the heads held visions of what they would like their schools to become, maintained an overview of the curriculum and informally evaluated initiatives. While heads in the 1990s have different tasks to do, underneath their day-to-day chores they continue to hold a strong and, perhaps, controlling interest in their schools.

Two primary heads who were pessimistic about the changes were Stone (1989) and Sedgwick (1989). These two were critical of the changes chiefly because they saw them as antithetical to their own beliefs about the purposes of education. By demonstrating strong and deep commitment to particular values they provide further support for the claim that headship is strongly concerned with values. Moreover, being passionate about their values, Stone and Sedgwick suggest there is an emotional dimension to headship, which only Acker appears to have reported, although Mortimore and Mortimore (1991:vii) allude to it. In other words, recent changes in education have helped to reveal how headship is not simply a technical matter but is concerned with social, moral and educational beliefs. Furthermore, some heads feel so committed to their beliefs that their work has an affective as well as an instrumental dimension to it.

Together, these descriptions have provided several insights into the nature of headship. However, some of the issues noted above arise from studies which were not strongly focused upon headteachers. Detailed, close-up studies of heads over reasonably long periods of time remain absent from the literature. Generally, we lack studies which provide 'thick descriptions' essential to developing an adequate picture of the work setting. As Blase says, we need more data on the processes of school leadership, the 'little stuff of everyday life' (1987:194). In terms of describing a head's work Wolcott's (1973) study of an American elementary school principal has not been emulated in this country.

Headteachers and Effective Schools

In recent years there have been a growing number of attempts to analyse and describe effective schools (see Gray 1981; Reynolds 1982; Purkey and Smith 1983; Reid *et al.* 1987). One characteristic commonly associated with effective schools is the quality of leadership provided by the head. This characteristic has been noted in North American studies (see Sergiovanni 1984; Hallinger and Murphy 1985; Manasse 1985; Burlingame 1987) and in reports in the UK (see Rutter *et al.* 1979; Mortimore *et al.* 1988). Moreover, it is a finding which HM Inspectors reinforce in their reports (DES 1977:36; 1990:12). For example,

> The leadership qualities of headteachers and the manner in which they fulfil their management responsibilities are key factors in determining the effectiveness of their school.
>
> (Scottish Education Dept. 1990:16)

It is not surprising then that the term effectiveness appears in the title of several articles (see Muse and Wallace 1988). Indeed, there is a taken-for-grantedness quality about both the notion of effectiveness and the idea that heads are key determinants of it in schools. The DES report on school management training, for example, includes the following statement:

> No two definitions of the effective school are just the same. Nonetheless, the list which follows clearly reflects both the inspection evidence reported by HMI and in other research work. Effective schools may be seen to have the following characteristics:
> - good leadership offering breadth of vision and the ability to motivate others;
> - appropriate delegation with the involvement in policy-making by staff other than the head;
> - clearly established staffing structures.
>
> (School Management Task Force 1990:5)

Two points need to be made at this juncture, one general the other specific. The first and general one concerns the concept of leadership. While numerous reports, commentaries and studies stress that leadership is a key factor in making particular schools effective, few provide a definition of the concept of leadership. The absence of a definition is worrying since the term is inherently hazy, slippery and complex (Bennis 1959:259–60, cited in OU 1988, E325, Block 2:15).

If leadership is difficult to define in a generic sense, in terms of schools it appears to mean the part played by the headteacher in exerting influence upon the school as an organization (Nias *et al.* 1989:95–7) and upon professional matters such as curriculum management (Hughes 1985:278–85). However, a weakness with this view is the way it restricts leadership to headship. Leadership is a term with much currency but little meaning.

Second, few school effectiveness studies have investigated effective primary headteachers. One reason for this is the dearth of studies in Britain which have focused upon effective primary schools. Only one study (Mortimore *et al.* 1988) has been undertaken into effective primary schools. This study, in line with other research into effectiveness, was concerned to examine the effects schools have on the pupils who attend them. Such effects are largely determined by measuring the educational gains pupils make. As such, 'the results of studies of school effectiveness are dependent, to a large extent, on the choice of measures of educational outcomes' (Mortimore *et al.* 1988:4). Moreover, there tends to be an assumption that when a school is measurably effective, by association its head must be an effective leader. Despite these conceptual and empirical difficulties, and the limited amount of work into primary schools, the findings of effective schools research are given serious attention. For example, Coulson (1986) has attempted to describe in the light of his work on primary heads what are the characteristics of an effective head. Bolam *et al.* (1993) have conducted a survey into heads' and teachers' views of effective school management and Southworth (1990) has examined the effective schools' literature and provided a synopsis of the characteristics associated with effective heads. Mortimore *et al.*, Coulson, Bolam *et al.* and Southworth will now be reviewed.

Mortimore *et al.* (1988) studied fifty schools in London and, from a detailed examination of 2000 children over five years, claim to have identified twelve key factors which contributed to school effectiveness. They are:

1   Purposeful leadership of the staff by the headteacher.
2   The involvement of the deputy head.
3   The involvement of teachers.
4   Consistency amongst teachers.
5   Structured sessions.
6   Intellectually challenging teaching.
7   The work-centred environment.
8   Limited focus within sessions.
9   Maximum communication between teachers and pupils.
10   Record keeping.
11   Parental involvement.
12   Positive climate.

(Mortimore et al. 1988:250)

Purposeful leadership of the staff by the headteacher involved the head: understanding the needs of the school and being actively involved in the school's work. These heads took part in curriculum discussions and influenced the content of guidelines drawn up in the school, but did not take complete control. They also influenced the teaching strategies of teachers, where they judged it necessary, monitored pupils' progress, ensured that teachers kept records of pupils' work and encouraged staff to attend in-service courses. These heads were seen as knowledgeable about classroom activities and pupils' progress. They were also described as 'not afraid to exert their leadership where appropriate' (pp. 250–1).

Elsewhere in their presentation of findings Mortimore and his associates offer detailed comments concerning the work of heads. In one section they report upon the heads' views of their role: 'The majority of responses noted fulfilling the needs of staff in terms of their cohesion, development and loyalty' (p. 41). The heads of the project schools were also asked to comment upon their work in terms of: the curriculum; influencing teaching strategies; decision-making; teaching; other contact with children; pastoral care of pupils; involvement with staff; staff appraisal and development; other contacts with staff; and contacts with parents and outside agencies (pp. 41–6). From these enquiries it emerged that effective heads influenced the behaviour of teachers in particular ways. For example, when teachers were required by their heads to produce forecasts of their teaching, the teachers generally spent more time communicating with pupils and talked to the whole class more frequently, both being aspects of teacher behaviour associated with effective teaching (p. 246). More effective heads also involved the deputy and staff in decision-making concerning school policies and guidelines (p. 247).

The research team also presented what they regarded as the main implications of their study for headteachers:

> In our view, heads need to have a very clear view of their leadership role. They need to be able to divide the decisions they are required to make into two groups: those which it is quite properly their responsibility to take and for which any attempt at delegation to a staff decision would be seen as a dereliction of duty and those which, equally properly, belong to the staff as a whole. In some cases it will be perfectly clear to which group a certain decision belongs: in others, it will be extremely difficult to decide. Mistakes will be made and the consequences — as when the

staff discover that a decision affecting their way of working has been taken with no opportunity for them to voice an opinion on the matter, or where there is a conflict of interests between individual teachers on the staff — will have to be suffered. However, if the head is perceptive and sensitive she or he will soon learn to distinguish which decisions are which.

(Mortimore *et al.* 1988:281)

Mortimore and his associates have provided a number of valuable ideas about the work of heads. However, although based upon some observational data (as well as much quantitative data), there is a noticeable absence of illustration. Also, the data concerning heads are rather piecemeal. There is no attempt to synthesize the data and so provide a rounded portrait of an effective head. The study provides data on aspects of headship, but not a portrait of a head, or heads, at work.

Coulson's (1986) set of seven characteristics associated with successful heads is a personal view based upon his study of how a number of heads conducted their work. Successful heads are

1 *goal orientated* — they have a vision of how they would like to see their schools develop; they give a sense of direction to the school; operationalize their goals through a long term strategy and at the level of their day-to-day actions;
2 *personally secure* — do not feel unduly threatened; some measure of disengagement from traditionally strong ego identification between head and school;
3 *tolerant of ambiguity* — can cope with frequent change and uncertainty;
4 *proactive* — entrepreneurial attitude, not always reactive;
5 *sensitive to the dynamics of power inside their schools* — seek out sources of power and support through informal networking, sensitive to informal codes of professional practice which govern teacher and head and teacher relations;
6 *analytical* — solve problems and understand the meaning of individual problems for the whole school;
7 *in charge of the job* — avoid being harried and swamped by demands, able to devote time and energy to activities which develop and sustain their individual visions.

(adapted from Coulson 1986:85–6)

These seven characteristics could provide the basis for further discussion and analysis. Unfortunately neither has been attempted. Coulson's characteristics have not been amplified or tested. They are simply a list of ideas generated from his knowledge of the literature, especially in the USA (see Coulson 1986:91–107) and his category analysis of English primary headteachers. While they are one of the more recent and research-based sets of insights they have not been developed.

Bolam *et al.* (1993) conducted a study into effective school management. Using union and professional association journals Bolam and his associates invited staff in schools to volunteer to participate. Those schools which signalled an interest were surveyed by questionnaire. Twelve schools were also selected to be visited in order 'to illuminate, deepen and extend the quantitative findings' (p. 3) concerning heads' and teachers' views of effective school management. Part of the project's report focuses on leadership and management (pp. 23–46), and Bolam and his colleagues set out the heads' views of themselves and the teachers' perceptions about school leadership.

Although all twelve heads of the visited schools 'espoused an essentially democratic approach to leadership' and none was autocractic 'in the traditional sense of management by dictat' (p. 25), five of the heads were prominent in the schools, being 'clearly influential, even dominant figures in their schools' (p. 26). All were 'very clear about the school they wished theirs to be' and 'they were determined to do all in their power to try to ensure that [their] objectives were widely endorsed by their staff and realised' (pp. 26–7). Bolam *et al.* set out, in the light of their findings, summarizing lists of the personal and managerial qualities which the teachers they interviewed and surveyed associated with effective school leaders (pp. 30–1). Later, in discussing their findings Bolam *et al.* comment, 'Having examined teachers' comments, the power of the traditional image of the headteacher, as, someone strong, dynamic and in charge comes across forcefully' (p. 43). In other words, effective heads are expected to be assertive, trenchant and potent figures. There is a tacit assumption that effective heads provide the vision for the school and shape the direction of the school. As Bolam *et al.* acknowledged, 'there could be no doubting whose voice ultimately counted the most' (p. 26).

Southworth (1990) has attempted to synthesize the literature concerned with effective leaders and primary heads including Coulson's and Mortimore *et al.* work. He notes several gaps in the literature (p. 12). For example, he argues that there is a need to investigate how heads convey their values to others and deal with differences between themselves and other members of staff. He also notes the need to consider the effects of school size upon the work of heads.

Southworth draws upon the literature to produce a list of sixteen features which form an initial outline of what an effective primary headteacher appears to look like (see Appendix 2). The list is presented as an interpretation of and selection from a number of references (ILEA 1985; Coulson 1986; 1988a; DES 1987; Mortimore *et al.* 1988; Southworth 1988a; Nias *et al.* 1989). While the list is a useful summary of thinking in the 1980s, it also serves to show that there is a 'noticeable lack of in-depth, refined or longitudinal studies' (1990:15). Indeed, he concludes that the study of leadership in primary schools 'is in an embryonic state' (p. 15), a conclusion which remains valid today since this chapter highlights the gaps in the literature and holes in the research focusing upon primary heads.

Issues Arising from the Literature

In this section I will discuss the main issues arising from the foregoing review of the literature. The issues can be grouped into three sets; content, method and theory. I will discuss each set in turn. There are three content issues to note. The first concerns the main theme within the literature while the second and third concern issues absent in the literature.

The main theme to emerge from the texts is the power of the head. Primary heads are seen to be very powerful figures inside the schools they lead. They are perceived to be possessive about their schools (Coulson 1976; Nias *et al.* 1989); are regarded as holding a 'formidable concentration of power' (Alexander 1984:161);

exercise control over the form and direction of development in their schools (Campbell 1985:109); and are believed to be one factor, admittedly amongst a number of others, which determines the effectiveness of the school. By contrast, there is a marked lack of attention paid to other staff who hold senior positions in the school's hierarchy, such as deputy heads. The sheer amount of attention devoted to heads in school management texts implies the central importance of heads to the work of the school.

While 'the according of massive responsibility and power to the primary head is a constant in all recent writing on primary schools' (Alexander 1984:161), and continues so to be (see DES 1989; Alexander, Rose and Woodhead 1992), those who draw attention to this feature of headship (see Coulson 1976; 1978; Alexander 1984; Campbell 1985; Southworth 1987) frequently fail to provide a definition of power. In other words, although the concept has been raised and discussed, the failure to define terms means the discussion lacks analytical rigour and depth.

The second content issue concerns the lack of attention devoted to differences in school size and their possible effects upon the work of heads. Although primary schools range in size from below fifty pupils on roll to schools with over 600 pupils (DES 1992:134), discussions about headteachers generally fail to take variations in school size into account. In particular, there is a failure to attend to the nature of headship in small schools where the headteacher is responsible, for the major portion of the working week, for a registration class of pupils. No major studies appear to have been conducted into headship in small schools. The tendency generally to speak about primary headship infers a sense of uniformity which is not matched by the variations in school size. Nor has uniformity been demonstrated since no comparative studies have been conducted into the effects, if any, of school size upon the work of headteachers.

The third point centres upon the lack of any substantive account of what it feels like to be a headteacher. The felt-experience of headship, while a topic of interest in the USA (see Blumberg and Greenfield 1986, 2nd ed.), has not been paralleled in this country although glimpses of this aspect of the work can be detected in Sedgwick (1989), and the need for headteacher support groups has long been recognized (Southworth 1985). Even so there is a lack of knowledge concerning what it feels like to be a headteacher. It seems inadequate to note that heads have considerable power without developing this theme further by enquiring into the experience of headship. How do heads emotionally respond to being responsible for the school, held accountable for the whole institution and exercising power over others? By not studying these aspects of headship the inference is that they are of little importance and influence. Until these and other related questions are examined, the affective dimension of headship will remain unexplored. Indeed, until such matters are addressed we might be 'taking the actors out of the play' (Huberman 1988:120).

The second set of issues are concerned with methods. I have noted the absence of any major study investigating primary school heads, of any survey data across a large sample of heads and of any longitudinal studies. Consequently, the data available on headteachers are confined to individual reports and small-scale investigations. Questionnaires, interviews and structured observations are the most common types of inquiry. Only Coulson (1986), Acker (1988) and Nias *et al.* (1989) have undertaken qualitative studies using participant observation. The data bases of all these studies give rise to two interrelated issues.

First, any emerging picture of headship is not based upon a comprehensive study or set of studies but is, rather, constructed from a number of diverse and limited studies. It cannot be said with any confidence that the research permits an overview of primary headship. Just as in the fable of the blind men and the elephant, where each individual having touched a part of the creature (the trunk, a leg, an ear, the tail) claimed to know the nature of the whole, so our knowledge of headship is confined to portions and restricted to particular aspects.

Second, there is a paucity of detailed observational studies. There is no substantial, close-up study of a headteacher at work. No ethnographic study into headship has been undertaken, apart from in two cases where the data on heads was part of a larger investigation (Acker 1988; Nias *et al.* 1989). Moreover, no fine-grained study has been conducted over a reasonably long period of time. Views of heads' work are based upon data collected over short periods of time. These studies present a static and analytic view which are essentially snapshots of heads at work. There has been no attempt at a more synthetic approach which might provide a moving picture of the fluidities of managerial work in its different guises, or which might indicate the diversity and variation in managerial jobs (Hales 1986:93).

Qualitatively and quantitatively the research base for understanding primary headship is neither abundant nor ample. In particular, the empirical foundations of our knowledge about headship are incomplete. Until the generalized picture of headship is tested by greater knowledge of more heads and/or fuller descriptions of heads at work, developed over long periods of observation, then our conception of headship must be regarded, at best, as partial.

The third set of issues concerns theory. There are two points I wish to make. First, a large number of the reports and studies adopt ideas from other investigations and settings, yet the authors do not address the issue of the transferability of these insights. Also, there is a tendency for particular concepts to be applied in an uncritical manner. For example, leadership style is treated as unproblematical. Moreover, whichever theoretical concepts are adopted by writers interested in headship, the tendency is for the concepts to be applied to heads rather than the reverse. The concepts, such as typologies of styles have not been tested for their relevance to or validity for primary headteachers. Furthermore, there is little or no attempt to develop *grounded theories* (Glaser and Strauss 1967:3) about headship and this compounds the unidirectional nature of theorizing about headship.

Second, much of the literature concerned with primary headteachers and management is dominated by a particular form of rationality. Bartlett (1991), for example, argues that school management and, specifically, the management of change is dominated by a form of rationality which is characterized by

> a complex division of labour, stable authority channels, power centralised at the apex of an hierarchical system, one-directional communication, impersonal relationships, standardisation and an assumed value neutrality. These features affect the dominant rationality of organizations in Western culture. This rationality may be described as bureaucratic.
> (Bartlett 1991:25)

According to Bartlett a bureaucratic rationality treats educational issues and dilemmas as problems that can be resolved through the application of 'precise standards and sophisticated engineering' (p. 28). Bureaucratic rationality is principally concerned with efficiency and effectiveness in managing the organization.

> Every bureaucratic organization embodies some explicit definition of costs and benefits from which the criteria of effectiveness are derived. Bureaucratic rationality is the rationality of matching means to ends economically and efficiently.
>
> (MacIntyre 1985:25)

Foster (1989) offers a slight variation on this theme by referring to this form of rationality as bureaucratic-managerial. He argues that the bureaucratic-managerial form produces a particular model of leadership which

> normally describes the way business and other managers and scholars of management talk about the concept of leadership. This model contains a number of assumptions. Among them is the assumption that leadership is a function of organizational position; the 'leader' is the person of superior rank in an organization. This assumption is almost universally held among management writers and forms the basis for the various models of leadership which have been developed in the last thirty years. A related assumption is that leadership is goal-centred *and* that the goals are driven by organizational needs.
>
> (Foster 1989:43)

The pre-eminence of a bureaucratic rationality means that formal models of management (Bush 1986:22–47) have mostly been applied to both primary schools as organizations and the work of primary heads. Consequently primary headship has tended to be conceived in terms of role theory (see OU 1981, E323, Block 4:54–7) and there has been an absence of alternative studies and commentaries. For example, Bush (1986:48–108) has suggested that there are four other models of management theorizing (democratic, political, subjective and ambiguous). As an antidote to the single, unchallenged model of rational leadership it is necessary that some studies into primary headship apply and explore some of the concepts and assumptions within the alternative models.

Together these three sets of issues show that our knowledge of primary headship is partial, untested and confined within a single set of theoretical assumptions. The literature shows there is a need for further work which addresses the deficiencies in our knowledge and understanding of headship.

A Response to the Literature: Questions to be Addressed

In this section I will briefly present the way I have responded to the weaknesses in the literature. The presentation will act as a summary of the key points in this chapter, will articulate how I initiated this study and will provide a prelude to the next chapter which considers the methodology of the research I have conducted.

Recognition of the deficiencies in the literature acted as a spur to my inquisitiveness concerning primary headship. Consequently, I began to devise a number of questions which I believed further research needed to address. The questions I constructed were:

- What does the work of a headteacher look like over the period of a term or longer?
- Is there an affective dimension to the job?
  If so, what are the characteristics of this dimension?
- How does a head think about his or her work?
- Does a head possess a great amount of power?
  How does a head exercise his or her power?

As I formulated these questions and reflected upon them, I realized that to discover answers to them I would have to undertake a piece of research myself. Sifting through many of the issues embodied in the questions I was posing myself I came to the conclusion that although it was not difficult, given the meagreness of our understanding of headship, to identify issues where further knowledge would be useful, perhaps the best approach would be to undertake an open-ended piece of research which would provide:

- an empirical basis for testing the validity of the claims and ideas outlined in the existing literature concerned with primary school headship and leadership;
- a data base for generating ideas and concepts grounded in the practice of a head or heads.

To achieve these goals I decided to undertake an enthnographic study of a single headteacher, over the course of a school year. I elected to do this because I wished to:

- attempt to provide a detailed portrait of a headteacher in action by observing what s/he does;
- attempt to present a rich portrait which described what the head did rather than a category list of what s/he should be doing.
- describe what s/he experienced in terms of feelings about her/his work;
- capture some of the tensions and challenges s/he might face;
- record the rhythms and patterns of her/his work over the period of a school year;
- discover what other members of staff thought about the head's work.

In setting out these areas of interest I simultaneously decided upon a particular research method, namely participant observation. I was influenced in my choice of methods by two factors. First, previous experience as a participant researcher (see Nias *et al.* 1989) persuaded me that this was a useful method. Also, not only was I familiar with it but, because participant observation was underrepresented in the research studies concerned with primary heads, I believed it served a purpose in counterbalancing the bias towards self-report and questionnaire methods.

Second, Wolcott's study (1973) of Ed Bell was an inspiration because he had undertaken a similar study to the one I was then preparing for. Yet, as noted above, no comparable study of a primary head had been conducted in this country. Moreover, Wolcott's research method was similar, though not identical, to the one I was considering. In other words, I believed Wolcott's work might act as a guide and general model along the way.

This chapter has presented a review of the literature concerned with primary heads, and noted the weaknesses as well as major findings. In presenting the deficiencies in the literature I have gone on to set out the directions for this study since it was undertaken, in part, as a response to the limitations. While some flaws exist in terms of the scant data base upon which to construct insights and theories, others are attributable to the methods used to study headteachers. Mindful that any study needs to defend its methods I now turn to this task in the next chapter.

Chapter 2

Methodology

In this chapter I will describe how I approached and conducted the research which forms the basis of this book. The chapter is divided into three sections. The first section focuses upon ethnography, case study and educational enquiry. The second section looks in detail at how I conducted the research. This section is broken into six sub-sections which deal with access and entry; the informant; fieldwork; recording data; data analysis; writing. The third section highlights four things I have learned from conducting the research.

Ethnography, Case Study and Educational Enquiry

In this section I shall explain my understanding of ethnographic enquiry to make explicit the assumptions upon which this research is based. By definition ethnography is descriptive (Woods 1985a:52). An ethnography is 'a "picture" of the way of life of some interacting human group' (Wolcott 1975:112). Yet ethnography is not wholly descriptive since analysis is also present, to varying degrees, in ethnographic studies (Seymour-Smith 1986:98). Derived from anthropology, ethnography

> is concerned with what people are, how they behave, how they interact together. It aims to uncover their beliefs, values, perspectives, motivations and how all these things develop or change over time or from situation to situation. It tries to do this from within the group and within the perspectives of the group members.
>
> (Woods 1986:4)

Therefore, while an emphasis will be placed upon description, this will not exclude analysis. Moreover, description and analysis are not the only aims. Ethnographers also strive to understand another way of life from the native's point of view (Spradley 1980:3). Ethnography, then, is the description and analysis of a community or group which seeks to present with understanding the natives' perspective. As such there are four related points to note and discuss.

First, Woods, Wolcott, and others (see Rabinow 1977:151; Peacock 1986:146) make it plain that ethnography is fundamentally concerned with understanding groups and cultures. However, this study is concerned only with an individual, although his cultural setting is recognized as important. Therefore, this research will not, by itself, provide sufficient description to understand the culture of headteachers, if such a phenomenon exists. Rather, this study, like most accounts labelled as ethnography, is only a 'contribution towards the ethnography of some culture-sharing human group' (Wolcott 1975:112). As Wolcott goes on to say, to sub-title the study of a single elementary school principal an ethnograhpy (Wolcott 1973) is presumptuous: a study of one principal is not a study of them all. The study of an individual is a

> tiny part of the growing literature that only collectively will constitute the ethnography of American schooling. My use of the sub-title is intended to signal to a potential reader the manner in which the research was conducted and the framework in which the completed account appears.
>
> (Wolcott 1975:112)

What I have attempted, then, is not an ethnography of English primary heads, but an ethnographic *approach* to studying a single headteacher.

The second point concerns description and interpretation. Ethnographers place particular emphasis on describing, often in detail, the social interactions and settings of the subjects they are studying (Hammersley and Atkinson 1983:8; Spradley 1980:73–84). Like certain visual artists, the ethnographer 'works with great care at capturing both the general and essential characteristics and the finer points which underpin them' (Woods 1985a:53). One aim of ethnography is to provide a 'thick' description of the subject and settings observed (Geertz 1973), whose virtue is verisimilitude (Stenhouse 1982:267). Yet description is not an end in itself. The intention is not to present

> merely surface detail. The ethnographer is interested in what lies beneath — the subjects' views, which may contain alternative views, and their views of each other. From these the ethnographer may perceive patterns in accounts, or in observed behaviours which may suggest certain interpretations.
>
> (Woods 1986:5)

Indeed, interpretation is both inevitable and necessary. It is inevitable because the ethnographer always labels and categorizes his/her observations and these reflect his/her own situation and consciousness, as well as that of the actors observed.

> Description is also interpretation, for one categorises and labels — indeed, constructs — his data even as he 'records' them. . .The impossibility of making a carbon copy of reality and therefore the necessity of interpreting even as one describes is true in all sciences.
>
> (Peacock 1986:66–7)

Third, interpretation is necessary because ethnography is essentially concerned with the *meaning* of actions and events to the people we seek to understand (Spradley 1980:5). The ethnographer especially wants to record and report 'the meaning the actors themselves assign to events in which they engage' (Wolcott 1975:113), as well as the meaning of symbolic forms such as language and appearance (Woods 1986:10). The ethnographer aims to represent the reality studied in all its various layers of social meaning, seeking to give a thorough and faithful description of the relationship between all the elements characteristic of the chosen topic.

Understood in this way, ethnography provides an alternative view to that of the positivists (Geertz 1983:19–35; Peacock 1986:68–70). Ethnography is located within the perspective of naturalism and is often associated with symbolic interactionism which rejects the stimulus-response model of human behaviour built into the methodological arguments of positivism.

> In the view of interactionists, people *interpret* stimuli and these interpretations, continually under revision as events unfold, shape their actions. . .
> According to naturalism, in order to understand people's behaviour we must use an approach that gives us access to the meanings that guide that behaviour. . .As participant observers we can learn the culture or subculture of the people we are studying. We can come to interpret the world in the same way as they do.
>
> (Hammersley and Atkinson 1983:7)

Yet, in addition to studying people ethnography means *learning* from people. In order to discover the hidden principles of another way of life and the rules — largely implicit — that guide the subjects' conduct (Woods 1986:10), the researcher must become a student and the subjects become the teachers (Spradley 1980:3–4).

Fourth, description and interpretation facilitate the discovery of meanings which, when explicated, can be used to test existing social theories about how groups and individuals are thought to behave. Although ethnography is often used to generate and develop theories (Woods 1986:153; Strauss 1987:5), it can also be used to test theory (Hammersley and Atkinson 1983:19) and in this study that is another of the aims.

It is common for ethnographers to report their research in a case-study mode. Indeed, according to Yin case studies are often confused with ethnographies (1989:23). Yet case study is a research strategy in its own right. Hence, in conducting an ethnographic investigation of a single headteacher which will be reported in a case study, I need to say not only what I mean by ethnography, but also what I understand by case study.

Yin (1989) argues that case studies can be exploratory, explanatory, or descriptive (p. 15). While the boundaries between these three types are not clear and sharp (p. 16) and overlap occurs, it follows from the discussion of ethnography that in this research the case study is largely a descriptive one, albeit with the riders (above) about analysis and interpretation applied. I also find Yin's technical definition helpful. A case study is an empirical inquiry that

- investigates a contemporary phenomenon within its real-life context; when
- the boundaries between phenomenon and context are not clearly evident; and in which
- multiple sources of evidence are used. (1989:23)

Yin's definition makes explicit the fact that case-study research is the examination of a particular phenomenon such as an event, a process, an institution, or, in terms of this research, a person. Also, case studies are concerned with contexts. As Walker (1986) says, the case-study worker collects information on biography, intentions and values which allows the researcher 'to capture and portray those elements of a situation that give it meaning' (p. 189). Moreover, the researcher uses evidence from a number of different sources. Such evidence helps the researcher avoid too strong a reliance upon any single source and facilitates an examination of the particular phenomenon from other angles and perspectives.

It follows from this definition that case-study research needs to reflect a number of operational characteristics. Moreover, given that I am undertaking an ethnographic study, the characteristics also need to be consistent with the canons of qualitative research. These canons have been set out at length by Lincoln and Guba (1985) and can be summarized as follows: The research is conducted in a natural setting. The researcher is the primary data-gathering instrument and uses his or her tacit (intuitive, felt) knowledge. The researcher, by using qualitative methods, eschews random sampling in favour of purposive samples. Inductive data analysis is preferred and emerging theory is understood as grounded. The research design emerges and unfolds, as against being preordinately designed, and outcomes and interpretations are negotiated with the human sources from which the data have been chiefly drawn. The research is reported in a case-study mode. Interpretations of the data are based upon the particulars of the case, rather than in terms of lawlike generalizations, and the researcher is tentative about making broad application of the findings because realities are multiple (1985:39–42).

Generalizing from a case study is regarded by some researchers as problematic. Critics typically state that single cases provide 'a poor basis for generalizing' (Yin 1989:43). There are two ripostes to these critics. First:

> such critics are implicitly contrasting the situation to survey research, where a 'sample' (if selected correctly) readily generalizes to a larger universe. *This analogy to samples and universes is incorrect when dealing with cases.* This is because survey research relies on *statistical* generalization, whereas case studies (as with experiments) rely on *analytical* generalization.
> (Yin 1989:43; author's emphases)

In analytical generalization the researcher attempts to generalize a particular set of findings to some broader theory (p. 44). The researcher does not seek to enumerate frequencies, rather the goal is to expand and generalize theories (p. 21).

Second, although ethnographers do not accept the positivists' notion of causality, they nevertheless retain a need for explanation in order to answer the question, Why? (Lincoln and Guba 1985:151). As Woods (1986:153) acknowledges, ethnographers are always seeking to explain. While the explanations will be grounded in particular cases where local conditions make it impossible to generalize statistically, *working hypotheses* can be tentatively advanced for both the situation in which they are first uncovered and for other situations (Lincoln and Guba 1985:124). However, the researcher's explanations and hypotheses need to be plausible imputations of what was found in the case setting.

It is possible to combine these two points. In studying a single case, in this instance a primary head, I do not seek to generalize to all other primary heads. Rather, I wish to examine one head in order to explore and, perhaps, expand theories about primary heads and leadership. Moreover, any conclusions I draw from the case study do not warrant inference to a larger population because that is to confuse statistical generalization with analytical generalization. Instead, the conclusions I offer are not truths, but only working hypotheses about headship.

I now wish to turn to the idea of educational enquiry. It is necessary to do so because ethnography originated from anthropology and has subsequently been adopted as a research tool by sociologists. While ethnography is now commonly used in educational research (see Burgess 1985), 'much ethnography feeds the paradigms of anthropological and sociological work' (Adelman 1985:42), and

> I would contend that the majority of ethnographic researchers who have worked in educational settings have done so as sociologists, endeavouring to test a priori hypothetical constructs in particular cases.
>
> (Adelman 1985:42)

Indeed, Woods begins his book on ethnography in educational research by saying that a great deal of educational research

> has not been done for teachers. Rather it has been generated within a body of knowledge related to one of the disciplines such as psychology, sociology, philosophy and its theoretical interests.
>
> (Woods 1986:1)

Now this is not to say that such research is irrelevant to education. Rather, it is to say that if a study is intended to be an educational study then researchers

> must be concerned with the nature of ethnographic fieldwork in *educational* settings, taking educational settings to be distinctive in their accommodation of concerns with curriculum, pedagogy. . .
>
> (Adelman 1985:37; original author's emphasis)

In other words, educational research needs to contribute to education as a discipline and not to some other concern. Research is not educational simply because it has been conducted in a school or on an educational site. Nor is it educational research if it only tests or develops theory for other disciplines. Educational research should aim to contribute to educational theory and practice.

What I wish to make clear is that I regard this study as *educational ethnography*. This is not to change what I have already said about the aims of ethnography and case study as a research tool, but it is to make explicit the purposes of the study.

In regarding this study as an educational ethnographic case study I wish to draw attention to two related points. First, although the study will involve uncovering and describing the subjects' beliefs, motivations, relationships, forms of organization and rules of conduct, my intention is not solely to produce a study *about* practitioners, but also one *for* practitioners. This distinction derives from Stenhouse (1982:269) who was concerned that research should be of benefit and interest to those who are studied. A major goal in undertaking this research was to develop insights which had practical value for teachers and headteachers and addressed issues and problems that they recognized and dealt with. In other words, the research is not an end in itself.

I cannot deny a selfish motive in the work since, in part, the study reflected a desire to obtain a further qualification. Yet I primarily undertook the work to improve my understanding of primary headship in order, through my work with heads and teachers, to share with them my ideas. This sharing process aims to strengthen teachers' and heads' critical awareness of their work in schools and how others, such as myself, interpret their actions. Just as Woods (1986) regards ethnography as a valuable tool for looking inside schools, so I regard this study as an attempt to get inside headship for the benefit of teachers and headteachers.

Second, this enquiry is neither research for its own sake, nor sociology for its own sake (see Adelman 1985:40), because it addresses educational issues and seeks to develop practice. As Adelman says:

> a major criterion of whether this work (ethnographic research) is educational would be whether it tries to illuminate educational practices and provide information for the wide range of people who would make practical decisions which would lead to adjustment or change and, hopefully, improvement.
>
> (1985:42)

The purely descriptive traditions of ethnography had no intention to help practitioners. By contrast, and in line with Adelman and others, I regard this study as not only helping heads and others understand their practice, but also contributing to improving their capacity to do their job (Stenhouse 1982:269). Ethnography can contribute to education as a discipline. Ethnography can test and develop educational theory. It can also play a part in strengthening the actors' professional understanding and serve to improve their educational practice.

To sum up then. The detailed case study of a single headteacher is intended to provide a rich portrait of what the subjects did, as well as how and why. Using this picture the meanings of his actions will be explored, particularly in respect of how he conceptualized headship. In turn, his conceptualization of headship will be further analysed with the intention of developing a hypothesis concerning the nature of primary school headship. Any outcome from the case study must take the form of a hypothesis because a single case does not warrant inference to a larger population — the case is not a sampling unit — and because the study aims for analytical generalization. The hypothesis will be used to re-examine and, if possible, expand theories concerned with school leadership. Furthermore, the research is intended to serve heads and teachers and those who play a part in their development. The enquiry is concerned with the interests and issues that headteachers face. The study strives to make a contribution to educational theory and practice and not to anthropology or some other discipline.

Having set out my views on ethnographic case-study enquiry in education, its aims and audiences, I have also indicated the ground rules for this research. In the next section I will try to show how I followed these rules as far as I was able.

Research Methods

I shall set out how I undertook the research in six sub-sections. Throughout, I shall try to show that the methods I used were consistent with the operational characteristics of ethnographic case-study research noted in the previous section. In addition to describing what I did and why, I shall critically review the methods I adopted.

The Search for a Setting: Access and Entry

Locating a headteacher who was willing to be the subject of the study was the first and crucial step. Clearly I had to find a case to study. The search for this person took many months. At the outset I identified four criteria for selection. These were that the headteacher

- worked in a school with between 150–250 children on roll;
- did not have a full-time teaching commitment;
- had been headteacher of the school in which he worked for a minimum of three years;
- was male.

These criteria were devised in order to study an experienced head of a school of medium size, who undertook managerial duties during the day and was familiar with his present school. The final criterion was chosen because I wanted to conduct some shadow studies of the head and believed it would be easier for me and the subject if we were of the same gender. Also, I might, at times, find it useful to contrast the subject's experiences with my own, when I was a head, in which case, the elimination of gender as a variable seemed sensible. From the outset I wanted to be clear that this was a study of a male, by a male and to be reflexive about the gender of both subject and investigator (Delamont 1992:34).

With these criteria in mind I then spoke about the idea of the study to several heads. Where I sensed interest I ventured to ask if they would be willing to participate. Although I did not lack interested heads, each worked some distance from my home. Fieldwork in a previous research project (Nias *et al.* 1989) had taught me that days in the field are long and compiling fieldnotes in the evenings prolongs them. Adding between one and two hours for travelling makes days in the field protracted and impractical when the rest of one's work and life are taken into account.

At the same time, I was also trying to solve the problem of finding time to do the fieldwork. Naïvely I had hoped to accommodate the fieldwork within my teaching and other commitments at work. However, after two abortive attempts to create some slack in my work I was, at Easter 1988, contemplating delaying fieldwork until I was granted some study leave. Finding the time to do the research is a problem common to other studies (Woods 1986:20) since ethnography is especially demanding in time (Wolcott 1975:117).

Fortunately, I did not have to delay fieldwork. A submission to the Economic and Social Research Council (ESRC) to undertake research into Whole School Curriculum Development in Primary Schools (WSCDPS) was accepted, with funding from the first of June 1988 (ESRC ref. no. R000231069). The proposal required one day a week, over one academic year, to be spent conducting fieldwork in a school. The budget for the project allowed for my time to be bought out of the University of Cambridge Institute of Education where I worked. The project was ethnographic in approach and overlapped with my intention to study a single headteacher since WSCDPS aimed, amongst other things, to examine the nature and location of leadership in primary schools and to do so by participant observation and interviews. I was satisfied that the two projects were compatible and that it was feasible to conduct the fieldwork for both studies simultaneously. However, as the project team contacted schools and negotiated access to them, I elected to say nothing to prospective schools about my own project, although my co-director was aware of my wish to undertake both studies at the same time, in the same school, if possible.

Access to the schools (for WSCDPS) was negotiated. Using the project team's extensive knowledge of and dealings with schools and supplemented by consultations with colleagues and Local Education Authority (LEA) officers, team members contacted a number of heads. These heads were perceived to be working in schools which were characterized by a high degree of staff collaboration. The nature and purposes of the research were described. Where heads expressed an interest in the project one of the team then visited the school, provided a fuller description and discussed implications. Those heads who remained interested, as long as they were in settings the project team judged to be appropriate, were asked to discuss the possibility of the school's involvement with all the staff. Given no dissension, they were to organize a staff meeting at which one of the team would describe the research and answer questions. At the end of this process a short list of six schools was drawn up from which five were selected.

When the project team met to allocate schools to each other, I reiterated my interest in combining the two studies. Just two out of the five schools met my criteria for this study and my colleagues kindly assented to my request to undertake fieldwork at one of them, which I have called Orchard Community Junior School (all the names of schools, locations, and personnel have been changed).

In early July 1988 I visited Orchard School. Ostensibly I went to meet all the staff and reacquaint myself with the headteacher, Ron Lacey and the deputy head Dave, both of whom I previously knew. However, I was also casing the setting for my own study. At this point my concerns were the receptivity and openness of the staff to the WSCDPS research and the nature of Ron's response to me. The staff I judged to be comfortable with the idea of being involved in research. I estimated they were sufficiently at ease with the idea of being researched that a proposal to extend it would not be unsettling. Ron and Dave were very welcoming.

Orchard is a designated community school and I was concerned to gauge the effects of a community role on Ron. Separate conversations with Ron and Dave suggested that the community role had some impact upon Ron's work, but mostly after school. During the school day the Community Development Officer (CDO), who had an office on site, usually dealt with matters. Neither Dave nor Ron believed that the community aspect of the school markedly altered the work of the headteacher.

The first visit to the school took one afternoon. Before I left I raised with Ron the idea of focusing upon him in detail. He did not object to this nor appear to be discomforted by the idea. Conscious that Ron was the gatekeeper for both projects and anxious not to disturb the WSCDPS project, I proceeded cautiously when broaching the idea of my specific research into headship. I spoke only generally about wanting, at some future time, to study a headteacher. I was, of course, sounding Ron out in case I later felt confident to suggest he be the subject of such a study. If he saw through this charade he nevertheless went along with it, saying he thought such a study could be useful. He had also spoken, unsolicitedly, about the Primary School Staff Relationships project (Nias *et al.* 1989), saying how, since his attendance at one of the dissemination conferences, he had sometimes wondered what the heads of the host schools had experienced. He appeared to be curious rather than uncomfortable. I asked if I could return to talk further about some possible close-up study of himself and he agreed. We set a meeting for the following week. I left feeling that negotiating access was indeed a balancing act (Hammersley and Atkinson 1983:72).

At the second meeting Ron appeared to have warmed to the idea. Emboldened by his response I explained what I wanted to do; why I wanted to do this (to increase my understanding of headship and to attempt to qualify for a PhD for which I was registered); and how, using, for example, shadow studies; interviews; observation; time sheets; dialogue. Throughout I made it plain that I was describing something I hoped to do, that it was not incumbent upon him, because of WSCDPS, to enter into this additional agreement, that no tacit contract existed and he personally was under no obligation to me to agree. I was, of course, delighted when he agreed to the project.

An ethical code (see Appendix 3) had been agreed for WSCDPS. Ron and I felt this should also apply to this study of his headship. Ron raised the possibility of me having access to material he regarded as confidential, yet which might be included in a thesis stored in a university library. I promised him that the thesis would be available only on restricted access. He was satisfied by that. Also, in now translating the thesis into this book Ron has cleared this text for publication and agreed to the removal of some specific pieces of data regarding third parties which neither he nor I felt should be made public. He felt that other guarantees of anonymity in the ethical code were sufficient to protect himself, the staff and the school.

I believed the ethical code and the agreements reached with Ron safeguarded his rights, interests and sensitivities. He had been made aware of the objectives of the research. His privacy was protected by anonymity and, while the use of tape recorders had been signalled he knew he could decide whether or not he wanted them used. Transcripts of interviews would be compiled, made anonymous and returned to him for clearance, as would the eventual case study. I did not feel I was exploiting him, since he knew from the outset that I might gain a further qualification. Indeed, we spoke about what might be a fair return for him (Spradley 1980:24). We both felt that, as the key informant, he too might gain new insights and understandings. I also undertook to make any reports emanating from the research available to him, prior to release elsewhere and to provide him with a copy of any completed thesis and book. These undertakings and safeguards are in accordance with those adopted by the American Anthropological Association (see Spradley 1980:20–5). Like Woods (1986:29), I believe that the best way to develop trust is to have an honest project. Moreover, I was conscious that the building of trust is a developmental task and must begin from the very first contact and continue unabated throughout the term of the enquiry (Lincoln and Guba 1985:256).

In line with this last point, Ron agreed that I should speak to the staff about my study of him. Since I was due to talk about the WSCDPS project at a staff meeting in July, we decided I would say something then, which I did. The staff appeared unperturbed by the announcement, which I took to mean not a lack of interest, but an acceptance of Ron's judgment. As one teacher said in conversation afterwards, 'If Ron's willing to go ahead, fine.'

In making an entry to the site I had been aware that negotiating access and collecting data were not distinct phases of the research process (Hammersley and Atkinson 1983:56). I had already been alerted to Ron's awareness of confidential information, of the staff's possible trust in (or deference to) Ron's judgment and, perhaps, Ron's interest to learn about being researched.

The Informant

Ron was the *native* I was studying and the research was aimed to elicit his vision of his world. I wanted to uncover those concepts which he used effortlessly and naturally to define what he saw, felt and thought about his world (Geertz 1983:56). In order to achieve this Ron had to be the strategic informant (Schatzman and Strauss 1973:87) in two senses. First, he provided information about the staff, the school and its context. Second, he shared with me knowledge about himself and his work. There are five points to make about Ron as informant and my relationship with him.

First, because of my background (primary school teacher, former junior school head) we had some professional experiences in common. Moreover, working with heads on In-service Education and Training (INSET) courses meant I was still involved with headteachers. Anthropologically I was in a strong position: I could speak the subject's language (Wolcott 1973:12) and could not be excluded in this way. Since fieldwork should be conducted in a group's primary language (Rabinow 1977:70), I felt well placed to develop a rapport with Ron and the staff.

Second, because Ron and I had previously worked together during his secondment to look at an aspect of headship, we were not establishing a relationship but re-establishing one. Already knowing Ron was both advantageous and disadvantageous.

One particular advantage was that Ron was not only familiar with headship as a practitioner but also as a student. Potentially this made him a first rate informant since he was likely to be reflective about his work and his peers, and more self-conscious than defensively self-justifying (Rabinow 1977:73–5). Of course, this was a stroke of good fortune rather than part of some plan. Nevertheless, serendipity plays a part in research development and ethnographers need to be flexible since their research design emerges and develops and because it is not fully designed in the pre-fieldwork phase (Hammersley and Atkinson 1983:24, 28, and 40). Once it was agreed that Ron was to be the subject of this study, I considered how to capitalize upon his involvement.

Prior to fieldwork I decided to ask Ron to try to use a tape recorder to make an oral diary of his work. I hoped he might devote a few minutes each week to recording what he had done at work and his reflections upon it, believing the data might shed some light on the affective dimension of headship — issues such as what irritated him, made him unhappy or gave him satisfaction and upon his interests. We discussed the idea at the start of term and Ron agreed to try.

However, he quickly felt the business was too contrived and artificial. In my wish to take advantage of Ron I had failed to take account of his habits. While I knew that using a tape recorder was novel for Ron, I failed to recognize that Ron did not keep a written journal or diary, nor complete the school's log book. It was alien for Ron to keep records since he did not commit his observations to paper or anything else. He stored most of his observations about the school and his work in his head. If I had been less impulsive I might have been more sensitive to the informant's customs. As it was, I turned an advantage into a selfish demand.

What did transpire from this clumsy attempt to capture his observations was a willingness on the part of Ron, to share with me, during our conversations, his observations about the school. As the fieldwork progressed he developed a habit of spending time talking with me about what he had done, or was concerned about, or was planning to do. These talks were informal, when we sat in his office with the door open, or in the staffroom, swapping stories. Usually I contributed by talking about my work: where I was going that week, who I was meeting. I tried hard, but did not always succeed, to avoid initiating topics. In this way Ron became a dialogue partner where I played a more passive role than he and where I tried not to steer the direction of the conversations.

Third, a disadvantage of knowing Ron was that he might have had particular expectations of me. I felt it was likely that he would regard me as either an expert, or a critic (Hammersley and Atkinson 1983:76). Having worked with him during his secondment and guided his reading on headship, it was possible he saw me as an expert. Also, because I would be watching him at work, he might feel I was appraising his performance — something he once acknowledged. Early in the fieldwork he said,

> I'm attempting to resist asking for a second opinion. . .I'm dying to say, 'Was that alright? You know, did I come across O.K.?'
>
> (Interview 13.9.88)

My response was to emphasize the fact that my study of him was to learn from and with him and not to judge him. This seemed to allay his concern, although Ron was never one to be overtly anxious. Nevertheless, over the next weeks, I endeavoured to eliminate any evaluative comments from me, about his work, during our conversations. Over time I believe Ron was reassured that the study was not explicitly evaluatory and, to judge by the material he shared with me, I feel he became relatively open. However, this episode points to the fourth point, namely my impact upon Ron.

Like Wolcott (1973) with Ed Bell, I cannot imagine that my presence did not produce some changes in Ron's behaviour, although I am at a loss to give specific evidence of such changes (1973:13). No one ever said to me that Ron had changed during the course of the fieldwork. I speculated about the extent to which he was screening material from me, but, since at times he surprised me with his candour, I was not unduly concerned.

Like other ethnographers I recognized

> that the very act of observing or focusing the attention of inquiry to aspects of behaviour can make *any* aspects of behaviour a sensitive one. . .As behaviour becomes self-conscious, it frequently becomes the source of concern, apology, defence or self-ridicule. I do not know how frequently events towards which I turned my attention subsequently became the focus of more self-conscious behaviour.
>
> (Wolcott 1973:14)

It seemed unavoidable that Ron's self-consciousness would increase since my wish to discover Ron's perspective on some aspects of his behaviour would have channelled his attention. However, while I accepted that observation would inevitably influence behaviour, I believe my marginal position prevented my part-time presence from becoming overly obtrusive when he dealt with others.

The fifth point focuses on the affective dimension of my relationship with Ron. During the first term of the research I realized that I enjoyed Ron's company. We shared a common interest in football and I enjoyed his humour. Privately I respected his patience with others, his energy and commitment. His selflessness and consideration for others, including myself, was affecting and I recognized that I began to feel well disposed towards him. Also, I gauged that he felt similar sentiments towards me. If a rapport was developing I did not wish to destroy it.

However, despite feeling that we could become friends, I did not wish a friendship to develop during the research. The kind of trust which could have grown within a friendship would undoubtedly have benefited the research (Rabinow 1977:142–9), yet it was a trust I might have kindled for instrumental reasons, and the friendship would have been essentially exploitative. Moreover, the growth of friendship between the two of us would have been too marked a development in the school and, perhaps, unhelpful to others.

Therefore, conscious of both a warmth towards Ron and a desire to maintain a distance, I tried to model my behaviour on that of other staff. I always knocked on his office door and sought no privileges because of my association with him. Indeed, I may well have done more than my share of washing up in the staffroom and classrooms and of following instructions from the staff. I also took comfort in the sentiment expressed by Schlesinger (1978:xv), in the preface to his biography of Robert Kennedy; if it is necessary for a biographer to regard his subject as evil then I am not qualified to be a biographer. Rather, the researcher must remain alert to the interpersonal relationship which exists between self and subject. Affect as well as reason can play a part in the field. Surprisingly, little has been written about affection and little in the way of warning has been issued concerning the dangers of researcher and subject developing a bond which transcends the research enterprise (see Delamont 1992:137).

In the Field

In this sub-section I want to focus on how I presented myself; participant observation; solicited and unsolicited accounts from informants other than Ron; documentary data; tensions in the field. I intend to focus on these five in order to show how I gathered data about the case, the context and how I collected information from a number of sources.

During the 1988–89 academic year I spent thirty-five full days in the school and ten half days. I also visited the school on nine other occasions (to observe a staff selection event; talk to Ron; attend an Autumn Fayre; watch the Christmas concert; attend Governors' meeting) and met Ron seven times in the evening (once on his MA course; once at a headteacher's retirement party; five times to interview him).

Visiting the school three times before the commencement of participant observation in the school enabled me to see how staff dressed and how I might blend in, since how one presents oneself is important (Delamont 1992:133). I dressed like the male teachers: sweater, collar and tie, slacks. I followed their habit of being jacketless, not least to preserve Ron's distinctiveness in (mostly) wearing one. One factor in my favour was the presence in the school of four male teachers (head, deputy, two classteachers), plus a male caretaker, alongside five women teachers and four women ancillary staff. My presence neither unduly altered the gender balance, nor created an unusual male presence. In terms of age I was younger than Ron and one other teacher, the same age as another, and older than all other teaching staff. I felt it was better for me to be younger than the head I studied believing seniority in age creates its own hierarchy.

The greater proportion of my time in the field was spent as a participant observer. In line with the definition of case study, this enquiry should take account of the school as a context for the head's work and draw upon the staff's perceptions and knowledge. Participant observation is the most suitable method for achieving these goals as my previous research experience and Wolcott's (1973) work had shown. However, although on occasions I focused strongly on Ron, I was not convinced that Wolcott's (1973) approach was entirely appropriate.

Wolcott describes himself as a *participant-as-observer*,

> a role in which the observer is known to all and is present in the system as a scientific observer, participating by his presence but at the same time usually allowed to do what observers do rather than expected to perform as others perform.
>
> (Wolcott 1973:7–8)

This role made Wolcott a constant companion of his subject. As his subject's 'shadow' (1973:13), Wolcott risked being over-identified with him in the eyes of others in the research setting. It also prevented the researcher from directly experiencing the authority of the principal. For my part I was rather more a participant than Wolcott.

There are few roles open to an adult to adopt for participation in primary schools and for this research they were restricted to teacher and/or ancillary helper. During the course of the fieldwork I performed both roles. I taught alongside the members of staff, moving from teaching unit to unit (the school being an open plan design). I was generally compliant with the teachers' instructions. At their invitation I would teach groups, attend to individual children, hear readers. I undertook ancillary tasks — fetching and carrying, cleaning up. When staff were absent I acted as resident supply teacher. If staff gave me advance notice I would share my ideas for activities and join in planning. I attended staff meetings, INSET days, year group meetings and went on educational visits. In this way participation gave me access to the staff's interests, the issues in the school and the ways they regarded Ron.

By participating I hoped to achieve two things: credibility and experience of Ron's leadership. I was aware that I had to establish myself in the school (Delamont 1992:125). Although I could speak the language of primary school teachers and was generally familiar with their concerns, I did not forget that I was an outsider, being a transitory member of the school's staff (see Rabinow 1977:18) and knew I would have to prove myself to them as a teacher. I believe I established my credibility during the first half-term. I demonstrated that I could manage groups of children, produce acceptable results and fit in with teachers' professional norms.

I was also subjected to Ron's management of me as a teacher, for example, when he requested I take a class one afternoon. Also, as I worked in the teaching units, I was visited by him and Dave, and gained a first hand impression of their scrutiny of my work. By experiencing his authority I was able, to a degree, to be under his influence, issued with instructions and directed by him. These experiences I recorded and drew upon since they gave me clues as to topics to pursue with Ron and other members of staff.

As Rock (1979) says, the point of participant observation as a methodology is that it

> uses the self of the sociologist as a tool to explore the social process. . .its justification stems from the definition of knowledge as an on-going practical activity and from the argument that sociologists cannot know by introspection or surmise.
>
> (Rock 1979:178)

Participation in the social process enables the accumulation of explicit knowledge, tacit knowledge and subsidiary awareness, which can only come from direct experience (Pollard 1985a:221). Therefore, unlike Wolcott, I attempted to find out directly and personally what it was like to participate in the school as a member of Ron's staff.

Distinctions between participant observer and observer participant are not easy to sustain (Hammersley and Atkinson 1983:95–6). Yet I concur with Rabinow that observation is the governing term in the pair since it situates the ethnographer's activities.

> However much one moves in the direction of participation, it is always the case that one is still both an outsider and an observer. . .In the dialectic between the poles of observation and participation, participation changes the anthropologist and leads him to new observation, whereupon new observation changes how he participates. But their dialectical spiral is governed in its motion by the starting point, which is observation.
>
> (Rabinow 1977:79–80)

Keeping observation as the governing role was one defence against going native (Woods 1986:38), that is, over-identifying with the respondents and losing the researcher's twin perspectives of his own culture and research outlook (Delamont 1992:34). To avoid feeling at home I tried to treat whatever I saw or heard about as anthropologically strange (Hammersley and Atkinson 1983:8). Although I had been a member of the occupational culture and retained close links with primary teachers and schools, individual schools are sufficiently idiosyncratic to make one conscious of differences existing amongst them. Moreover, each school's organizational culture is unique (Nias *et al.* 1989:181). Therefore, and certainly initially, it was not too great a challenge to regard the school as strange.

When there is protracted contact with the same individuals and their culture it is possible that what was once strange becomes over-familiar (Delamont 1992:40). Inquisitiveness is then drawn out of the researcher (Everhart 1977:13). At the same time, participation can become too absorbing, so that the observer is busily immersed in tasks and has too little time to observe what else is happening. Ethnographers, in order to generate creative insight, need to maintain a more or less marginal position (Lofland 1971:97). Indeed, occasionally, a surplus of spare time can aid the ethnographer's endeavour since fieldwork is a dialectic between the immediate and the reflective (Rabinow 1977:34 and 38). For these reasons I tended to devote more of my time in the field to acting as an ancillary than as a teacher, particularly once I felt I had established my credibility. As an ancillary I usually had some time to watch what was happening around the school during teaching periods.

Participant observation involves a number of dualities: immersion/marginality; going native/feeling strange; inside knowledge/outsider detachment; the immediate/the reflective. These I think of as options which the researcher can adopt at different times in the fieldwork. Sometimes it was helpful to allow myself to be immersed in something, as when teaching a group of children and then later, at a distance, to examine what I had done and how Ron had been party to this activity, for example, what comments he had passed about my teaching and how he had learned about what I had done. By employing different stances I was able to defend myself against feeling at home and from creating an inhabitable niche in the field and staying there (Hammersley and Atkinson 1983:104).

Regarding the dualities of fieldwork as options means that the researcher needs to seek some balance between them. Balance is an important principle during fieldwork. Not only do researchers need to consider the different options open to them, but also they need to take account of the different kinds and sources of data. In addition to my observations, I collected insider's accounts and documentary data.

All staff provided insider accounts when I interviewed them during the summer term to elicit their views on Ron and headship. However, there lingers the feeling that I should have interviewed staff a second time, seeking to probe more deeply and widely. Yet I was aware that the process of interviewing staff caused a temporary alteration in our relationship, and I was anxious to disturb the field as little as possible. By deciding upon a single round of interviews, I hoped to be able to revert to participant observation and so to continue to gather unsolicited accounts from informants and others. I believe I achieved this.

One oversight in the collection of data concerns my failure to formally interview the school's secretary, Judy. I was aware that she prized efficiency more than social relations, preferring to work through breaks in order to complete her tasks by the allotted hour, rather than spend time in the staffroom. I elicited useful data from observing her and her interactions with Ron. Yet she escaped from being interviewed. I can only offer my preoccupation with other matters, my then close contact with Ron, who was willingly sharing his observations with me and the fact that Judy was taken-for-granted, as reasons for this omission. While reasons can be found, they do not excuse such blinkeredness.

In addition to Ron two teachers were valuable informants: Dave the deputy head and Sarah, unit leader in the third year. Dave I saw as someone who enjoyed sharing his views with me on the school, its history, development, current staff and Ron's work. He was frequently to be found in the staffroom, being a smoker (smoking was permitted only in the staffroom or Ron's office); since the staffroom was my base, we were often in one another's company. Moreover, we tended to meet there at the start and end of the day. Thus, it was not unnatural for conversations to develop on the basis of 'How are things going?'; 'What is happening today/tomorrow?' Both Dave and I initiated these enquiries, hence neither had a monopoly on the questioning.

I worked alongside Sarah more than any other teacher. Although initially I tried to distribute my time equally amongst the units, I later elected to focus on the third-year unit for a while. In part this was to observe the induction of a new teacher, but also to benefit from Sarah's openness. Along with Dave, she was the longest serving teacher on the staff. She sometimes spoke about the past and how the school had changed. Whenever I asked her for information she answered directly and, I felt, frankly. She was someone who spoke her mind.

Useful as Dave and Sarah were, I was nevertheless conscious of needing to avoid too strong a reliance upon the same sources. However, as settings primary schools are akin to villages, rather than cities, and anthropolgists have recognized how difficult it can be to cultivate and change informants in villages. I attempted to overcome this problem by working in every classroom and openly, in the hearing of others, asking questions and seeking advice, especially when the status of newcomer and novice legitimated these appeals.

Over time I asked as many staff as possible for comments. I did this for two reasons. First, to build up a range of perceptions and feelings from individuals from which I could draw inferences (Hammersley and Atkinson 1983:112) and so I could draw upon their multiple realities (Lincoln and Guba 1985:76 and 296). Second, solicited accounts can be regarded as less valid than volunteered comments (Hammersley and Atkinson 1983:110). By asking the same questions of different participants, I sought to check the frequency and distribution of responses and, in turn, to compare these to volunteered accounts and observations of behaviour (Becker 1958:252–3).

At an early stage I decided not to investigate previous staff members' views of Ron, even though they would have provided another perspective. I made this decision because their accounts could not be supported by observation data, nor could I guarantee being able to find staff whose perspectives were chronologically synchronized and thus related to the same periods, in order to corroborate (or not) one another. Also, many former teachers were widely dispersed around the country. I decided, therefore, that the expenditure in time was too great a cost.

I also elected not to interview the school governors and parents, even though there is a good case for including their views. Data from governors might provide useful material for an analysis of their expectations and role conceptions of a head-teacher, thereby illuminating concepts such as approachability and pupil discipline (Elliott 1981a:46–52); headteacher accountability to governors (Elliott 1981b:163–77); and insights into professionalism, individualism, community and democracy (Gibson 1981:189–210). Although these concepts would inform and enrich an understanding of headship, it was my judgment that attempts on my part to solicit the views of the governors and parents would have inhibited Ron's relationship with myself and my relations with the rest of the staff.

However, I quickly discovered that a parent governor, Wendy, was a frequent habitué of the staffroom and was a person who related easily to me. When, during the first term of the fieldwork, Wendy was elected chair of the governors, I felt more comfortable with my decision not to formally interview the governors and parents. If I should need to seek either or both groups' views, Wendy provided a fallback. Moreover, since my contact with her was established and regarded as natural by both the staff and Ron, then any consultation I might decide to make would not be extraordinary or unusual.

I also made use of documentary evidence. I studied the school's official documents, such as curriculum policy statements, syllabuses, school brochure, staff handbooks, job descriptions. Ron provided me with copies of his reports to Governors during the period of fieldwork and of newsletters to parents. He also gave me access to his in-tray, so I could record material arriving by post and I studied the staffroom notice board. Informal and personal documents which I read included notes, cartoons and jokes posted on the staffroom notice board, some of the personal letters Ron showed me, for example, letters of thanks from parents and visitors and the notepad on which he jotted *things to do* each day. He did not keep the school's logbook up to date (it was out of date by several years), nor a journal or a diary, other than to keep a record of appointments.

I did not use questionnaires, nor did I ask Ron to fill in timesheets. I had intended to use timesheets, but he had a strong aversion to them, having in the previous year been asked to keep them for an LEA audit of heads' use of time. So strong were his feelings I decided it would have been counter-productive to have insisted he complete some for me.

There is another aspect of fieldwork to note. Upon entering a setting the researcher may become involved in the social divisions and politics that exist in the community (Rabinow 1977:92). Despite my efforts to share out my time with every teacher and avoid being over-identified with Ron, I was undoubtedly caught up in the web of relations that existed in the school, not all of which were positive.

Tensions existed amongst two pairs of teachers. These developed during the first term of fieldwork and arose because of newly appointed staff and new pairings of teachers. Spending time with Ron enabled me to gain access to how he tried to resolve these tensions. Yet my proximity to Ron may have influenced how staff regarded me. I did not attempt, for the first two terms, to solicit from other staff information about these problems. That way I hoped not be seen as prying. On the other hand I did note unsolicited remarks. Two of the protagonists (one from each of the pairs of teachers whose relations were strained) were willing to talk — one with anyone who would listen, the other when she and I were in private conversation. Of their partners, one spoke only when interviewed by me, the other only mentioned the problem in an oblique way during the interview. Generally, my stance was to avoid an advocacy position (Wolcott 1975:119) and to preserve an edifice of neutrality in my language. However, my contact with Ron and Dave probably marked me as one who was acquainted with the leaders' perspectives.

Recording Data

At the end of each day in the field I made extensive fieldnotes at home. Using a tape recorder, I spent between forty and ninety minutes recalling all that I had seen or heard. I never broke the habit of making fieldnotes on the same day as working in the school since I was anxious to minimize memory decay. Even so, fieldnotes were supported by coded jottings made during the day. I usually had a stub of a school pencil with me and a piece of folded paper on which to make notes, each chosen for their apparent ordinariness. If something caught my attention, I would scribble the essence of it ('Ron and parent') since this was sufficient to enable the events to be recalled later (Delamont 1992:119). Occasionally, when an uttered phrase seemed valuable, I would write it out verbatim. I preferred to make notes in private to avoid looking too much like an observer. I found some privacy by being last out of the staffroom, going to the toilet, or loitering in a corridor. If I had a few moments to myself, I would use them to scribble something.

I overtly took notes in the second and third terms when Ron began to brief me, usually after school, about matters which were concerning him. The bulk of these were unsolicited because he took to calling me in for a talk, or to show me something he had received in the mail. Towards the close of these encounters I would make a note of the topics covered. Sometimes, with Ron's permission, I would take in my small cassette tape recorder and let it run while we talked.

I also made notes overtly in three staff meetings, otherwise I relied upon memory and jottings. These three meetings I judged especially significant and wanted to capture the flow of the discussion and the contributions of individuals. My aim in making notes was to record as faithful an account of the day's observations as possible, since I knew the research depended upon the strength and accuracy of this material (Woods 1986:45). However, data collection was not unconnected with analysis since as part of my fieldnotes I included interpretive asides (Smith 1979:327). For example, in an early fieldnote I included this observation:

> Ron, in talking about his reflections on the staff meeting and his views about the 'mini-crisis' in the school today, wondered where a head might get job satisfaction from. He did accept that the great bulk of his satisfaction ought to come from within the school, but he also speculated as to whether, in fact, it was possible to get any kind of job satisfaction from people outside of the school, such as LEA staff. Perhaps today was a little indicator of the loneliness of the long-distance head?
>
> (Fieldnote: 13.9.88)

I appended this and other ideas to the fieldnotes for two reasons. First, putting them at the end meant they did not break the flow of description, which in itself was an interpretation of what I witnessed, since the description was mediated by the observer. Second, it was easier to retrieve these asides if they were always located at the end of fieldnotes.

My intention to record as faithful an account as possible was possibly impaired by the affective dimension of data collection. Others have reported that personal feelings are involved and how there is a constant interplay between the personal and emotional on the one hand, and the intellectual on the other (Hammersley and Atkinson 1983:166–7). In my case, the research was influenced by feeling either bored or totally fascinated. For example, there were periods, of up to one hour, when I felt I was only hanging around. These occurred towards the end of the fieldwork, usually between 4.00 and 5.30 p.m., when Ron was out but expected to return to school. Alternatively, there were moments when events unfolding before me were absolutely compelling. Such feelings can lead one to regard a day's fieldwork as 'not very useful', as in the case of feeling bored, or 'good' because something interesting occurred. Either judgment can colour the recording of the day's events in one's fieldnotes. Researchers need to be self-conscious about the interplay between emotion and observation, since feelings can permeate fieldnotes. While the method is not that of 'objectivity', researchers 'need to be disciplined in their subjectivity' (Adelman 1985:42).

Interviews with Ron were conducted throughout the fieldwork. Those conducted at my home tended to be longer and more probing than those in school. Ron decided the location and timing of the planned interviews since it was important they fitted into his life (Hammersley and Atkinson 1983:125) as well as mine. I aimed to make the interviews into 'conversation pieces rather than inquisitions' (Simon 1982:240); occasions when we engaged in some informal, free flowing process where he might be himself (Woods 1986:67). Although the interviews were semi-structured, insofar as I prepared a list of topics to raise, there was scope to discuss matters arising and for both of us to be reflexive (Hammersley and Atkinson 1983:113).

Later interviews focused upon his life history because this seemed a logical extension to the enquiry and offered 'historical and subjective depth to an approach which tends to suffer from rootedness to situation' (Woods 1985b:13). These interviews came after the fieldwork in the school. I sought to build upon our now established relationship, believing he would be less inclined to present a front. I was tacitly encouraging him to be himself, at least in the sense that he shared and contrasted his own experiences (Woods 1985b:20) of teaching and headship. As with the rest of the study, Ron was generous with his time when interviewed.

I should acknowledge that on occasions I tended to ask leading questions. In interviews Ron was both a slow respondent — there being many pauses while he marshalled his responses — and elliptical in his answers. Sometimes he used metaphors to try to make a point, sometimes he was, to my mind, vague. In my wish to be clear about what he was saying I found, in the transcripts, that I fell into the trap not of summarizing what he was saying, but of asking a question with the answer implicitly attached to it. Subsequently I have tried to check his responses in these circumstances against other corroborating data before drawing upon the data.

Interviews with the staff were conducted in May and June 1989. Each teacher was interviewed once, for approximately one hour during the school day. Placing the interviews in the third term meant we had become accustomed to one another. Again I tried to make them conversational, but the one-off nature of these interviews, coupled with my wish to raise some specific issues, resulted in only partial achievement of this aim.

During interviews with the staff, and sometimes with Ron, I played a more dominant role than otherwise (Hammersley and Atkinson 1983:126). Although conducted in a conversational manner, I pursued my concerns as well as theirs. Interviewing enabled me to test some of my observations and those of participants, while some of the comments gathered during the interview also tested my observations (Stenhouse 1982:226). All interviews were transcribed and returned to interviewees for correction and clearance before being filed and used when the case study was constructed.

Analysing the Data

I have already acknowledged that in ethnography the process of data analysis occurs more than once (Skrtic 1985:193). Analysis begins in the pre-fieldwork phase, in the formulation and clarification of research problems and continues into the process of writing (Schatzman and Strauss 1973:108). While analysis is ongoing, it is possible to think of it occurring at several levels. Skrtic suggests there are three levels of analysis. The first level occurs in the field and aids subsequent data collection. Second level analysis takes place as the data are organized and categorized. Third level analysis occurs during the process of writing the case-study report (Skrtic 1985:193–4). In a general sense these three levels describe the process I adopted for analysing the data.

Level one analysis took the form of the interpretive asides mentioned in the previous subsection. They were speculations and indicated the possible direction of future enquiries (Woods 1986:124). At the end of the fieldwork phase, when data analysis became the dominant activity, these speculations sometimes helped to stimulate ideas for categories.

Second level analysis involved immersion in the data, the generation of categories and their validation (Hopkins *et al.* 1989:64–5). My approach to analysing and organizing the data closely matches the approach Ball (1991) has described. All fieldnotes, transcripts and documents were read and reread. While reading I made notes trying to trace connections or feel for ideas. From these notes I then began to classify and categorize the data. At that point I was concerned to order the data in a succinct way (Woods 1986:125), since the data were of a considerable volume.

The identification of categories was a central element in the process of analysis (Hammersley and Atkinson 1983:169). The categories served two purposes. First, they enabled me to cluster the data and organize them. Second, they acted as elements of an emerging structure for the case study. Some of the categories were folkterms (p. 178). For example, the section in the case study called *confidential information* was initially called *dangerous material*, a phrase Ron used.

In addition to emergent ideas, I applied a number of concepts identified in the literature concerned with headship or leadership in educational institutions, such as educative leader (Duignan and Macpherson 1987); Management by Wandering About (MBWA) (Peters and Austin 1985). These acted as sensitizing concepts (Hammersley and Atkinson 1983:180) and made me look again at the data. The categories were constantly refined. Some grew in significance, others shrank, became elements in another, or were deleted. Contradictions and negative instances also appeared, and these further helped in the process of clarification (Nias *et al.* 1989:7).

To establish the trustworthiness of the findings, both for myself and others, I sought to triangulate the data, that is, I took steps to validate particular pieces of information against at least one other source and/or method (Lincoln and Guba 1987:283). I also checked whether inferences being drawn were corroborated by solicited and unsolicited statements, and whether the inferences held over short and long-term temporal cycles. Matrixes were used to establish answers to these questions.

Another technique for establishing trustworthiness was member checking (Lincoln and Guba 1985:314). A first draft of the case study was returned to Ron for comment. Factual errors were noted and his comments received. His concurrence with the description and analysis of his approach to headship (see Chapter 4), as well as his recognition of the validity of the propositions (Schatzman and Strauss 1973:134), marked an important point in the development of ideas. I was, of course, pleased to find he accepted the portrait. Moreover, it helped me to feel secure with some of the ideas, especially those to do with power.

Throughout the process of constructing and drafting the case study analysis continued. Ideas were jettisoned and several early attempts to find a structure were discarded. Also, the ongoing processes of sifting and checking produced a distillation (Woods 1986:121) of concepts. Despite setbacks, periods of doubt and uncertainty, and moments of utter confusion and despair, there was a sense of development.

Yet the development of the case study was not unidirectional. There was considerable backtracking and revision to the ideas I formulated. As I searched for other ideas, by reading and reflecting upon the data, I tried to incorporate new ideas or fresh insights. Nor was progress evenly paced. There were times when I made no progress, because I could not see a way forward or because the process had to give way to other commitments. Yet there was generally a sense of making headway.

The case study is an analytic description (Burgess 1984:182) of one head-teacher's work. While an aim of ethnography is to provide a holistic picture of a way of life (Peacock 1986:18–19), such holism is an impossible ideal since the researcher cannot see everything and must select and emphasize (p. 19). By re-garding the case study as analytic description I hope to make it plain that the case study is a selection from, and an interpretation of, a person's work.

I undertook this research with two broad aims. First, to test the validity of the ideas in the literature concerned with primary headship. Second, to create a data base for generating ideas grounded in the practice of a head. In other words, the research is both verificatory and generative (Lincoln and Guba 1985:333). Here I must admit to being taken by surprise at the imbalance between these two goals. I did not anticipate that the research would verify existing ideas about primary heads to the extent it has. I expected that an enquiry which did not set out with a specific hypothesis, and which sought to arrive at propositions by inductive reasoning, would generate more original insights than it appeared to do!

The finding that Ron was powerful was one I reflected on at length. I appre-ciated that the data were themselves constructions (Lincoln and Guba 1985:332), and that they may have been mediated by me so that the data were unconsciously tailored to match my own predilections. This was a puzzle which questioned my own integrity as a researcher and, for a spell, made me insecure about the findings. I re-examined the data closely. Yet, eventually, I was satisfied with the internal validity (1985:291) of the case study. Moreover, I was reassured that it was a picture which Ron himself validated.

After much scrutiny, I believe my reconstruction of Ron's headship is faith-ful. Moreover, it is in accordance with Lincoln and Guba's ideas about establish-ing trustworthiness. They argue that findings, and the interpretations based upon them, are more likely to be credible if the researcher can demonstrate a prolonged period of engagement; provides evidence of persistent observation; triangulates by using different sources and methods; and guards against going native and having premature closure (1985:307).

In effect, the process of analysis made it apparent to me that I had a preference for a generative enquiry while having to accept that I was closer to a verificatory one. Yet, when I began to seek an explanation as to why Ron was powerful, I then began to move towards the generation of propositions.

The search for an explanation of my interpretation of Ron's headship needed to be nourished by new material. I therefore read as much as I could on the topics which emerged from the case study. As Delamont (1992:4) says, reading widely is an important task for the ethnographer. I was struck by Ron's sentiments about his work resembling those of teachers. From studying Lortie (1975) and Nias (1989a) I began to develop hypotheses about Ron's occupational identity, and teachers' and heads' assumptions about power.

The hypothesis I advance in Chapter 5 is a working hypothesis (Lincoln and

Guba 1985:124) since it is a tentative finding, being based upon a single case and particular conditions. Regarding the outcome of the study as a working hypothesis means the research is less concerned with theory building than with the application of theory. Theory building

> carries with it an imagery of the careful construction of layers of generalisations, firmly cemented together by accumulated empirical observations ...It is naive to suppose [such a view] has much relevance to social science. . .because of the traditional problems of control of variable influences, replication of observations and so on.
>
> (Giddens 1987:43)

Instead of theory building, I regard this ethnographic study as the application of theories (Hammersley 1992:22), because I draw upon identity theory and Gidden's structuration theory, and the testing of theories about headship and leadership.

Ethnography which aims to find tentative explanations and resolutions (Agar 1986:20) to the cases studied, and applies theories to deepen the analysis, is not mere description. While the researcher needs to be concerned with representing the case, description is enriched by the application of theory, or theories, during the process of analysis and so the researcher delves beneath surface appearances and deepens understanding.

Writing the Case Study

I have already said that writing is a third level in the process of analysis. However, I have chosen to separate writing the case study from the previous sub-section because I want to focus specifically upon it, albeit as a part of the wider process of analysis.

So far I have defined what I take case study to mean, said that it is an analytic description and acknowledged that it is an interpretive presentation and discussion of the case (Stenhouse 1978:37). Lincoln and Guba (1985:360) argue that a case study is the best means for summarizing the data and displaying them for review. Also, a case study seeks to offer a measure of vicarious experience for the reader. It is a thick description of the case and the context and is a vehicle for demonstrating the interplay between inquirer and respondents (358–60).

These characteristics I have attempted to embody in the study of Ron, believing it to be a detailed record of the experience of an individual within a given framework (Seymour-Smith 1986:32). The study is my account of Ron's work at Orchard School during one school year. It is a slice of life (Lincoln and Guba 1985:214), but it is also a translation (Skrtic 1985:197) of Ron's work by me. As such the account is congruent with the nature of ethnography and naturalistic enquiry as set out in the first section of this chapter.

The process of writing the case study was challenging for two reasons. First, I had to deal with both description and interpretation. Second, I had to clarify in my own mind what kind of writing I was attempting. Each of these challenges will now be considered in turn.

Handling both description and interpretation at the same time was not straight-forward. For one thing there was a need to resolve structural issues, such as the organization of illustrative data and the integration of analytic and interpretive comments. Eventually I resolved these matters by organizing my interpretation of Ron's work into two parts. The case study itself is the first part of the inter-pretation. In the case study I organize data around a series of themes which aim, incrementally, to construct a portrait of Ron's headship. Towards the end of the account the themes are synthesized, and I present my interpretation of Ron's concept of headship.

The second part of the interpretation is not part of the case study, but forms the major part of Chapter 5. Here I explore Ron's approach to headship in greater detail and the finding that his headship was an occupational identity is further analysed.

This two-part presentation of the interpretation is not wholly satisfactory, but I have adopted it for two reasons. First, the process of compiling the case study acted 'as a mid-wife to perception' (Eisner 1979:191). The case study caused me to look deeper and in greater detail at Ron's work. Second, although I incor-porated the idea of identity into the case study I recognized that the whole concept of identity needed to be further and more fully explored.

As I was resolving these structural issues, I was also trying to deal with the issue of how to approach ethnographic writing. I found little guidance in the literature. A review of the texts concerned with ethnographic writing and case-study construction was generally unhelpful. Writing is frequently neglected in methods books (Delamont 1992:50), and the literature is not good in transmitting ways to write case studies (Lincoln and Guba 1985:215), although Woods (1986) and Wolcott (1990) are exceptions to these generalizations. Far more attention has been devoted to fieldwork techniques and to issues of validation than to writing.

I recognized at the outset that the case study was a form of narrative in the sense that narrative displays the goals and intentions of human actors, it is the primary way through which humans organize their experiences into temporally meaningful episodes, and it is a mode of reasoning and representation (Richardson 1990:20–1). Moreover, from Richardson I recognized that the case study used three different forms of narrative: the everyday; the autobiographical; and the biographical. The everyday narrative articulates how actors go about their rounds and accomplish their tasks. The autobiographical narrative is the telling of one's own story and how one's past is related to the present. Biography is concerned with the ability to empathize with the life stories of others and with the retelling of the other's life (1990:22–4). While it is possible to regard these as different forms of narrative they do, in fact, overlap. Hence, it is possible to regard the case study as a record of Ron's everyday life in the school, supplemented by knowl-edge about his professional autobiography, which he told to an interviewer who has written it up as a biography.

During the process of writing the case study I became increasingly interested in the biographical form. From an early point in the construction of the case study, I began to consider the case study of Ron as a form of *portraiture* (Mueller and Kendall 1989). Initially, I regarded portraiture in purely visual terms and tried to apply the concepts painters might use, such as likeness; background and fore-ground; figure in a landscape; light and shade. Some of these proved useful meta-phors and were incorporated in the text. I did not, however, develop this line of thought because following my reading (for pleasure!) of Alison Lurie's (1988) novel, *The Truth about Lorin Jones*, I next began to regard the portrait of Ron as biography.

The account of Ron's work is in some respects similar to a biography of his professional life. I had details of his background and career, observations of him at work, accounts from himself, his wife and staff. These data were not dissimilar to those used by biographers and I wondered if the canons of writing a biography might inform the construction of the case study.

Further impetus for this line of enquiry came from an observation by Smith *et al.*, 'Biographers know that through a person's story they can shed light on the stories of others, too' (1986:22). Not only does this statement reflect one of the aims of this study, namely to know more about headship by studying in detail one headteacher, it also suggests that biographers have something to offer ethnographers. I therefore sought to discover more about writing biography.

Clifford (1970) shows that the concerns of a literary biographer parallel those of ethnographers. Data must be checked for authenticity with the biographer remaining rigorously sceptical (p. 69), constantly checking (p. 72) and corroborating evidence (p. 80), while scenes should be described to the best of the biographer's abilities (p. 81). Clifford raises the problem of dealing with the biographer's involvement: what are the biographer's motives (p. 99); and should a biographer be personally involved with his/her subject (p. 104)? He raises the question of how' much should a biographer tell (p. 114); which facts are significant; the dangers of 'overloading the backdrop' (p. 117); and ethical questions concerning privacy and confidentiality (p. 119).

Furthermore, Clifford offered useful advice about how to approach writing a life. He describes his biographical writing as 'artistic scholarly'. This involves exhaustive research but, having assembled the evidence, he proceeds as

> an imaginative artist, presenting the details in the liveliest and most interesting manner possible. There is not conscious distortion of evidence . . .[but] the biographer may be as imaginative as he pleases. . .in the way he brings his materials together.
>
> (Clifford 1970:85)

Here Clifford is alluding to the biographer's need to deal with such problems as: chronology (p. 90); the creation of a semblance of life created out of facts, ideas and words which give an illusion of living (p. 91); and thematic continuity (p. 94). These are also problems for an ethnographer.

Clifford's notion of imagination is challenging, until understood in the sense offered by Berger (1960:51), that imagination is not, as is sometimes thought, the ability to invent, rather, it is the capacity to disclose that which exists (see also Geertz 1988:140). More than anything Clifford's title *From Puzzles to Portraits*, reveals the problems of presenting an account of someone else's life and work. The process is indeed a puzzle out of which, hopefully, a portrait emerges.

Clifford, along with Smith (1990) and others who are interested in life history (Goodson 1980; Woods 1985b), teacher biography (Aspinwall 1986; Goodson and Walker 1991), and portraiture (Mueller and Kendall 1989), confirm that there are methodological matters to learn from biographers. Pursuing these matters further, I found Denzin's (1989) monography, *Interpretive Biography*, illuminating.

Denzin shows how some of the assumptions and conventions of the biographical method, such as gender and class; family background; starting points,
are Western literary conventions which shape how lives are told (1989:17–19).
Denzin develops this by arguing that when a biographer purports to be giving real
details of a real person's life, she or he is 'only creating that subject in the text that
is written' (pp. 21–2). In other words, only the representations of experience can
ever be captured (p. 69), which tends to result in two things. First, the inherent
ambiguities and complexities of life situations seldom appear in the analyst's text
(p. 69). Second, experiences are not reported, 'only glossed, narrative reports of
them' (p. 69). Denzin suggests that writers of biography and ethnography should
be conscious of the mediated nature of their accounts and texts; alert to the dangers of presenting an overly tidy analysis; and aware that since the report is of a
segment of a life in progress, no biography or portrait of a life is ever complete
(p. 46) and is only 'a search for a partial, not a full identity' (p. 82). These warn-
ings I attempted to keep in mind when writing up the case study.

The work of Denzin and others, (see Geertz 1988; MacLure and Stronach
1989) highlight three related issues. First, case studies are texts and as such they
may benefit from greater awareness of literary concepts such as story and narrative. Moreover, where a case study is an account of part of an individual's life,
attention should be paid not only to the selection, editing and reduction of evid-
ential material, but also to the idea

> that lives are written from within a culture and an ideological stance and
> that the ways in which an account of a life is assembled will depend upon
> such things as the temporal and cultural context in which it is written,
> the biographer's predilections.
>
> (MacLure and Stronach 1989:8)

The case study of Ron is a product not only of the research paradigm and methods
but also of the author and his context.

Second, Denzin shows that everything a biographer handles is mediated. The
same is true in ethnography. Fieldnotes, informants' comments and interviewees'
responses are all mediated. When the researcher comes to work with this material,
she or he is always dealing with secondary percepts. 'Data are, so to speak, the
constructions offered by, or in, the sources; data analysis leads to a *reconstruction* of
those constructions (Lincoln and Guba 1985:323; authors' emphases). What a case
study offers is, at best, an interpretation which does not 'tell it like it is' but,
rather, attempts to 'tell it as it feels to be in it' or 'tells it as it phenomenologically
is' (Stenhouse 1978:34).

Third, all the issues discussed thus far — fieldwork techniques, analysis, interpretation, biographical data — fundamentally rely upon the process of perception (see Abercrombie 1969; Vernon 1962; Ornstein 1975). Although many of the
writers cited in this chapter explicitly address such issues as the social construction
of reality, multiple realities and mediated data, few devote much, if any, attention
to the psychology of perception.

Observation is not merely looking, and reporting is not simply writing, they
are the product and a part of the process of seeing. Moreover, because the ethnographer is the principal research instrument, what is observed and written relies
upon that individual's schema because his or her frames of reference will influence

what is observed and how it is interpreted (Abercrombie 1969:46–94). As Berger's work (1972; 1982) shows, there are ways of seeing and ways of telling and both are predicated upon perception. Indeed, it follows from this subsection and the previous ones that researchers need to be self-conscious about the part they play in the collection, organization and reporting of data. Texts, like the data from which they are constructed, are inevitably seen through an author-darkened glass, yet the darkening can be minimized by authorial self-inspection for bias or subjectivity (Geertz 1988:145).

Research and the Researcher's Development

Smith (1979:325) says every researcher has a personal tale to tell. The tale I want to tell concerns four related things I have learned from the process of conducting the research. First, I learned that fieldwork is not a smooth process (Hammersley Atkinson 1983:166). Indeed, it is often emotionally taxing and draining, because it is open-ended and uncertain. For example, early in the first term of fieldwork Ron announced to me that he had applied for a job and was to be interviewed in two weeks time. Having devoted much time and energy to setting up the study I felt unhappy at the prospect of it disappearing along with Ron's departure from the school. I remained anxious about the survival of the research until Ron explained, a week later, that he would not be able to leave the school until after the Easter term; that would have enabled me to gather data for two terms which might have been sufficient for a shorter study. Nevertheless, I was concerned that if he was successful, it would alter the character of the study. As things turned out, the research was not truncated by his promotion, although I continued to feel uncertain about the exact period of fieldwork until the end of January, after which time any resignation would only have taken effect from the first of September.

Second, my principal aim in undertaking this study was to improve my understanding of headship. In other words, the research was based upon my interests and for that reason I was personally involved and strongly committed to the study. Moreover, I now recognize I needed to be strongly committed because ethnographic enquiry is demanding. It is tiring, because days in the field are long. The process of conducting the research involves uncertainty, doubt and frustration. The research process is also an intellectual labour involving a capacity to handle data and the ability to identify ideas and concepts. Also, the researcher needs will power to complete the analysis and write up the findings. Unless the enquirer has a strong commitment to the study, the arduous nature of the process of enquiry can blunt his/her appetite and interest and even, in some circumstances, defeat him/her. In short, personal involvement is vital. Unless the researcher is motivated by and committed to the project in a way that virtually ensures an emotional attachment, the project could easily falter because of the demands the research makes upon the individual.

Third, as I have noted on several occasions, I might have improved upon the way I conducted the research. For sure, I sometimes chose inappropriate courses of action. However, I also made several decisions because I was still learning. For example, while I elected to conduct some life history interviews, it was only later that I realized how rich these had been and how, with greater foresight I might have explored Ron's occupational identity more carefully. Yet, at the time, I was developing my understanding of life history interviews and was not prescient enough to realize their value. In short, the experience of conducting the research has been a learning experience for me.

Fourth, the one thing I have learned most is how micro-studies, such as this one, are far from being merely concerned with the inconsequential trivia of day-to-day life. 'Some of the features of mundane social action are deeply implicated in the long term (and large scale) reproductions of institutions' (Giddens 1987:44).

Summary

In the first section I argued that the research adopts an ethnographic approach to constructing a case study of one male headteacher at work in his school. The case study is a contextualized, analytical description of the headteacher and includes my interpretation of his conceptualization of headship. Findings from the case study are working hypotheses and serve analytical generalization and not statistical generalization. The study aims to contribute to education as a discipline and not some other interest or discipline. The study is about practice in education and is concerned to strengthen and improve practitioners' understanding and practice.

In the second section I described in six sub-sections how I conducted the research. First, I stated how I identified a head to study, secured access to him and his school and gained entry to the setting. Second, I explained how I aimed to elicit this head's view of his work. Third, I set out how I operated in the field, focusing upon participant observation, interviews with staff, unsolicited and solicited accounts from key informants and documentary data. Fourth, I described how I made fieldnotes, used interpretive asides and conducted interviews with the subject and the staff. Fifth, I explained how I analysed the data and justified the trustworthiness of the analysis. Sixth, I focused upon writing the case study, and drew parallels with portraiture and biographical writing.

In the third section I highlighted four things I have learned from undertaking the research.

In the course of this chapter I have been critical of my approach. While decisions were made in good faith at the time, as I developed and gained experience in the field I recognized that some aspects might have been improved.

I have also identified a number of research issues which I believe need greater attention. These are the affective dimension of fieldwork; ethnographic writing; the process of perception and its effects upon research.

Having set out how I conducted the research it is now appropriate to turn to the case study.

Part II

The Case Study and Reflections

Chapter 3

Case Study of Ron Lacey

Section 1: Ron's Background and Context

Ron Lacey, headteacher of the Orchard Community Junior School, is the subject of this study. During the period of the fieldwork (1988–89) I collected material on his professional and personal background. Moreover, during the Autumn term of 1989 I conducted two interviews with Ron where I asked him to talk about his professional and personal background. Much of the following draws upon this material.

Ron: The Professional

He was trained as a teacher at Westminster College, Oxford, 1960–63. He studied Education, English and History 'because I did these subjects at 'A' level' (interview). Ron's recollections of College were slight. He could recall little about the courses, or the books he read. Nor could he say very much about his teaching practice schools. He took a Junior education course —

> just a junior, full stop, course. Looking back on it there was supposed to be a lot of things happening in Oxfordshire in the 1960s which never really seemed to impinge at all on the college. There were a lot of heads, I think, who were very influential over a long period of time, who were at that stage in their first village school or before they moved into their new open-plan school. . .I think there was one at Banbury who became nationally quite well known at that time.
>
> (Interview)

When asked why he had wanted to become a teacher he said:

> I suppose it goes back to when I was at school myself (a public Methodist school). I think it was sort of suggested that teaching might be something to consider when I was about 17. I seemed to think it sounded quite a nice idea and so that's really it. I mean it was a Methodist link from one of the Methodist public schools into a Methodist college, so it was almost a natural transition from school into the college.
>
> (Interview)

Ron began his career in a junior school in Walthamstow, teaching 'what we called a second- and third-year C stream' (interview). Ron believed the teachers were very good, but the head less so. At the end of that year he moved to Southlands Junior School in Crawley New Town, Sussex. He taught there for four years. The move to Crawley was prompted by his family moving there. His wife-to-be, Kate, started her teaching in Crawley that year. They had met at college and married at the end of her first year of teaching. '(Southlands) was a nice school to work in. There was a very enthusiastic staff who got on very well together' (interview).

While in Crawley Ron became involved with the Nuffield Science Project, a major curriculum innovation at the time, and this may have helped him gain a graded post at Ford Junior School in East Anglia in 1968. Initially the graded post was for 'something like RE and Boys' Games' (interview). In his first two schools, 'there were no curriculum meetings ever. . .some staff meetings, but they were about Christmas, Sports Days and day-to-day life of the school really, that's all' (interview).

Ford school though was quite influential,

> it did have regular meetings, the head was a very, very strong presence, an authoritarian-type headteacher. He was also very concerned about his staff, he tended to look after them very well and very perceptively. In a sense. . .he enabled curriculum meetings to take place. I suspect it was an act of trust and nerve, to allow people to talk about things together and make decisions together and develop. He allowed new things to happen in the school. It was deemed to be a good school at the time.
>
> (Interview)

Ron was more aware of the Headteacher of Ford School than the other heads he worked for. Indeed, they became personal friends when the Head moved on to become a College of Education lecturer. They still keep in touch.

Ron's wife, Kate also taught at Ford school and she described it thus, after first saying Ron was very ambitious:

> He very quickly looked for promotion and got a graded post for Boys' Games. He was in a school where he was encouraged to think career-wise. I think that could have been quite a significant school. . .the head was a very charismatic person, great sense of status but made everyone feel very valued. . .and he [gave you] a real sense of worth. I think he had a gleam in his eye that Ron was going to be somebody, do something, go somewhere and I think he just kept on kicking him until he got somewhere. I think he [the head] sort of elevated him [Ron] in the school, although he was just a graded post. I think he [Ron] had a very high profile in the school and Ron was very quick to match that expectation. . .it was that school which fostered professional development.
>
> (Interview)

While at this school Ron was directly involved in developing team teaching, although he also acknowledged that it was allowed to happen only with the head's approval. Ron had visited a local small village school with Ford's deputy head and the LEA primary adviser. 'We'd been very impressed with the work that we had seen going on in that school. . .they were team teaching in an open plan way' (interview). The LEA adviser encouraged Ron and the deputy to try something similar at Ford and the two agreed. The LEA 'provided quite a bit of money for structural alterations and furniture' (interview) and their two classrooms became linked. They worked together for two years.

Around the same time, Ron was rather imprecise on the timing, he became Head of Department which was then a Scale 3 post and a further promotion. He was awarded the post for Science, although he felt his main task was only to organize the science cupboard. He also became involved with the setting up of the Teachers' Centre and undertook some practical courses in physical education and swimming. He had by now taught all the junior ages though he had no infant experience. In his last year at Ford School he was acting deputy head. The headteacher was seconded to study full time for an Advanced Diploma in Education. The deputy and Ron were temporarily promoted to fill the vacant head and deputy posts.

By 1970–71 Ron had been teaching for seven years and had worked in three schools; been promoted three times, albeit temporarily in the third instance; been involved in a major curriculum project (Nuffield Science); was known to the local primary adviser; contributed to the establishment and development of a Teachers' Centre; was actively participating in team teaching in an open classroom setting and benefiting from LEA sponsorship for this initiative; and was on good terms with his school's acting headteacher and headteacher, the latter of whom was encouraging and developing Ron. In the post-Plowden years that would have been an impressive curriculum vitae. Furthermore, given the general tendency in several LEAs at that time to appoint young (male) teachers to headships in primary schools, Ron (then 27) was well suited to taking the next step on the career ladder.

During one interview I put it to him that he must have been seen as in the vanguard of development and he agreed he probably was (interview). Moreover, Kate, when asked why she thought Ron wanted to be a head, replied: 'He was (and is) very ambitious, that's the kind of person he is' (interview). Perhaps, then, it is not surprising that he was appointed in 1971 to be the headteacher of a small village school, Dillington Junior Mixed Infant (JMI) (Aided) in a neighbouring LEA.

Ron and his family moved into the school bungalow which was next door to the school. He was the youngest head in the school's history and his predecessors had all been school mistresses. According to Ron, the school was quite run down and under threat of closure. Just two miles away a new town was being built and a larger school was opening. Moreover, 'a lot of the children had gone to (another) school' (interview). His new job had been negotiated in the school's corridor with the principal LEA adviser. Having been told he was going to be offered the job the adviser asked would he accept it. Ron replied that it depended on how long the school would survive. He felt he did not want to take it on if the school would close in a year. The adviser guaranteed Ron three years so he accepted the offer.

Ron was a teaching-head in a school with approximately forty-five children on roll. There was just him and another (woman) teacher. On arriving in post the incumbent colleague retired, so Ron appointed a successor. Together he believed they redeveloped the school, clearing away years of accumulated, but now defunct, equipment and materials. The drift of the children to other schools ceased and the school's viability became more certain. Indeed, the school remains open today.

When asked about the dual role of head and full-time teacher he suggested he had not found it onerous, partly because he received two mornings' relief from teaching. During the fieldwork phase of this research Ron would occasionally mention Dillington. We both knew Ron's successor, who remains to this day the school's headteacher, and several times Ron spoke of this man's happiness, commitment and success. Ron also attended a 200-year anniversary at the school. Generally, he noted the school's continued survival and always spoke of the school with affection. He also compared, in terms of extra demands, headship there and then, to headship now:

> It was not particularly demanding. . .there were very few school-type meetings evening wise. I mean at Dillington there was just one Governors' meeting a term. That was all really. . .quite different to now.
>
> (Interview)

In 1975 he moved to the headship of a larger, five-teacher school. This was in the same LEA, but some seven miles from Dillington. The school, Thorn Parochial Primary School, was located in a village and had been recently built to house children from a cluster of surrounding villages whose schools were closed. For Ron it was a very different school to Dillington. Yet:

> I probably enjoyed Thorn as much in some ways. The people and their families, the staff were quite different in some ways; the deputy head had been head of one of the small village schools which had closed. . .We picked up the whole cross-section of the villages. Longfield village had been very feudal, tied cottages and farm labourers still. Thorn, developing new houses then, new estates, in-filling, people coming in. . .Kingswood, again a mixture, but beginning to see the influx of professional people. It was very nice and Kate came back into education at that stage; she ran a playgroup five mornings. Beautiful site, near the church. . .I still think of families doing things together at the school.
>
> (Interview)

Three years and two terms later, in 1978, Ron became headteacher of The Orchard Community Junior School. Again this move took him to a larger, two-form entry school, initially with over 200 pupils. It was a brand new, purpose built, open plan school in an expanding suburb on the edge of a town. However, when Ron began his headship the new school building was not completed. The Orchard School actually opened in September 1978, somewhat inauspiciously in the playground of a neighbouring school, the children and staff being housed in seven mobile classrooms. The teachers and children moved into their new premises the following spring (March) and the school was opened officially in June 1979.

Ron stayed at The Orchard School until the end of 1989. He was headteacher of The Orchard for longer than he was a classteacher in his first three schools, and for longer than both his previous headships combined. In 1988, when this study began, Ron had been a headteacher for seventeen years. He remained at The Orchard School until he left to become a Primary Adviser in an LEA in 1990.

During his third headship Ron attended local, short in-service courses. In January 1989 he began a two-year, part-time MA Course in Education. He had experienced a one-term secondment in Spring 1987 investigating his LEA's induction programme for newly-appointed primary headteachers.

Until he applied for LEA advisers' posts he had always been successful in applying for jobs. Each of his headships was the first post he applied for. Thus he only knew appointment; during 1988 and 1989, however, he experienced disappointment since he applied for seven local authority adviser/inspector posts before securing an appointment.

Why did He want to be a Headteacher?

When I asked Ron why he became a head his answer focused on two things. First, others had encouraged him to seek promotion, especially when he was acting-deputy at Ford school. Second,

> I suppose you want to see your thoughts about teaching, those you actually put into practice in your own classroom, put into practice on a wider scale in some way.
>
> (Interview)

Kate answered the same question in this way:

> He [Ron] wanted to do his own thing, even do his own thinking, make his sort of statement about the way children learn, presumably he wanted his own school, to see it through to the end.
>
> (Interview)

These comments suggest two things. First, Ron followed a conventional career path, particularly for a man, because the concept of career used in common parlance describes a commitment to promotion (Ball and Goodson 1985:22). This conception is an institutional one since it regards career in terms of organizational structures (hierarchical structures) and rewards (monetary recognition) (McLaughlin and Yee 1988:23). In other words, Ron's career was vertical and staged (Smith *et al.* 1986:29). A vertical path tends to be a common route for men's careers. Studies of teachers' careers show that many women teachers' careers are constructed, in both objective and subjective senses, in different ways to those of many male careers (Ball and Goodson 1985:22), being more lateral than vertical (Nias 1989c:401). Ron's career might also be a gendered one because he was encouraged by a male headteacher and all his headteacher role models were men.

Second, Ron was impelled towards headship by his wish to have a wider influence and greater responsibility. This desire, to see his own thoughts and practice emulated on a wider scale, is a theme which reoccurs at later points in the study.

There is a third feature to note. Ron's recollections of college days included the idea that there were certain Oxfordshire heads who first worked as heads in small village schools, later in larger open-plan ones. Ron's career path replicates these patterns. Also, Ron's career appears to reflect his male role models (the head of Ford school and the head of a small, open plan village school he visited) who were innovators and developers.

Ron: The Person

Ron was born in 1942. From his birth his mother was plagued with ill health. For his first ten years Ron was cared for either by his father — or more usually — paternal grandparents. His mother spent long periods of time in hospitals. Originally living in North London his grandparents moved to Norfolk to seek a better climate for Ron's mother. Methodism figured large in Ron's early life:

> I'd been brought up with it, I suppose. My father became a Methodist minister when I was about nine. I was living with my grandparents anyway at that stage and they were Methodists themselves. My life with them really revolved around Methodist Church on Sunday, Sunday School in the afternoon and sometimes going out with my grandfather, who was a lay preacher. This was in Norfolk, of course, so I went out with him to the villages to preach, etc. It was school during the week and going to the old people's club, which grandparents helped to run on a Friday afternoon, directly after school, and then going to the cinema every Friday night.
>
> (Interview)

In 1953 he was awarded a scholarship to attend a boy's Methodist boarding school in the west country. Ron described this school as an awful place:

> Every part of your life was regimented. When you sat, when you slept, when you stood, there was no freedom at all.
> Certainly the life style in that school was totally at odds with what I had known and what I went back to in the holidays. . .[Also] there was a very definite feel about not being from a monied family. A lot of people came from abroad, a lot from Malaya, some from Hong Kong. . .I think it was a tremendous shock moving from the extremely protected environment living with my grandparents; I wasn't allowed to have a bike because it was dangerous. . .So it was a tremendous shock, literally, going from one part of the country to another.

Ron felt this school and its ethos affected his political outlook.

> I think there are things that gradually over the years have come to be clearer, certainly my political views have, probably as a reaction. . .I think the whole idea of public school ethos, of developing a social elite, responsible, able to make decisions, stand on your own two feet and play the game, and all that sort of crap really, you accepted it while you were there. . .Only at a later stage has it helped to define your own (contrary) views, I think.
>
> (Interview)

At College he met Kate and they married in 1965. They lived in Crawley teaching in different schools in the town. Later, in 1968 they moved to East Anglia and having found a home they each found a job. Teachers were in such short supply they could pick and choose jobs. In the end, they both taught in the same school, Ford.

At college and public school Ron felt Methodism had not featured too strongly. Indeed, he once said that while he was brought up in it, that was not the same thing as being part of it (interview). He and Kate had been involved in a church while in Crawley and when he worked and lived in Walthamstow. Usually Ron produced plays. Also, while living near Ford School, they had both attended a small Methodist Church, yet 'the church connection was beginning to wane a bit at that stage' (interview).

Kate told me that they just 'dropped' the church,

> he started off being involved in the church because his father was a Methodist minister. Then he got rather more cynical about the whole thing, from within, from knowing what goes on from within the church structure. He gets very cynical about organized religion, as I do. . .I think he's sort of grown away from it.
>
> (Interview)

Their daughter was born in 1969 and Kate stopped teaching to rear her. Later, after their son was born, Kate returned to teaching, initially running a play-group in Thorn School hall. Between 1968 and 1978 they not only lived together and moved houses in pursuit of Ron's career, but they also worked together quite a lot. By 1988 Kate had become an advisory teacher in a different LEA to Ron's school. Their daughter began a university course and their son was attending a comprehensive school.

Physically Ron is neither tall nor large. He is relatively short — five feet five inches tall and slim in stature. He is clean shaven and has a good head of greying, brown hair. For work he dressed in a jacket and slacks, sometimes a suit. During the day he would discard his jacket and work in shirtsleeves. He always wore a tie, he rarely loosened his tie and collar. While always clean he was not immaculate in his dress. By mid-morning he could appear a little creased and tousled. Sometimes his shirt became loose around his waist. Often his hair looked windswept. If he was going out of school, or receiving a visitor, he had a habit of combing his hair and straightening his dress, as if he knew he needed to.

Ron did not use spectacles. He did smoke, something like twenty filtered cigarettes a day. He smoked only in the staffroom and his office, if alone. He never expressed a concern about smoking and his health. He did not appear to worry about the habit, although his wife chided him about it. When he visited my house to be interviewed he always asked permission to smoke.

Ron's interests were football, music and art. He often attended the local football team's league matches, supporting his town team. His interest in music stemmed from childhood. He had learned to play the piano and sang in the school choir. At his home a splendid grand piano resides in the lounge. He still sometimes plays, but I never saw him play in school. Both his children are musical, playing in orchestras and groups. His wife is artistic. Ron shares this interest enjoying photography in particular. From time to time he showed me photographs — most memorably of Swiss mountains (1989) and Monet's garden (1988) which he and Kate visited on holidays. Ron often placed art books on display around the school. He also enjoyed reading and occasionally produced for the staff books, poems and snippets from newspapers, either in response to topics raised in the staffroom, or as stimuli for meetings.

He is a modest man, not prone to self promotion. Nor does he appear overtly emotional. Kate described him as reticent and added, 'He's not one to make a meal out of low spots or high spots. He doesn't actually come home exhilarated or debilitated' (interview). He kept his emotions under control. I never saw or heard about him losing his temper with adults or children. Neither did I see him upset or overtly disturbed by events. He was apparently equable and calm. He usually understated his feelings. I came to appreciate that when he said he was a little unhappy about something, it meant something had registered on his personal Richter scale.

He spoke in a soft, quiet voice which made tape-recording him difficult. He often paused before he responded to others. His voice was almost even in tone. Perhaps his most obvious characteristic was humour. He frequently smiled, often he giggled — in delight — especially when listening to children's accounts. He laughed a lot and enjoyed humourous stories and anecdotes, but he did not tell jokes. However, he liked cartoons and witticisms in the press.

Ron is not a self-centred person, and is apparently more interested in others. He listened to others, rather than spoke of himself. He always asked, 'How are you?' When he spoke on the phone he usually finished the conversation by saying, 'Take care.' I only witnessed him being abrupt with a person once. An encyclo-paedia salesman failed to recognize that he was not going to make a sale. Ron first used humour about being financially broke and then, when that did not succeed, walked away with a perfunctory goodbye.

It was entirely in character that he was not effusive when he was appointed as an adviser. His first action, on returning home that very evening, was to dash off to watch a football cup match. Later, when he informed me, he said he felt quite neutral about it, as if he had still to comprehend what it meant. Yet he had pursued just such a promotion over eighteen months and had made seven applications.

Ron did not live in the vicinity of the school. He lived in a bungalow, in a village some nine miles from the school. Each day he drove alone to and from work.

The Orchard Community School

The school was a purpose built community school set in spacious grounds. The local community was a dormitory suburb of the town. In the immediate vicinity of the school there were no industrial or commercial companies. The pupils came from owner-occupied houses. The majority of the children lived in the neat, modern, semi-detached, three-bedroomed homes on the housing estates which surrounded the school. There was little unemployment in the area and few signs of deprivation. The catchment area of the school was predominantly prosperous and white; there were no significant numbers of pupils from other ethnic groups. The proportion of children on free school meals was low and the Educational Welfare Officer (EWO) was not a frequent visitor to the school. There was no school uniform; in the main children wore fashionable clothes.

The building was designed in three sections. The main entrance foyer led to the school's administrative area (secretary's office, head's office, staffroom, stock-room), school hall and canteen, and the community area. The latter area formed a second section made up of a meeting room, coffee bar, toilets, small hall and Community Development Officer's (CDO) office. The third section was the teaching area. This consisted of four units, each unit accommodating a pair of classes. There were eight full time teachers:

First year unit:	Marion; Helen
Second year unit:	Dave (Deputy Head); Jean
Third year unit:	Sarah; Michael until Dec 1988; from Jan 1989 Graham
Fourth year unit:	Marie (INSET Co-ordinator; Scale A postholder); Ken

The first named in each pair were unit leaders charged with keeping an oversight of the unit's work, plans, equipment and their partners. In the year of fieldwork there were 198 children in the school. In addition to the four units, there was a library area and quiet room. At the rear of the school was a swimming pool and a mobile classroom used for music.

The open plan design meant it was possible to see into three of the units relatively easily since they did not have doors. The one unit that did have doors also had large glass 'port holes' cut into them. The units were all carpeted, except in the vicinity of the wet areas which were a feature of each unit. These were located in the centre of a unit and made up of double sinks, storage cupboards, craft tables and display boards/walls. The teaching units were separated from the administrative section by a pair of glazed doors. These ensured the administrative area was rather quiet, although it was not unusual for children to be found there.

The teaching staff were aged between 25 and 45. Ron was the oldest. Additionally, there was a caretaker (Len), cleaner (Barbara, Len's wife), secretary (Judy) and ancillary assistant (Madge). Everyone was called by first name except when children were present. The school was well cared for, being tidy and clean. There was a good range of equipment and materials: audio cassettes, musical instruments, good stock of books, range of papers and craft materials, glue guns, vibra saw, two micro-computers, TV and video monitor, plus reasonable storage space. At no time did I hear complaints about inadequate resources.

The school's organizational structure consisted of children grouped into classes according to chronological age, the unit pairings, and delegated staff responsibilities (deputy, INSET co-ordinator, unit leaders). Unit pairings and staff responsibilities relied upon staff being able to work together. Unit pairs were expected to plan together. Staff also met together each week for curriculum meetings. Working as a (teaching) staff group and chaired by Ron, staff discussed, reviewed and developed the school's curriculum. Typically they took an aspect of the curriculum and talked about possible developments, shared individual judgments, or looked at children's work. During 1988–89 they considered reading, reading records, computers, a school-wide marking policy and code, topic work, National Curriculum Council proposals for English and Science, and project plans to celebrate the school's tenth anniversary. Each teacher was issued with a curriculum file which contained the school's policies. In Ron's office there was a filing cabinet where he held copies of all documents and discussion papers from the time the school opened and a record of the 'types of input' (i.e. involvement of LEA advisers, external speakers) which had informed the staff's work. Curriculum review and development was an integral part of teaching and there was an expectation that all staff would participate. Moreover, there was a tacit assumption that through these discussions staff would contribute to their own and the school's development. In short, staff and curriculum development was built into the structure of the school.

Development was something which keenly interested Ron. He had a strong sense of knowing where the school was coming from, not least because by 1988 he was the only professional member of staff to have been in the school since it opened.

> The school's coming into its tenth year now and during these ten years we've had different phases in the school, we've certainly had different phases of staff and a lot of staff have gone within a short period of time.
>
> We have two new people starting next September (1988). In the past newcomers, I think, had somehow looked over their shoulders to a residue of pioneering elements that was either still here — in terms of people, or in terms of what they had produced. At the start of life in the school there were very strong written curriculum and policy statements, some of which are still going, some of which have become dinosaurs over the last few years, but even going back three or four years, there was still a feeling these were the principles upon which the school had been established by these pioneers, who had a reputation for incredibly long hours of work in the early years of the school. I think it's only about now that that feeling has disappeared. I don't think people are looking over their shoulders.
>
> I think the stability of a team which was there at the start of this year has generated its own challenges. I think cosiness is perhaps too strong a word for it; I think if we said, at the end of this term, what I would like to do is to gather together a whole range of what you regard as really high quality work across the curriculum, there would be some, but there would not be uniformly as many examples as we have seen in the past.
>
> (Interview)

For Ron the school was a changing context not a static one.

> there's never been a static period. There's never been a time when I felt that things had come to an end. . .When I think about the phases of development within a school, I don't tend to think about year groups of children or particular years, I think of it in terms of the team of people we had at that particular time.
>
> (Interview)

This was probably because The Orchard School had prospered in the past from a throughput of teachers. Independently, Ron and Dave told me:

> In the past the school had relied on career-minded young teachers whose ambition helped the school to develop. They would be people who came for a scale post and worked for three or four years in the school with that post before moving on to a bigger job. Or they were people looking for scale posts and worked hard in the school in order to earn a scale post elsewhere.
>
> (Fieldnote)

A teacher described it thus:

> I think this school feeds on people passing through and hammering away
> for a few years and then going on — I think it feeds on that and it needs
> the dynamism.
>
> (Interview)

Yet in 1988–89 Ron and Dave felt that pattern no longer held. After hearing
them talk about this I made the following note:

> [The present staff] are older than previous staff groups and the [new]
> salary structure which has replaced scale posts with fewer A allowances
> [meant] no one could now be bidding for a scale 2, no one would come
> into the school on the basis of wanting a scale 2. The lack of a career
> ladder seemed to be inhibiting school development.
>
> (Fieldnote)

Some of the staff also thought the school had altered. This teacher had worked in
the school for four years.

> I feel the school's much more settled than it used to be for some reason.
> I think maybe that's to do with the staff we have at the moment. I feel
> as though it's a bit more conventional. The school feels more traditional
> than it did.
>
> (Interview)

Ron's long and close acquaintance with the school meant he was the school's
historian — he held the institutional memory. This helped him compare the past
with the present and thus he could gauge development. Moreover, he saw part of
his work as acting as the school's leading developer:

> I think the new developments would come from myself initially. I think
> I allow a degree of autonomy within the structure providing it's under
> fairly close scrutiny. I would challenge the ideas quite stringently.
>
> (Interview)

Of course, as leading developer Ron was not only emphasizing his longevity and,
perhaps, desire to control continuity and change, but he was also maintaining his
position as the founder of the school (Nias *et al.* 1989a:102). Indeed, staff acknowledged that this was Ron's school, since they spoke of it as his school, or of what
Ron wanted.

As the school's founding headteacher he was not the sole creator of the school
— that would deny the contribution of significant others (especially, it seems, the
first deputy). Rather, Ron was the architect of many of the school's policies and
practices. When asked what it was like setting up a new school, he said,

> I think there are two or three strands in that. The first is there's no
> comparison between the previous head and the new head. Obviously
> there's an advantage in having a brand new building and you're able to
> make choices about what to buy. The greatest advantage, the greatest

69

difference to the schools I'd been head of previously, was the fact that you were able to appoint all new staff.

Clearly, the building itself has direct bearing on how we would want to see it work. The pairings are critical to how people work together. I think it would have been very difficult in an open plan school, which also had a community expectation on it, to have members of staff who were uncomfortable working with other people. And with other people being in and around their working area, whether it be parents or anybody that's in. . .Every day is a public day. . .so comparisons are always very clear to anybody that comes, either parents, or teachers, or inspectors, or anybody.

(Interview)

Of course, the visibility of staff also enabled Ron to witness how well staff were developing and performing. However, his comments also suggest that he was very aware that the school as an organization was made up of people.

Ron's Beliefs: Words, Deeds and References

Education is a value-laden enterprise, as those who have examined the ideology of primary education have shown (Alexander 1984:13–20; Campbell 1985:20–3). More recently, adult behaviour in primary schools has been perceived as governed by norms which, in turn, can be taken as an expression of values derived from deeply held beliefs which emanated, in part, from the headteachers of the studied schools (Nias *et al.* 1989a:10, 97–9). Primary schools are value-laden institutions. Moreover, given the association of a set of beliefs with a school's headteacher (Coulson 1976:275–6), it is important to consider what a headteacher believes. However, first it is necessary to define belief.

A belief is any simple proposition, conscious or unconscious, inferred from what a person says or does, capable of being preceded by the phrase 'I believe that. . .' The content of a belief may describe the object of belief as true or false, correct or incorrect; evaluate it as good or bad; or advocate a certain course of action or a certain state of existence as desirable or undesirable.

(Rokeach 1968:113)

When the totality of one's beliefs are considered in their content and structure, one has a belief system:

The belief system is conceived to represent all the beliefs, sets, expectancies or hypotheses, conscious or unconscious, that a person at a given time accepts as true of the world he lives in.

(Rokeach 1960:33)

I do not intend to map Ron's belief system. Rather, my aim is to focus upon his educational, social and moral beliefs as disclosed in the school, or in connection with his work.

I learned about Ron's beliefs from four sources. I asked Ron, on different occasions, to talk about his beliefs. Second, I studied the school's documentation

— statements of aims and the like. Third, I asked the staff to describe his educational aims and values. Fourth, I observed Ron at work and identified clusters of consistent behaviours which I took to be indicators of what he believed in.

When I asked him what were his beliefs in terms of primary education he said,

I have a great aversion to prejudice, to intolerance and to the class system we have in the country, which is linked to insensitivity to people and a lack of caring and equal opportunities.

(Interview)

Ron often spoke of quality in education by which he meant.

I think there's quality of relationships between children and children, and children and adults, and adults and adults. The quality of individual children's achievements and collective achievements. The learning environment itself should be conducive to enabling the quality of the relationships to develop.

(Interview)

On another occasion he was talking about the INSET cluster group of schools.

'One of the things about the cluster group is that we all share the same sort of philosophy, like this stuff here,' and he picked up a letter from the head who had been acting as spokesman for the cluster group. The head had set out his rationale for the cluster and there were five statements of belief:

1   A deep concern for the spiritual, social, emotional and intellectual well-being of every child in our care.
2   A belief that all individuals, both children and adults, respond best and and find personal fulfilment when they and their contributions are valued by the group.
3   That children learn most effectively in well planned, stimulating environments where, for the most part, the learning opportunities are based on active, open-ended situations springing either from the children's own developing interests, or from the teacher's knowledge based on experience as to what interests and challenges children.
4   Above all, that each child's engagement with the learning task should be meaningful and that attempts to learn should be met with critical dignity and self respect of the child.
5   That with mutual help, trust and support, teachers will continue to develop through monitoring and appraising their own work and that of their colleagues.

I asked, 'Do you agree with the cluster's aims?'
'Oh yes,' said Ron. And I could tell he wholeheartedly approved of that statement.

(Fieldnote)

The aims of the school were expressed thus:

Education Aims of the Orchard Community Junior School

The aims of any school are essentially a declaration of intent for the staff as a whole and in a general form indicate the tone, ethos and quality of the school. The simplest expression of aims for this school are as follows:

1 To recognize that the primary school years are not solely a preparation for the future, but stand in their own right as an important period of any person's life.
2 Children should acquire a wide range of skills and techniques in the fields of language, i.e., reading, writing, speaking, listening and mathematical skills that are useful and relevant to them, both in the school and in the community of which they are a part.
3 As part of the school community each child should learn social and moral values that give them respect for, and a sensitivity to other people by acquiring an attitude of tolerance and care.
4 To develop creative abilities in each child through experience of music, art, literature and physical activities.
5 To develop a spirit of enquiry that enables each child to come to a clear understanding of his or her own world and by doing so help them to a wider understanding of the world around them.

I also asked him about the types of experiences the school was trying to provide for the children:

Ron: I think it's types of experiences which recognize there will be an emphasis on individual development throughout the four years they're here.
GS: What are your ideals?
Ron: Individual children?. . .I can see the ideals in lots of situations throughout the day, there was a tiny one this morning. There were two children in the second year using a vibra-saw for cutting out a polystyrene block and they hadn't used it before. They'd been shown how to use it and they were doing it together, totally unsupervised, the teacher wasn't watching, hovering, over them. They were talking while they were doing it and the level of concentration was incredibly high. Just to actually watch the face of the child moving his tile around was quite fascinating. I think that's a good situation because it showed all sorts of things: it showed a certain trust in the ability of the children to follow through an instruction; to do it with care; to work with other people, other children, because the other child who was there, waiting to have her turn to use the machine, was quite absorbed in what the other one was actually doing; and they were discussing it together. It was a good experience, I think, for those children. Literally, I'm talking about thirty seconds this morning, but it was right and I suppose in a sense one could interpret that as working out an ideal. . .I think children should have a wide range of different experiences. I think for the children to benefit from those experiences

and to move on to another experience there has to be a continuity throughout the whole year of the school. Some elements of that have to be agreed and written down for the teachers (as plans and records). . .There has to be, I think, opportunities for surprises in what the children are doing and I think there's got to be opportunity for achievements which exceed the teacher's expectations. That's very general, you could be even more general, with broad generalizations about recognition of individual potential and talk about the academic and social development.

(Interview)

When I interviewed other staff no one doubted that the school as a whole reflected

- a child-centred approach to learning
- individual differences
- first-hand, experiential learning
- cross-curricular project work

Teacher: Our main vehicle for learning is cross-curricular projects. . .and as far as possible our learning is based on first-hand experience.

(Interview)

Teacher: [It] comes down to this phrase we keep using, cross-curricular, child-centred, which he [Ron] obviously does want.

(Interview)

Working in the school I was constantly aware of these beliefs underpinning the staff and children's work. My fieldnotes contain numerous references which threw them into relief. For example:

Ron was making himself some coffee at the sink and two children came in to return a cup and Ron said to one of the children, 'I liked your poster I saw the other day. I thought it was very good.' The child smiled brightly and they continued talking about the poster until the two children had to leave.

(Fieldnote)

Marion came in and told Ron how well C. had done this afternoon. 'She worked very hard,' said Marion, 'very hard indeed and very well.'

(Fieldnote)

Jean says to the child doing a shield, 'You need to work from a picture, not just make one up from your head.' Then Jean says to me, 'He [meaning the child doing the sword] is at least working from his rough book, from a sketch of a sword he had seen.' The message seems to be that there has to be a connection with firsthand experience, and in my mind, I noted; firsthand experience rules.

(Fieldnote)

Additionally, there were few exercise books, children worked in rough books and, following a process of marking, correction and redrafting, copied out their written work onto individual pieces of paper. Children mounted their own work. Few textbooks were in evidence, even fewer in use. Some worksheets were used, principally for mathematics. There was a strong emphasis on display and each Friday there was a showing assembly which celebrated the children's work.

The weekly, after school staff meeting always commenced with Ron asking staff if there was anything any teacher wanted to report on an individual child:

> 'Could we just check if we need to concentrate on any individual children that we all ought to be made aware of? Fourth year unit?' he asked.
>
> 'No one to mention,' said Marie.
>
> 'Third years?' Sarah named one child who was now wearing glasses. Second years had no one to mention.
>
> 'First years?' Marion reported that a child who'd had a headache was now wearing glasses, but the headaches were recurring. She also spoke of a child who doesn't speak English and how well the child is fitting in. Ron pursued this a little further and suggested ways of helping this child.
>
> (Fieldnote)

Such reports always preceded curriculum discussions and I inferred that individual children took precedence over curriculum review.

The cross-curricular emphasis was demonstrated in many ways. Teachers' planned projects which encapsulated a range of curriculum areas. Discussions, especially during May when the staff looked at the NCC Science document, revealed concerns about the long term feasibility of cross-curricular work since the National Curriculum was seen as a threat to it. Classroom displays showed how an overarching project, such as movement was developed in a variety of curricular areas, such as science, art, maths, CDT, music.

Ron projected his beliefs in several ways. On the very first day of the school year staff met together for an INSET Day. At the start of the meeting Ron began by telling the story of two children he had taught:

> They were little anecdotes, smuggled into which was the fact that today he was celebrating twenty-five years in teaching, and he talked about two children he remembered in his very first class. Ron then went on to say he'd reflected on those children and what they'd meant for his career, his teaching, and wanted those reflections to signal the kinds of reflections that he felt all teachers went through, or should go through at the start of a year; learning from the past, as it were, for the future.
>
> He also read an extract from Christian Schiller's book. It was Schiller's letter to Len Marsh, where Schiller likens change to the movements of an earthworm, which is not only slow and serialized, but it's also at ground level. He made great play about needing to see oneself at ground level, and as a very valuable person at ground level. Then he took Schiller's writing as a useful piece of reflection in itself. I wondered at the time if, in fact, this was the head operating as philosopher for the group.
>
> Ron also spoke of a couple of themes that he could identify in the last twelve months in school and in education generally. There was a

sense of people feeling that there was the beginnings of a loss of individual autonomy and the need for collective uniformity. He felt that perhaps teachers were now beginning to learn to step to a distant drummer. He implied that Mr Baker, [then Education Secretary], was that distant drummer. But he also went on to say that he felt schools needed Pied Pipers. 'In fact children need Pied Pipers, they don't respond to distant drummers.' In that sense he wanted teachers to reflect so that each of them can be in Schiller's term 'pioneers', or perhaps in Ron's terms Pied Pipers. Ron also said that he felt the school had snaffled more than its fair share of good teachers — pioneers.

He was, throughout this talk, signalling, symbolizing probably, values he felt appropriate for the year ahead, if not for the years past and stimulating the staff to use their own skills and understandings and awareness, to develop their own work and expertise. It was a talk which valued individuals he said, and he didn't want to lose those individuals' perspectives. 'Our planning has got to reflect our individual aspirations,' he said.

(Fieldnote)

Ron's use of Schiller was no accident it now seems to me. As I came to know Ron I discovered he was a member of NAPE (National Association for Primary Education), was interested in Robin Tanner's work (both educational and artistic) and had attended, during 1982–83, Len Marsh's course for primary headteachers which looked at primary schools in terms of both practice and philosophy. Speaking of the course Ron said,

I found it thoroughly enjoyable, fascinating and very exciting. [It] was very, very good. It was a lovely year. I think it helped clarify your beliefs, in some way they were verbalized for the first time.
GS: How long have you been in NAPE?
Ron: About six or seven years, from that course.

(Interview)

Ron also said his interest in Schiller and Tanner stemmed from that course. When I put it to him that Len Marsh and the course were influential he said,

It's to do with beliefs isn't it? [Pause] That's what it is, it's personal and professional beliefs, it's where those two match together and they match in writings like Robin Tanner's *What I Believe*. . .I think it's when the personal and professional beliefs coincide. . .I think it's inspirational, it moves beliefs into conviction. They're [Schiller, Tanner, Marsh] saying the sort of things [I believe] in a better way than I could ever say it. . .you think that's it. It's a mixture of heart and head probably.

(Interview)

I looked up the Schiller extract Ron referred to in that first formal meeting. My eyes lighted on

The movement of change is not a steady advance on an even front; nor is it a series of charges after brilliant ideas. The major force in the movement is the patient and persistent pulling of pioneers, scattered far and wide, each at work in his or her own school, determined to find a way in which the children shall live and learn more abundantly.

and later

The metaphor has changed. It is pleasanter to think of a pioneer than of a worm. But the movement in each image is the same: the movement is on the ground because it is on the ground that change in our schools takes place.

(Schiller's letter to Len Marsh; in Griffin-Beale (Ed.) 1979:xvi–xvii)

Schiller believed that lasting change in education stemmed not from advisors and researchers handing down prepackaged innovations, but from individual pioneers modifying their classroom practice in response to observations of their own pupils (Griffin-Beale 1979:xiii). Did Ron see himself as such a pioneer? I believe he did. His awareness of the Oxfordshire heads in the 1960s and his attraction to the ideas of Marsh, Tanner and Schiller seem to be mutually reinforcing. Moreover, in his own work he tried to live out his beliefs and convictions.

There was a close correspondence between Ron's educational beliefs and the teachers' classroom activities, and staff attributed this congruence to Ron. Staff saw Ron as providing the school's guiding beliefs:

Teacher: I suppose he [Ron] must put the ideas (interview).
Teacher: I quite often think that Ron sort of steers it [the school] the way he wants it to go. . .I think he knows what he wants.

(Interview)

Ron not only explicitly stated his educational beliefs, he also exemplified them in his actions. For example, earlier Ron was quoted as having an aversion to insensitivity to people and this probably accounts for his manner when dealing with people, something staff readily appreciated.

Teacher: 'I think Ron has incredibly brilliant, unmatched, interpersonal skills.

(Interview)

He knew all the children by name. New staff were overtly encouraged to contribute at staff meetings; I was invited to join in on the first day. During the school's Tenth Anniversary Assembly Ron insisted that the caretaker, his wife and Madge (the ancillary) joined him to cut the cake (fieldnote). He regularly thanked people. At the close of a meeting with the Inset coordinator, Marie, he said, 'Thank you for going to last night's meeting' (fieldnote). On another occasion, having gone to watch an away inter-school football match he phoned me at home, 'to say thank you for coming to watch the soccer match' (fieldnote). He always concluded telephone conversations with a 'Goodbye, thanks for calling' (if they had) and 'take care'.

He was a member of the staffroom — taking his coffee with staff, often washing up cups for staff.

Ron arrived, said 'hello' as he went into his office, then some minutes later came into the staffroom and went to get some coffee and then circulated around, quietly saying 'Hello, good morning' to everyone.

(Fieldnote)

He was patient with people. I recall only one occasion when he was overtly irritated with someone and he expressed regret to me the next day (fieldnote). He had a lot of self control. He also displayed few signs of status. He had his office, but no special car parking space, no reserved chair in the staffroom — indeed he most often knelt on the floor — and when he entered the staffroom no one's behaviour manifestly changed.

Spending time with staff, both collectively and individually meant he could take into account their needs and concerns. Moreover, this extended to all who played a part in the school:

From 3.10 p.m. to 3.30 p.m., there were three parents, one of them a Parent Governor talking with Ron. It was a mixture of conversation and organizational arrangements to do with after-school events and activities; it was all conducted in an atmosphere of friendliness and cordiality.

(Fieldnote)

The deputy CDO arrived and asked Ron for some advice, a point of information. He said to her, 'Are you alright?'

'Yes,' she said. Ron finished his writing and came into the staffroom. 'Coffee?', he asked me.

'Oh, yes please,' I said. We just chatted over a few points and he said, looking out of the window, 'Oh, good. Mavis is coming. Have you met Mavis?'

'Yes,' I said, 'She's the crossing patrol lady isn't she?'

'Yes,' he said. 'Did you know she got an MBE at the January awards?'

'No, I didn't.' I said, 'I imagine she's pleased.'

'Oh yes. Very pleased,' said Ron. 'It's made her life.' And he went out and I could hear him making a fuss of her, congratulating her, telling her how pleased he was.

(Fieldnote)

I phoned Ron and asked how he'd got on at his interview for an adviser's job. He'd not got it, he said. He didn't sound too depressed and he talked about the questions they had asked him. Four jobs were on offer and six candidates had been called, but in the end only two appointments were made. He told me he wouldn't be in very much on Friday; would it upset my day very much if he wasn't around? 'No,' I said. It struck me as being remarkably considerate to remember my need while facing what must have been some disappointment. He went on to say with some irony, well, he wasn't too disappointed, it was the Parent Teacher Association (PTA) meeting that night.

(Fieldnote)

His humour has already been noted, but he was often telling stories in the staffroom. On the matter of swimming he said:

I have a London County Council book from 1910 which has photographs of children lying on desks being taught swimming strokes and underneath it says, 'You can teach children to swim in elementary schools providing that they do not go in the water!'

(Fieldnote)

He enjoyed, more often than not, the absurdities of life.

Like those pioneers who inspired him he tried to bring together his professional and personal beliefs and live them out, on the ground, in the school.

Section 2: What Did Ron Do?

There were several strands to Ron's work as a headteacher. Each week involved a number of relatively permanent points, (such as fixed appointments and timetabled commitments — showing assembly, staff meeting, Monday's meeting with caretaker and CDO), but there were also numerous unexpected meetings with people who arrived without warning. Ron was frequently meeting people; some meetings were informal (chance encounters in the foyer, corridors, car park, etc.), others formal occasions with agendas (staff meetings). He dealt with an extensive range of people (teachers, ancillaries, parents, children, community representatives, LEA officers and Inspectors, welfare, social and medical agencies, heads of local schools, staff and students from local Higher Education (HE) college, sales representatives, maintenance staff), all of whom usually wanted to talk with the head, but who also wanted Ron to focus on different things.

Meeting people sometimes took a short time (often less than five minutes), while others needed longer (something around ten to fifteen minutes) and a few meetings were of a relatively long duration (an hour or more). Ron met people before, during and after school. Some meetings and tasks were important, others he regarded as trivial. Some he found interesting, others mundane. A few meetings were private and took place in his office with the door closed. The great majority were public meetings with others, on the threshold of his office, or the staffroom, as well as in the staffroom, foyer and teaching units, where he was within earshot of colleagues and others on site.

The content of his meetings and tasks varied. He was involved, for example, with curricular matters, child and adult welfare, staff development, judgments on performance (teachers, children, governors, curricular materials, ancillary staff, self) health and safety, administration (salaries, timetables, funds, returns), buildings and plant. Some things were urgent, most appeared not to be pressing.

His work involved a range of media: face-to-face talk, telephone conversations, incoming mail, writing letters and reports, touring the school and watching and listening to what was going on. He was assisted by the school's secretary and ancillary who usually dealt with the mail and telephone calls. Ron also had installed an answering machine which helped to free him from sitting by the phone when the secretary was off-site. It was usual, though, for him to work in his office after some absence (touring the school; off-site activity) and to review any recorded messages.

Ron did not have a timetabled teaching commitment: he told me he found he couldn't keep to the timetable, he would start things with children, but then be unable to complete them in the allocated times and sessions (fieldnote). He did, though, cover for teaching staff if they were ill during the day, attended half-day or shorter meetings, or when no replacement could be arranged for them.

Ron was a member of a number of groups: the school's staff, community associations, the school governors, local primary heads, LEA working party, INSET cluster, LEA primary heads.

Encounters in School

Although Ron did not always know who might visit him he expected callers most days. The periods around the beginning and end of school (8.45–9.15 a.m.; 3.15–3.45 p.m.) were times when parents often called. In the morning Madge (ancillary) and Judy (secretary) were on hand to act as receptionists, although they tended to deal with the telephone while Ron dealt with visitors. Ron was usually available and his approachability no doubt encouraged callers:

> As Ron was describing to me the trip to Holland, between 3.20 p.m. and 3.40 p.m. he was constantly interrupted. A parent came in enquiring whether there was a rota for the swimming and who would be holding the pool key? Another parent brought in letters about the play scheme and handed them to Ron. A third parent did exactly the same with a letter, but Ron then enquired how the minutes of the PTA committee were coming along. Another parent made a brief enquiry about a lost jumper and Wendy, the chair of governors, arrived. She asked for the school's key for the swimming pool, explaining that she wanted to plant some flowers in pots before she went home that evening. There was also an incoming telephone call, which Ron took.
>
> (Fieldnote)

From his arrival in school (usually around 8.30 a.m.) until after school started Ron was also in demand from staff.

> At 8.59 a.m. — Ron was having coffee in the staffroom. He was kneeling on the floor the other side of one of the low coffee tables, chatting to Dave and me. We were talking about the National Curriculum when Graham arrived. 'You wanted a word,' said Graham.
> 'Oh yes, I think it's about records and the folders on the children,' said Ron. Before he could say anything else, Ken arrived and asked, as he walked in,
> 'Will there be a staff meeting a week on Monday?'
> Ron said to Ken, 'Dave and I are going to look at that today, we'll let you know later.'
> The chair of governors, Wendy, then arrived and as Ken left she came in and sat down next to me. Ron said 'hello' and signalled did she want some coffee. She shook her head. Ron turned back to Graham.
> 'I'll be with you in a minute,' he said to Wendy. 'Now,' he said to Graham, 'I think we need to also have a word about the trip.'
> At that point, Len, the caretaker appeared. 'I'll have to phone Jack Day,' he said, 'and then the Police, that young girl last night was nothing but a nuisance. She kept running in and out slamming doors and she came over to our house and banged on our door. Imagine that,' he said, 'banging our door! I'll contact Jack Day.'
> 'No,' said Ron quietly, 'I'll do that.'
> 'She's nothing but a nuisance,' said Len, in a state of considerable agitation and he went on to repeat about the girl banging on his front door. 'I'll contact Jack Day,' he said. (I took Jack to be the supervisor of the evening class.)

'No,' said Ron firmly, 'I will do that.' Len again repeated the incidents of the night before; children running in and out of school and banging on his door and what he was going to tell Jack Day; and how he had told the Police last night about it and that the Police will follow it up.

Ron, fixing his eye firmly on Len, repeated, only this time with meaningful insistence, 'I'll contact Jack, leave it to me Len.' Len did not seem placated by this and discontentedly muttered on. Len repeated the incident's description four times and each time Ron repeated his view that he would contact Jack.

Then a parent signalled from behind Len that she wanted to speak to Ron. Ron went to talk to her about some problem with her daughter's health. When Ron returned, Wendy stood up to speak to Ron. They wanted to talk in private so they went off into his office. Graham was still waiting for his time with Ron. Len remained in the staffroom. All of this lasted four minutes and one could see Ron dealing with multiple incidents, each pressing, each immediate and each impinging directly upon himself.

Although at the outset Dave (deputy) had been present, within the first thirty seconds the school bell had gone and he had gone off to do his teaching. It was a small example of a headteacher dealing with many things at once.

(Fieldnote)

Clearly many individuals sought Ron's attention, often at the same time. Moreover, these individuals looked to Ron for information and for him to resolve their problems.

At the end of the Christmas term the CDO resigned and the post was vacant for two terms. The assistant CDO took over many of the responsibilities, but Ron also dealt with some matters.

I've seen the CDO's former deputy four times this morning and, I'm dealing with a transport issue for the over-60s group and that means there'll be an extra meeting at 10 o'clock on Monday morning to sort this out. There are other community groups' concerns to settle and even quite mundane matters, like trying to find a room (in school) for the Lion Football Club manager's meeting. I don't regard it as a separate part of my job, it's an additional part.

(Fieldnote)

Problems could come in all guises:

Madge came into the staffroom and asked Ron, 'Is it alright if D comes in with "pink eye"?' There was some discussion as to what affliction "pink eye" might actually be and whether it was contagious or not. The school's nurse, Betty, was in school. Ron suggested Madge should go and ask Betty so she did.

Wendy also came in before 9 o'clock and sat down. 'I've a confession to make,' she said to Ron. 'This form I am supposed to have filled in and sent off, about a meeting in a local high school, well I haven't,' she said. 'In any case, you need to sign it. Will you sign it and then it'll look like it's your fault.' Ron took the letter from her without saying anything, but he smiled.

(Fieldnote)

Some problems centred around staffing. Staff were sometimes ill, and/or absent and cover for their classes had to be arranged. Staff also left the school and new staff needed to be appointed. At the same time, other events were also happening so that the pace of Ron's work was sometimes hectic:

Ron was talking about the last four days before half term. 'It's going to be a busy week,' he said. 'Dave won't be in on Monday morning, we've got interviews on Thursday, we've got a posse of students in from college as well on Thursday, about eighteen or nineteen. If we're not careful we might appoint one of those instead of one of the real candidates.' He giggled. Ron said he would be out some time during the week as well. He also said that this week had been fairly busy. Jean's been off all week with a bad case of 'flu, Marie hadn't been well, but had returned on Monday.

Clearly there's a sense of busyness in his life and of keeping things going in the face of disruption from unexpected absences.

(Fieldnote)

Ron was surrounded by people he could turn to. All staff were willing to receive unexpected callers (most usually parents). Madge and Judy did most to help with callers who needed small points of information or help. Where the matter was perceived to be more important, if Ron was unavailable, then Dave took the lead, but upon Ron's return Dave would always brief Ron. In other words, although Ron was assisted by his colleagues, they recognized he needed to know what was happening.

Ron also tried to meet staff on a formal basis. 'Ron said he was going to have a meeting with Marie at lunchtime about the Inset coordinators' meeting she had attended; she wanted to update him' (fieldnote).

Nor were all his dealings with parents unpremeditated.

After three o'clock Ron saw another parent, a mother, in a family where the children had been physically abused; the middle child was in local authority care, and the youngest child had just been admitted to the school today. Ron wanted to see the mother in order to establish some ground rules about the care of the child.

(Fieldnote)

On two occasions (3.11.88; 6.2.89) and different weekdays (Thursday, Monday) I shadowed Ron before, during and after school. Data from the shadow studies confirm both that his work involved dealing with the needs and wants of individuals and groups associated with the school, and that he initiated numerous contacts of his own. In other words, he was not entirely reactive, nor always at the mercy of all who arrived to see him. He went out to see people, making and sustaining his own contacts.

On both days when I shadowed him (and most other days I was in school) Ron spent time in the staffroom, ate lunch with colleagues on the teachers' table, visited the teaching areas, talked to children, teachers and parental helpers and toured school during lunchtime keeping an eye on what was happening:

10.15 a.m.	Ron goes into 4th year unit. Speaks to individual child.
10.15	Ron into 3rd year unit, joins in some groups. . .
10.25	Ron going round each table/activity group looking at what the children are doing. On one table the children are looking at live locusts. . .
10.27	Ron sits on some floor cushions to talk with a student and child. The [student's] tutor joins Ron; the two talk. . .
10.32	As Ken walks by on his way to playground duty Ron approaches him and they talk: they discuss the student who is presently experiencing some difficulty with some pupils. Ken offers his opinion; 'She should try not to worry.' They discuss tensions of teaching experience.
10.35	Ron goes to staffroom; on the way he picks up a paper trimmer left lying across a pathway. He leans it against a wall.
10.39	Ron stands in staffroom. He is still and silent, smoking a cigarette.
10.41	Picks up a letter, hands it to Marie. 'Isn't it lovely?' They giggle over the contents. It is a letter from the CEO to all INSET co-ordinators about the costs of meals which some have been claiming. Ron, kneeling, joins a discussion with Madge and others about printing ink.
10.45	Ron goes into the office, talks to Marion after she's phoned a parent. He is soothing, calming.

(Shadow Study Notes 18.11.88)

Some of Ron's time was devoted to reading (notes from parents, proof reading reports he had written, mail, catalogues and requisition forms). He spent time talking with Judy and Madge in their office, and on other days he was seen visiting kitchen staff in the canteen. Len often used the staffroom so the two tended to meet there. Ron's daily work pattern had its costs. When I once asked him what he had done during the morning he said, 'I don't know really. Bits and pieces. A bit of this, a bit of that' (fieldnote).

Fragmentation was one feature of his work and this could lead to him leaving undone things he later felt he ought to have done:

4.29 Ron said to me: [I] didn't see the lst year students before 12.00. . . should have done.

(Shadow Study: 3.11.88)

Feeling 'detached' was also a danger, because it was less satisfying:

'I feel I've been involved today, some days I feel detached. [There have] not [been] many interruptions or things from the office, or visitors.' Dave joins Ron for a cigarette — communal fag?

'So have you had a good day?' says Dave to Ron.

'Yes,' says Ron, 'involved rather than detached. Ron said to me as an aside. My definition of a headteacher being detached would be more the management role; involved would mean more the professional, teaching role.

(Shadow Study: 3.11.88)

There are four points to make about Ron's encounters in school. First, in common with other studies, Ron's time in school could be characterized as hectic and fragmented, full of people-centred activities and unanticipated events and visitors (Clerkin 1985; Harvey 1986; Davies 1987; Acker 1988; 5–6, 8–13). Like the subject of Wolcott's (1973) study, the greatest part of Ron's time was spent in an almost continuous series of encounters from the moment he arrived at school until the time he left (p. 88). Second, it was essential to the smooth running of the school as an organization that Ron dealt with parents' and staff members' day-to-day queries and concerns. Third, meeting people face-to-face ensured Ron was not a remote figure but, rather, was active in the social network of the school. Fourth, his contact with the teaching staff, especially in terms of teaching and learning issues, helped Ron to feel involved in the professional work of the school.

Encounters Over Time

So far the picture of Ron's work has been developed from individual incidents of short duration. When Ron's work is looked at over a longer period of time it is possible to see his work in a slightly different light. For sure, Ron's work continually involved him in dealing with others, and these encounters were sometimes unpredictable. However, over the course of two or three weeks there would be some planned events and predictable meetings. Also, while Ron would most often be dealing with people, the content of these meetings was varied. Both these latter points can be seen in the following extract taken from an interview when Ron was describing to me, using his diary as an aide-mémoire, what he had been involved with over a two week period (27 April–15 May) and what he would be involved with in the coming days:

The 27th, we had the review of statemented children, one child will be moving into secondary school and therefore we had to update her statement in the light of what will be needed at the secondary school. Another child, who is not statemented, but still has special needs, is going into that school; that's meant working with the educational psychologist and the head of special needs at the receiving school, plus the parents as well. That took up a certain amount of time. In terms of the school meals supervisors, we actually lost two. We lost one right at the beginning of term, she got another job, and we lost another because her husband's very ill and she had to leave. So we went down to three. We're back to four now and we have another person starting next Monday.

We've had a liaison meeting with the heads of the primary schools in the area and secondary staff, the result of which was that the existing maths and English tests are going to be dropped. There have been working groups on English and mathematics, made up of primary and secondary school staff. They will produce a profile in terms of the core subjects of the National Curriculum which will be uniform throughout the schools and will be matched with the requirements of the National Curriculum in language and maths for use by next year's intake at the secondary school. The traditional English and maths tests will go, and be replaced by this. That was quite an interesting development.

It was also interesting because it was the first time that a lot of the newly appointed local headteachers were there. It was the first time that group had been together.

The community development officer post is due to be appointed on 23 May, which is a week tomorrow. I've obviously had to go through that with the Council. They had thirty-four applicants I think; we actually saw about ten and we selected a shortlist of five.

The Donkey Derby was on 7 May, which took up a certain amount of time towards the end of that week and was very successful, a good event. It probably cleared something like £1000 profit in the end. We had a lot of people, a lovely sunny day, the races were good, and a car boot sale, swingboats and that sort of thing. That was a good event.

Students have just started today. We have three students in school. They're postgraduate students doing their final practice. One of the students in the fourth year will be going on the visit to Holland. That exercise has taken up a fair bit of time over the last few weeks, doing the groupings, passports, E111 forms. We had a meeting for the parents last Wednesday night, saw we had all money from the bank, etc., but that's done now. That visit is tight [meaning organized] and is ahead of itself.

School photographer, boring I think.

Playground has been finished (tarmac extension laid).

Last Friday we had a meeting of the INSET cluster group, a head and coordinators' meeting which was looking at the conference we had at the start of this term and also looking at future developments. One of the things that came up at that meeting was the anxiety (amongst heads) about the LMS formula that's been used (to set schools' budgets). In fact we've got a meeting on Thursday with the heads of that cluster group and then another meeting with the head of Fields Infants, because she is one of the pilot schools for LMS. We want to match that budget formula with her experience.

We are preparing for Mavis' MBE award here next Monday afternoon, it's crossed lollipops, guard of honour, and tea for 130!

There's a festival meeting tomorrow night here. I'm chairman of that group, PTA meeting on Wednesday, Play Scheme meeting on Thursday afternoon, the MA [his course] in the evening, out in the afternoon at Uptown and then Fields School. There's a PTA disco here Friday night for children. I'm having my hair cut at 10.30 on Saturday. You don't want to know that, do you, really?!

Next week there's Mavis' MBE award in the afternoon, CDO interview on Tuesday afternoon in here. Governors' meeting on Wednesday and that's about it.

(Interview)

Arising from Ron's account are three points. First, Ron's work was varied and wide ranging. Over a two–three week period he dealt with these topics:

- children with special needs and their transfer to high school;
- lunchtime supervisors;
- liaison with high school;
- liaison with neighbourhood primary headteachers;
- assessment, pupil records and profiling;
- reviewing practices in light of National Curriculum;
- appointment procedures;
- fund raising;
- induction of students and allocation of students to classes and teachers;
- organizing a trip to Holland;
- parents' evening for children going to Holland;
- INSET co-ordination, review and planning;
- preparing for LMS;
- award ceremony organization;
- community meetings;
- personal inset (MA);
- preparation for approaching Governors' meeting.

In other words, Ron's work was diverse in its scope and required him to be conversant with a range of issues.

Second, when Ron touched lightly on some things (school photographer, PTA disco, governors' meeting) and dwelt longer on others (liaison with high school, local heads, LMS) he often was distinguishing between what he was more or less familiar with. Over this two–three week period Ron was involved with some things which he had experienced before and were well known to him (PTA, festival meeting, photographer), while others were new to him (LMS, National Curriculum), or changing (constituency of local heads' group, pupil profiles).

Familiarity stems not only from precedence, but also from recurring patterns in Ron's work. Ron was dealing with liaison with the high school and plans for September's Village Festival in the summer term because it was then timely to do so since there is an annual cycle to teaching, schooling and headship (Wolcott 1973:178–91).

In part, the annual cycle was made up of termly events (parents' evenings, governors and PTA meetings), seasonal activities (Christmas with its concert and parties) and regularized administrative tasks (parents' choices for high school completed during spring term; requisitioning within financial years; annual returns). To these events and activities some other fixed points can be added (teacher resignations and appointments by end of October, February, May for succeeding terms) and habitual patterns (settling in children new to the school in September; introducing next intake of children and parents to the school in previous June and July; determining unit pairs and allocation of teachers to classes during summer term). I did not plot the specifics of Ron's annual cycle though as the above suggests I was aware of it in a general sense. Its significance lay in providing some predictability to Ron's work.

The nature of his day-to-day encounters suggests a degree of uncertainty. He did not always know who he might encounter or what might happen, hence there was a degree of unpredictability in his daily work. Yet this was counterbalanced by both his programme of fixed points (weekly events in school and planned appointments) and a context which offered a relatively stable pattern of tasks. Ron's work might, in part, be varied, fragmented and unplanned, but some of it was also familiar, predictable and contingent upon the time of year.

Third, his work was not always conducted on-site. Indeed, over the year, he attended many meetings away from school (National Curriculum dissemination conferences, area heads' meetings, LMS briefings, Inset cluster meetings, case conferences). He was also a member of an LEA working party comprised of heads and LEA Inspectors which called themselves The Committee of Good Practice. They had undertaken to produce for the LEA a booklet on the primary school curriculum. These meetings, and many others, conspired to keep Ron away from school. While he believed, in retrospect, that he was away from school too much (interview) the fact remains that part of Ron's work took place away from the school site; not all his encounters were in school.

The Night Shift: After school Work

Not all of his work occurred during the school day. Ron usually arrived in school around 8.30 a.m. and left anytime between 4.00 and 11.00 p.m. Part of his work took place in the evening.

Ron made it clear to me on a number of occasions that I was not seeing his afterschool work. Ron said, 'I am quite conscious that you are only seeing my in-school work and that you need to see some aspects of the community work.' On another occasion he said to me, 'I am conscious you have not seen any of my work with the PTA or the governors.' Before Christmas, when he and I were talking about how we might consider his work during the spring term, he said, 'You will, of course, need to come and attend some governors' meetings' (fieldnote).

Though I did not attend all his afterschool commitments, I nevertheless was aware of them:

> Ron told me he attended his MA course (last night) and then returned to school, some time after 8 o'clock, in order to meet the governors of the newly opening school in the district. They'd asked him to talk about what he thought a headteacher opening a new school should look like, as a way of providing criteria for them to use when appointing the head of their school. It meant he didn't get home until almost midnight last night. I also know he had attended a PTA meeting on Wednesday evening.
>
> (Fieldnote)

> Before school Ron told me about his week. He said he had been busy. He had attended a PTA meeting on the Tuesday night, he had been interviewed for a new job all day Wednesday, and then the governors' meeting had gone on beyond 10.30 p.m. on Wednesday night. Thursday he had been busy with absent staff and Thursday night was his MA course. Today the students were in and he obviously had things to finish off.
>
> (Fieldnote)

'Are you staying for the disco tonight?' I asked Ron.

'Oh yes,' he said. 'I usually spend a good deal of the time going around the toilets and making sure the children are behaving themselves properly. If the exhibition isn't finished I may well find that I'll spend a good deal of time in there' [putting the finishing touches to it].

(Fieldnote)

On Sunday I visited the school in the afternoon because there was a craft fair. Arriving at the fair at about 2 o'clock Marie was seated at the entrance, selling raffle tickets. The fair was very busy and the hall, the quiet room and the small hall were all filled with stalls and visitors. Ron was there chatting and smiling, 'pressing the flesh' as politicians might say. He had a stall where he was selling his photographs taken in Giverney, France, of Monet's garden. . . .

(Fieldnote)

The most obvious effect of Ron's afterschool work was that he frequently worked well into the evening. It was not unusual for him to be in-school two or three evenings a week. He also put in time at the weekend. In short, Ron worked long hours. Early in the fieldwork I appreciated how many hours Ron worked, as the following note conveys:

I found Ron dressed in a track suit. At 5 o'clock, he was going over to the recreation ground to help set up tomorrow's village festival. 'What time will you get home?' I asked.

'Oh, I don't know,' he said, 'perhaps 7 or 8 p.m. is when I'll get away from here. The worst thing about tomorrow is that it's such a long day,' he said, 'I'll be on duty at seven in the morning, back here, and it'll go on till six or so.' Ron's work schedule is undoubtedly heavy. He's had five days in school, although part of one morning was spent as a representative of the primary sector on the LEA curriculum group, which is an added duty, rather than a relief from his present responsibilities. He will be working till 7 or 8 o'clock tonight, all day tomorrow. He'll probably get Sunday off. He's got a full week ahead of him next week. Staff meeting is on Monday, which seems to go on till almost 6 o'clock and next Saturday he's got an INSET day. He clearly puts a lot of time and energy into the job.

(Fieldnote)

Perhaps I should have added to this note that he often worked both a day and a night shift as well.

Ron worked with a variety of different groups out of school hours, but after the school's staff, the governors were the most important. Prior to the start of the school year Ron spoke of his 'anxiety about the governing body, about how strong it's going to be, I will be putting effort into the governing body to try and get them to work effectively' (interview).

He felt a need to do this because first, as a result of the 1986 Education Act, a newly constituted body was to be established in the autumn term and, second, Ron intimated he did not have a uniformly high regard for the calibre of the Governors (a comment passed in a staff meeting, Fieldnote). When the new governing body was constituted the members were not unknown to Ron. Some were survivors from the previous governing body, or they were stalwarts of other groups, like the PTA. The chair of governors, Wendy, was a surviving parent governor. Thus, there was no sharp break with the past.

I attended one formal governors' meeting, witnessed numerous visits by Wendy to the school and was in school for one of the visiting governors' excursions. Wendy's visits to school coincided with bringing (or collecting) her daughter. She was a regular frequenter of the staffroom. She and Ron kept one another informed of events. As the school year wore on Wendy made increasing references to the effects of the 1988 Education Act, (such as LMS, charges for educational visits, sex education).

I do not believe Ron perceived the governors to cause him any major difficulties. Relations were warm, the atmosphere in meetings convivial. They did not appear to question his personal authority, nor query the school's policies. I think they trusted Ron as an experienced and well established head both in the profession as a whole and their community in particular. The following fieldnote was made after I attended a governors' meeting:

> No-one challenged Ron. Everyone seemed to be supporting him and there was a good deal of interplay, often non-verbal between Wendy and Ron. I got a strong impression of the two of them working in concert. Indeed, on one or two occasions Wendy deferred to Ron saying: 'Do you think we have said enough about that, shall we move on?' and on one occasion Ron nodded and so we did. (The meeting ended at 10.05 p.m.)
>
> (Fieldnote)

Although the governors were not a negative force to be reckoned with I am not convinced Ron saw them as a positive power. He dutifully attended the meetings accepting that it was a necessary expenditure of a headteacher's time. He also recognized the governors' need for information about the school through his written report to them and their visits to the school. However, while he complied with his responsibilities he believed they did not take their share of the tasks. Ron expressed to me the feeling that the governors left him to do too much for them (interview). Dealing with the governors took up his time and, in the process, did not relieve him of work, but left him with more to do!

For example, when at the end of the summer term Ron reflected on the school year 1988–89, he spoke about how the requirements of the 1988 Education Act had not been shared by the governing body. Ron noted a reluctance by the governors to meet their new obligations because:

> it was seen as extra work and I felt that it rebounded back to me. . .I think it means that I personally have to answer and comply with and respond to a lot of information that comes in that is not officially my responsibility to do. We only have one delegated governor for any areas of responsibility and that is for LMS, he actually sees all the information that I receive. I see him every now and again and we talk about it and that's as far as its gone. The offer of having other meetings in between governing body meetings, to discuss what's coming, was not taken up. It's worth remembering that we haven't actually been able to have a nominated governor to make a school visit for two terms.
>
> (Interview)

The governors might not have been a hindrance to Ron, but neither were they much of a help to him in dealing with the initiatives and changes he and the school faced.

Dealing with In-coming Mail

So far I have placed a strong emphasis upon Ron's encounters with individuals and groups. While much the greater portion of his time was taken up with face-to-face meetings which were planned and unplanned, formal and informal, Ron also worked with documents. He wrote letters to parents and officers of the LEA, produced reports for the governors and completed a variety of forms and in-voices. If possible, he preferred to speak to LEA staff and others on the phone rather than write, but he could not avoid writing or dealing with documents. Typically he would deal with letters and forms in between his meetings and encounters. Sometimes he would set aside a morning to catch up on a backlog of material. If he was especially busy in the week and the evenings he would occa-sionally visit school on a Sunday afternoon to ensure he was up to date with the administration.

Although Ron attached little importance to the administrative part of his work, once describing it as opting out of headship (interview), he nevertheless was increasingly occupied by the arrival, through the post, of documents emanat-ing from central government. During the spring and summer terms in particular, letters and documents arrived on Ron's desk to inform him and others (staff and governors) of the organizational and educational changes created by the 1988 Education Act.

From time to time, Ron allowed me to rifle through his in-tray to examine his mail. During one such search in February I noted his in-tray contained five documents from the DES (*Second ERA Bulletin, Information on Teachers' Superan-nuation, Animals and Plants in School, ERA and Collective Worship, Charges for School Activities*); and eighteen documents from the LEA (covering PTA lettings, com-munity education, LMS newsletter, staffing survey, heads' meetings, property conditions survey, health and safety, swimming, libraries, pupil care conference, multicultural education, science education, the whole curriculum, competitive tendering, schoolteacher appraisal scheme). The in-tray also contained papers concerned with school insurance, the INSET cluster group, a six-a-side football tournament, hiring charges, invitation to a retirement, notes from Helen and Dave, and papers from the local council concerning a Buggy Club. Much of this material consisted of letters of two or more pages; some were longer documents. Ron told me that while a few had been there since the start of term, 'most had arrived in the last two weeks' (fieldnote).

There are three points to make about Ron's work with documentary mate-rial. First, it struck me that there was a lot for him to read and digest. Indeed, as the school year wore on and documents from the National Curriculum Council (NCC) and Schools Examination and Assessment Council (SEAC) began to arrive, he faced an increasing and accelerating reading load. Moreover, while much material continued to arrive from or via the LEA, some documents came direct from central government or its agencies. In turn, this meant that while he could ask officers of the LEA for guidance on some issues, on others he was responding to more distant and remote partners. Consequently, Ron felt he needed to read the documents from the DES, NCC, and SEAC more carefully than LEA material and, since there was an increasing amount of material from the former, it meant he was devoting more time to reading than either he previously did or, importantly, wanted to. Dealing with all the new information was a frustration to him because it reduced the amount of time and attention he could devote to other things (fieldnote and interview) which he regarded as more important to headship — a point I will return to in Section 3.

Second, from examining the documents mailed to Ron as head of the school, it was apparent that while he had a lot to read, he also had access to a lot of information, some of which came only to him, or which he received before others associated with the school. Furthermore, when his frequent encounters with personnel in the school and contacts with others who played a part in the school's life are added to the documentary data he dealt with, it is clear that Ron received or collected a lot of information, most of which he needed to process and often act upon. Like other managers, an important part of Ron's work was gathering and processing information (Hultman 1989:148).

Third, and arising from all that has been presented so far in this section, Ron met, was contacted by and dealt with a relatively diverse number of individuals, groups and agencies. It was characteristic of his work that he was at the centre of an extensive communication network (Coulson 1986:20) which included all within the school, groups close to the school (governors, PTA) and those beyond the school's immediate community (INSET cluster group, LEA, local council, government agencies). Indeed, so important to Ron's work as head were his networking and information processing that I will consider them more closely.

Networker: Gathering, Processing and Acting on Information

There were six overlapping aspects to Ron's networking. First, Ron did not gather or process every single piece of information that came his way with the same amount of interest or attention. Rather, he paid particular attention to and placed greatest emphasis upon what was happening inside the school. Second, as he kept open his channels of communication in the school, he also monitored what the staff and children were doing. Third, he consciously reflected upon what he saw and heard. Fourth, by keeping in touch with colleagues and monitoring their work he simultaneously influenced what the teachers did. Fifth, by gathering and processing information he was able to resolve problems and make decisions. Sixth, some of the information he handled was confidential. I will present each of these six aspects in turn.

Paying attention to the significant
I once put it to Ron that he dealt with a lot of information. He agreed, however, he believed he dealt with two kinds of information: the transient and the significant. The former was information that came in and required him to do something quickly (pass on messages). Dealing with that was only a matter of distribution and transferring information. The significant was

> what's happened in the school at a particular time, the feeling of how people are, how children are. . .When I say people I'm not just talking

about teaching staff, it embraces anybody who might be in school for any purpose at any one time. You think about these a lot, because if you don't you are going to say the wrong thing to somebody some time, the insensitive thing, or people are going to be slightly offended if you haven't remembered something they told you a fortnight previously.

(Interview)

As reported earlier, Ron toured the school and made time to wander around the units. These visitations were opportunities for Ron to find out what teachers and children were doing.

While I was rummaging in the cupboard I noticed Ron was wandering into the third year unit and when I'd finished getting what I wanted from the cupboard I saw him coming out of the fourth year unit.

Ron asked had I seen Marie's work on bottles? 'No,' I said.
'Come and have a look at it,' he said. We walked into the fourth year unit and he showed me the very fine writing the children had done and artwork using paint, pastels and pencils, of old bottles.

(Fieldnote)

In addition to visits during the school day he made use of time after school,

a key time is after school. . .it's when we talk about what's been happening in the day, we talk about individual pieces of work, work that has been around during the day. It was very interesting, [today] for example, to talk to the third year [staff] about the work they've been doing on structure.

(Interview)

When, later in the school year, Ron expressed frustration at being out of school more than he believed he should, he said his absences prevented him from doing things in school. I asked, what would he be doing if he were in school? He replied, 'I'd be spending a lot more time with the first year because there was a gap between the quality and the work that was going on in the two halves of that unit' (interview).

Ron's comments and my observations of him touring the building and talking with staff suggest five points. First, he was an active networker. He was frequently walking around school, talking to staff, keeping open the channels of communication between himself and staff. Second, in constantly meeting staff, listening to them and paying attention to them, he exhibited concern and consideration for them. Third, he maintained the network with such consistency that it became clear he placed a high priority on knowing what was happening in the school. Fourth, within school he put a high premium on finding out what the teachers and children were doing. Fifth, by taking a strong and active interest in classroom activities he demonstrated the importance he placed upon teaching and learning.

Ron might not have taught very regularly, but he signalled his continuing interest in the professional work of the school through his networking and by what he focused on when he talked with the teachers. In other words, his networking in the school enabled him to monitor what was happening.

Monitoring

Ron monitored what occurred in the school by both direct and indirect means. Both means were helped by the school's design. The open plan layout exposed staff to Ron's scrutiny of their work. The direct means were his personal observations of the teaching and learning and his conversations with children, teachers and others in the teaching areas (Madge, the ancillary assistant; parent helpers; students). Indirectly he heard about learning activities from the unit leaders or the deputy and INSET co-ordinator. There was a well established organizational structure in the school which created a network of formal reporting and informal feedback to Ron. Each pair of teachers planned together and gave to Ron their termly plans. He also met each pair to discuss their plans, although during 1988–89 this pattern did not always work because of other demands on Ron's time. If unit leaders had a concern they let Ron know. In one unit there was a teacher who was finding aspects of her work difficult. When I asked the unit leader if Ron had a clear understanding of what was going on she said, 'Yes, I think so, because I've spoken to him quite a lot about it' (interview). Information flowed into Ron:

> Ron told me that there had been a meeting between Marie and Ken, a unit meeting, last week when Marie had tried to review the week's work on the anniversary project. Ron said that Ken had been virtually silent, he'd said nothing, even to Marie's direct questions. I asked Ron if he'd been there. 'No, but Marie told Dave about it.' The inference was that Dave had told Ron.
>
> (Fieldnote)

And:

> For the last part of the afternoon I was in the fourth year unit mounting the children's work. I'd been busy for about twenty minutes when Ron came in. 'Dave says you've done some nice work,' he said. Clearly there had been an exchange of information between deputy and head and it was a small sign of the kind of feedback and the monitoring that goes on in the school.
>
> (Fieldnote)

Just one teacher once voiced to me her disquiet about such transfer of information. She did not like things being said behind her back (interview). Others saw it as a legitimate part of the head's work. One teacher said, 'I think Ron's a lot shrewder than you initially think. . .His job's to know what's happening in these units (interview).

And staff recognized that Ron was monitoring what was happening in the school:

> *Teacher*: I think he is all the time assessing and looking at gaps and where things can be developed. . .I think he is particularly perceptive.
>
> (Interview)

Teacher: He knows the kids and what they're capable of and he'll glance and take things in very quickly (interview).

Deputy: He knows everything that's going on in the school. . .He's always looking, watching, listening. . .He operates on a sort of information system, always listening and picking things up.

(Interview)

After some of his tours I invited him to share with me what he had perceived.

Ron had been worried (in the past) by Ken's tendency to be rather heavy-handed in discipline, but today was pleasantly surprised that Ken was using humour with the children. In the second year unit Ron noticed a large number of project books had arrived and he was concerned whether these books were of appropriate quality and whether they might create too heavy a reliance on books alone. . .He took [the books] as a sign that the planning of the project work in the unit might need to be more sophisticated than at present. . .Planning shouldn't just be concerned with identifying a topic, asking the library to find a bundle of books that go with the project and then utilizing those books as an aide to the teachers and the learners. . .

He'd been watching how the new pairs of teachers in their respective units were balancing and maybe there were signals there he ought to keep an eye on. . .

The kitchen staff were worried about low numbers at lunch. . .

(Fieldnote)

Ron did not passively watch or wait to be told things. He studiously sought out individual's views by asking questions. He was curious and enquired into what people did, thought and felt, as I experienced:

'Did you enjoy showing assembly?' asked Ron. Ron seems to ask quite a few leading questions. He's gathering data every bit as much as I am; his data is about what people feel and think inside the school.

(Fieldnote)

He used showing assemblies to find out what the children had done and learned. While rehearsing the children in his unit for the next day's showing assembly, Dave said to them:

Look, do you remember what happened with the third years at the last showing assembly? Mr Lacey asked some really hard questions, you will have to do better than you are now to answer those.

(Fieldnote)

Showing assemblies were clearly times when Ron monitored work in the units. When Dave and Jean's unit presented their work the children stood up to display and talk about specific items:

Throughout the whole proceedings, Ron asked questions of the children, 'What was the propeller made of? How old is a penny farthing bike?

When were they last used? Why were these bikes called penny farthings? Does anybody know what a farthing is or was? What is an autogyro? Are they safe? What were the tyres on these bicycles made of? Were they soft or hard? Did we call them pneumatic or not?' Just once or twice when none of the children could provide the answers, he asked the audience (all the other children in the school) and, less occasionally, he might ask for clarification from Dave. 'What is special about the colour of a Model T Ford?' he asked one of the children who had drawn a picture of it.

Ron would put in some humorous comments to lighten it all. For example, one of the children had done a drawing of an Austin Seven and had said that someone once drove one to the top of Ben Nevis and it took seven and a half hours. 'That's a long time,' said Ron at the end of the child's story. 'Do you think he stopped for petrol on the way up?' Many of the children in the audience, as well as from the second year, smiled at this and so did the parents sitting at the back of the hall. When Ron saw a drawing of a penny farthing he commented, 'You know this was the nineteenth-century equivalent of a mountain bike.' But the questions continued throughout...He would also ask questions about how the children did things...When examples of needlework were held up he said, 'You did initial drawings of them and what types of stitching did you use?' '

(Fieldnote)

Like Dave, other staff knew that Ron's questions were not only stimulants to the children to say more about their work, they were also ways of testing the staff as well and of setting high standards (teacher interview). Moreover, recognizing Ron was monitoring their work, staff were aware that he was a critical enquirer and they could detect his approval or disapproval. One teacher said,

He sort of allows a standard to be set somehow by praising, but not praising anything he doesn't like. I think he sets quite a high standard through that means. I think you can see that in showing assembly in that he will only praise what's good. He won't make a big meal out of something that's really fairly mediocre.

(Interview)

At the end of the showing assembly Ron said, 'We've seen some lovely work, science work, structured work, maps, photographs, a lot of maths work, poetry, factual writing, artwork.' He listed all areas of the curriculum that had been displayed in this work and he said, 'All that work is of a high standard.'

(Fieldnote)

In effect, he was a quality controller. I asked him once how he ensured that curricular decisions in staff meetings influenced practice. Ron said, 'You monitor it by discussing with groups what's happening...You also monitor it by seeing what's happening in the classroom and talking to the teachers' (interview).

On another occasion, when he, Dave and Marie agreed that more guidance needed to be given to the work of the staff, Ron told the staff in a meeting what his expectations were concerning the school's handwriting policy. As a further impetus to this Ron told me, in private:

I'll also be making visits to all the units this first half-term and I shall be looking at the work the children have done, looking at the relevance of activities, looking at the plans that the teachers have made. . . .I see these visits as inspections.

(Fieldnote)

Monitoring, then, involved judgments. Indeed, from numerous comments he made to me, it was apparent that when he looked at work in the school he was evaluating it. For example, when I asked him what he thought of the school's Christmas production for parents he replied, 'I thought the first and second year production was a competent top infant performance and I thought the third and fourth year production lacked cohesion' (fieldnote).

Sometimes he judged how things had been organized. For example, in this case, the Tenth Anniversary Exhibition:

I now wonder if it might not have been better to have stayed with the existing topics, rather than switching. The topic they chose, and it hadn't got anything to do with me, was perhaps too broad and the time scale was perhaps too tight.

(Fieldnote)

As the school year came to a close, he looked back over the school year. 'While talking generally to me, in his office he said, "It's been a disappointing year"' (fieldnote). And, on another occasion, while talking with Ron about the school's organizational structure, he said,

Take the fourth year for example. It seems to me that if we had had a very rigid idea of working together, then things there could have been very difficult indeed. We have also never had the situation in this school where all four units have all been working very closely together as pairs of teachers. There has usually been one unit at least where things haven't gone very smoothly. That doesn't bother me too much. I think over the whole year perhaps only one unit has worked closely and that will be the third year unit.

(Fieldnote)

Another time he spoke in terms of curriculum balance:

I don't think mathematics is particularly well taught, there are patches of it where it's well taught and by that I would look at the increase in three dimensional work, this year, which has been very significant. . .I also think the use of computers, in three of the four units has shown a definite improvement. Certainly more than last year. I think the range of the written work generally reflects good balance, but I don't think there has been a consistent quality throughout the school. Practical writing has been very good, but I don't think that the imaginative or creative writing has been as good as it has been. At the moment I see little evidence of children being read poetry.

(Interview)

Reflecting

Monitoring the work of individual teachers, the units and the school as a whole provided Ron with a lot of intelligence to process. Generally, he processed the information in a reflective manner. For example, every Monday, after school, staff met together for a curriculum development meeting. These began around 3.45 p.m. and were supposed to end at 5.30 p.m. since staff had an agreed guillotine. Some staff left then (usually Ken and Sarah) while others stayed on, thus the discussions might continue informally until around 6.00 p.m. Each meeting focused on one main topic, though occasionally two topics were considered. During the school year a range of curriculum matters were discussed: individual subject areas including National Curriculum core subjects; project planning; school policies; INSET.

Each week's agenda was important to Ron, yet it was not the only content of the meeting that interested him, but also the dynamic of the staff group. These meetings were the only formal occasion in the week when all the teaching staff gathered together and worked as a group. Consequently, Ron could observe how individuals behaved in the group; how unit pairs related to one another; how the group of staff functioned as a group; what each of these elements might imply for himself and others on the staff.

The first staff meeting of the school year looked at the staff's priorities for curriculum review. A lively discussion developed around mathematics, and some staff revealed marked differences in their teaching of maths (Ken and Marie). At the close of the meeting:

> On my way out I bumped into Ron who'd left the room beforehand as I'd hung around to pack up my briefcase and listen to people's reactions. He said there was obviously a lot to reflect on in that meeting and it would take him about two or three days to chew over what was said.
>
> (Fieldnote)

The next day Ron said,

> I find that [last night's meeting] quite a salutary type of meeting for all sorts of reasons. . .It certainly made me rethink the possible structures for both individual unit work and also, connected with that, it made me aware of the possibilities of friction within the unit. I thought it looked alright, the balance of opposites [in the units].
>
> (Fieldnote)

Some of Ron's reflections were prompted by my need to be updated on events I had missed. On one occasion he told me what had happened at a previous meeting. The first part of the interview described the subject content of the meeting — each unit pair of teachers, in turn, shared a range of children's writing. Later they looked at the attainment targets in the writing section of the National Curriculum English document. For Ron the meeting highlighted the need to develop a broader range of writing across the school (interview). After another staff meeting Ron said, 'It's got to be very carefully looked at' (fieldnote), meaning he would need to think about what had been discussed at the meeting.

Careful attention to what people were doing and thinking was not always something he did by himself. From time to time he involved Dave and Marie:

> Ron, Dave and Marie were in the staffroom talking about the links between INSET, teacher development and curriculum development. Ron said that this [autumn] term the [staff] meetings they'd held had not progressed as far as he might have hoped and that several meetings had become sidetracked by the concerns of Ken, and to some extent, Helen too. The side tracks were not so much diversions as necessary responses to individuals' needs. Dave agreed, but was unhappy at the pace of development. . .As far as he was concerned curriculum development this term had not been very good. He felt it was a wasted term. 'We've not wasted the term,' said Ron.
> 'I think we have,' said Dave.
>
> (Fieldnote)

Whether Ron reflected alone, or in the company of others, what he was doing was interpreting the intelligence he received and searching for meanings. He sifted through what he saw and believed was happening in order to make sense of this information and to understand what it meant for the present and future. Moreover, what he saw and knew at any one time was compared with his previous experience and knowledge of what had happened in school in the past. When he once spoke to me about making judgments about the school's curriculum, he said he collected evidence which he then:

> Weighed with the objectivity of history and precedent. . .In other words, the objectivity one brings to it is an accumulation, over the years, of what you have actually seen happen and how you know things could happen. . .Does that make sense?
>
> (Interview)

It makes sense in that Ron used his institutional memory to contrast the present with the past.

As Schon says, following investigations of the reflections of business managers:

> Sometimes, when reflection is triggered by uncertainty, the manager says, in effect, 'This is puzzling: how can I understand it?' Sometimes, when a sense of opportunity provokes reflection, the manager asks, 'What can I make of this?' Sometimes, when managers are surprised by the success of their own intuitive knowing they ask themselves 'What have I really been doing?'
>
> (1986:42)

Furthermore:

> Organizations. . .are repositories of cumulatively built up knowledge: principles and maxims of practice, images of mission and identity, facts

about the task environment, techniques of operation and stories of past experience which serve as exemplars for future action. When a manager reflects-in-action he or she draws on this stock of organizational knowledge, adapting it to some present instances.

(Schon 1986:42)

Ron drew upon his accumulated knowledge of the school to make sense of what was happening and to determine what to do next. He monitored not simply to judge how well he thought the school was performing, but also to gauge what next to do and where to put his efforts. While talking about whole school development and how he devoted attention to individuals, unit pairs and other teams, Ron added,

That's only after a lot of sifting. . .It's thinking about the observations that then determines what course of action you're going to take. . .I don't think I do anything that isn't considered even though, at times, it may appear spontaneous. That's not playing games, that's just the way I am.

(Interview)

While on a previous occasion he had said.

How you respond [as a head] will in many ways be determined by those perceptions picked up during the day. . .It means you have to do an awful lot of thinking about the job, what's happening, an awful lot of interpreting and making decisions.

(Interview)

For Ron, monitoring and reflecting were not ends in themselves, but rather, they were the means for determining what next to attend to.

Networking was influential
Generally, Ron's way of collecting information had an influence upon the teaching staff. I have already claimed that the teachers knew he was monitoring them and that they discerned what he approved and disapproved. For sure, the staff were aware that his contacts and dealings with them had an effect upon them, as they told me in interviews:

Dave: He sets an unsaid, undemonstrated, unspoken, unpractised expectation. How he does it I haven't a clue. But it's there all the time. It's partly historical. It's partly from his relationships with people. It's very, very rarely a direct, straightforward command and yet it's still there. And it doesn't matter who they are or what they are, that expectation stays the same. How it's done I have no idea, but it's there. He knows everything that's going on in the school. He knows the children individually for the most part. When he actually gets to know that I don't know. I assume when he's walking round the school. . .

(Interview)

Teacher: He's good at leaving people alone and letting them learn. He's good at praising when things are good. He's good at drawing arguments out of people when they're perhaps in a muddle as to what their argument is and allowing a forum of discussion.

(Interview)

Teacher: I think he does have quite a big influence on the staff in his subtle way. I think most people are just a little bit nervous of him. I feel it. As I said before, I think he knows exactly what he wants, the sort of approach he wants the staff to take towards the children, although he won't say anything. He doesn't come round and encourage a great deal, but I think he seems to somehow know what's going on.

(Interview)

Teacher: I think expectations of you as a teacher are extremely high, which in itself is very motivating. . .[and those expectations] they must start with Ron. . .I don't think, for example, that he would let you ever get away with unthought-out responses . . .He asks you to explain what you are thinking.

(Interview 26.6.89)

For his part, Ron was very aware that his contacts with staff were influential.

I think if I had to identify one key area of, if you want to call it, curriculum influence, it would be time spent between half past three and half past five, almost every day in talking to individual teachers or groups of teachers, not necessarily in a planned way, but sometimes in a planned way, about what they're doing and how things have been going.

(Interview)

Ron knew that meeting informally with his colleagues, in their workplaces, enabled him not only to find out things, but also to praise their efforts, offer support, seed ideas and steer teachers in directions he approved. I once asked him why he talked to staff.

I think its all sorts of different reasons. I think they value that time I give in terms of recognition of their efforts, that's one dimension of it. I think the second thing is that it's a time when they can show and talk about things they're particularly excited or pleased about, that we can share. I mean I talked with Helen about some writing she was getting mounted up from some of the children. So it's talking about the results of their day's craftsmanship. I think it's also an opportunity to develop that professional craftsmanship by discussion. Something that can be apparently mundane and trivial. 'I think we've got a book on it somewhere,' or 'Surely we've got some more of those in the school. I'll go and see if I can find them' — that type of exercise which is useful.

(Interview)

For Ron, networking — that is talking to teachers — was at the very heart of his work as head. It was one of the things he most wanted to do because he regarded his contacts and discussions with staff as one of the main ways he contributed to their professional development. Moreover, developing teachers was one of his sources of job satisfaction. 'I do put an emphasis on [developing teachers], more so probably than anything else, because that's what the job's about. There's nothing else for headship in a sense' (interview). When I suggested there were other things to headship, such as administration, he said,

> Oh bugger that!. . .it takes up time and if I'm feeling tired, as I have been in the last fortnight, I can go and have a tremendous choice, really. I can go close my door and do boring bits of paper all afternoon, drink coffee and feel I've done something useful, or try and kid myself I've done something useful.
> GS: But what would be 'doing something useful'?
> Ron: Not doing that! Anything but that. No, something useful would be spending time with some teachers and some children, talking to people, talking to children, talking to teachers.
>
> (Interview)

On another occasion he answered my question about what he found most satisfying in headship by saying, 'What individual children do. That's what gives me the greatest pleasure, [and] people becoming better teachers in the context of the school' (interview). Kate, Ron's wife, thought that Ron's highspots in headship would be

> to do with relationships with people, not major events, or the digging of the swimming pool or the Donkey Derby. . .It's when members of the staff have responded and something has happened in school through a member of staff that sort of *enacts* something he [Ron] feels about education, something's right, going on educationally, then that gives him an incredible buzz.
>
> (Interview)

Kate had heard, in the past, how teachers were appreciative of Ron's influence. 'His staff say to me, as ever so many have in the past, "We've learned all we know because of working with Ron"' (interview).

Recognizing Ron's wish to see teachers develop alters the character of his contacts with staff. Ron was not simply watching the teachers in a supervisory sense. He was observing them to see how he, or others, could help them develop. Ron consciously used his seemingly casual encounters with staff after school, not only to gather information about their teaching, but also to prompt the teachers and reinforce what he approved of. The school's internal communication network was used by Ron to receive information and to transmit his messages to the staff about teaching.

Resolving problems

By continually gathering information and carefully processing it Ron was able to keep abreast of issues and problems in the school and respond to them as and when he felt it best to do so. For example, throughout much of the year there were professional and interpersonal tensions between the teachers in two of the units. Ron periodically intervened in an effort to alleviate the difficulties. Yet he remained constantly alert to the tensions. He frequently monitored and reflected upon the situations as he saw them and heard about them.

As noted earlier, reflection helped Ron to make sense of what he perceived and aided him in deciding what course of action to take. He appeared to reflect quite a lot, perhaps because at any one moment he was dealing simultaneously with a number of problems. Some problems were immediate and specific (absent staff, pupils' lost property). Others, such as the interpersonal tensions amongst staff, or one teacher's poor performance during the spring and summer terms, needed a longer timescale to remedy. When Ron faced a long and complex issue he made active use of the internal network to consult with staff in order to help him resolve the problem.

One of the clearest examples of such consultation occurred during the summer term. The problem began when the LEA informed Ron that, for the coming school year, the teaching staff would have to be reduced from 8 to 7.6 teachers. Such a reduction would have dismembered the organizational structure of the school which was based on four pairs of teachers. Ron informed the governors and they and he appealed to the LEA district officer. At first, however, the officer was unsympathetic to these appeals. Ron therefore discussed the possibility of redeployment with all the staff together. Ken volunteered to be redeployed to his home town.

While Ken's redeployment was being arranged, the cut in staff numbers was rescinded by the LEA, with the proviso that a replacement for Ken be made only on a temporary basis. This change of heart occurred because, in the meanwhile, the LEA had offered Dave the acting headship at a nearby school for one term, to which the governors of Orchard school had agreed.

Ron now did not have to make an alteration to the structure of the units and classes. Instead he faced as, he said, 'one big problem. . .who to appoint as the acting deputy head' (interview). Ron saw three candidates — Marion, Sarah and Marie — all of whom he regarded as having the potential to become deputies. He was thinking of a two or three-way job share. All three were happy with the idea of job sharing, as he discovered when they all met together. Ron also 'acknowledged that it would be easiest "for me to come up with the decision".' 'So why did you consult?' I asked.

> 'I think I felt I ought to consult [and] I think it was useful to consult,' said Ron. 'I think the consultations have given a better perspective, have provided an indication as to the strength of feeling and one isn't always aware of that.'
>
> 'Have you found anything you didn't know about?'
>
> 'No, but it is the strength of feeling I found out about. It's to do with relationships,' said Ron, 'and status, and how people view one another in school. It's easy to make assumptions about people's perceptions and how they feel about things.' Ron switched to talking about the Holland trip then, but as I was leaving the room he said, 'If there had been a unanimous view on this deputy headship then I would probably have accepted that. But there isn't. It [the deputy headship decision] digs right at the heart of the school.'
>
> (Fieldnote)

Ten days later he had reached a clearer position based upon a three-way division of labour and the strengths of the candidates as he saw them. He had written out his proposal and he gave me a copy. It amounted to:

Marion: dealing with routine management and organization (assemblies, duty rotas)

Marie: taking responsibility for school-based curriculum development (helping plan curriculum meetings, links with her INSET role)

Sarah: helping to induct new staff and supporting them (including students on school experience, liaison with local college). She would also share responsibility for acting as first point of contact in Ron's absence.

Ron had given the proposal to the three teachers.

I asked them to think about it and pass on their thoughts to me today, and all three of them have done that this morning. Marie said she would like to do it, and wants to be considered as deputy. She would like a job-share with another, but the idea of a job-share between three she thinks is a bit cumbersome, so if I'm thinking of a job-share between three not to consider her. So the catch in that is if I wanted it to go three ways it couldn't, since she wouldn't do it. He smiled.

Marion had come in to see him and she had reiterated about not wanting to become a permanent deputy head. She felt a job-share was OK with both the others, but she said that there could be some interpersonal difficulties. Ron said he was aware of this, since he knows one colleague can be threatening. Sarah had said she did not want to work with one of the other two. Ron looked at me, 'Do you have an answer?' I remained quiet.

(Fieldnote)

After a long pause Ron spoke again, at first his comments were mainly a reiteration of the above. Then he dwelt a little on one of the three named teachers and the tensions he felt she sometimes created. Towards the end Ron said,

It's quite a puzzle this deputy headship. . .so I'm just going to think it through a lot more. It's desirable to decide as soon as possible; I think I've got to sort it out before the unit pairings can be determined. There's a self-esteem element that has got to be thought through in terms of how they see each other and how others see them. . .It's like 'Dungeons and Dragons' [a strategy game] really. . .every attempt to resolve it or come to a decision on it, every tentative possibility makes you see seven, eight, ten other problems. So you come up with a sub-proposal, or a compromise. He was biting his pen as he said this and he fell silent again.

(Fieldnote)

A week later and Ron told me that there was still some resistance to the three-way job share, but the time was now coming when a decision needed to be made and he was probably going to make it.

(Fieldnote)

In the last fortnight of the school year Ron announced a three-way distribution of responsibilities between Marie, Marion and Sarah. The decision was reported at a staff meeting and the three staff directly involved appeared to go along with the plan as did other colleagues. (However, as a postscript, Marie's initial reluctance re-emerged over the summer holiday and in September she was not party to the job share.)

Two points can be highlighted from this illustration of problem solving. First, this seemingly singular issue actually impinged upon a number of others. Unlike his routine tasks and the brief and immediate problems he encountered each day, this one was a *story* (Acker 1988:13); that is, a problem which carries on over time and is complicated with characters, action and episodes. Like the story of the potential staffing cut, the acting deputy's post would have widespread implications for other matters and Ron needed to think things through and weigh the relative strengths and weaknesses of his options. Also, in considering his options Ron was balancing different factors. He was taking into account the strengths of individuals, the effect of decisions upon individuals' self images and their esteem in the staff group, the viability of a job share. The process of consultation provided him with a lot of valuable information and exposed the complexity of the problem.

Second, in the absence of a consensus he was prepared to go his own way, which, perhaps, accounts for his persistence with a three-way job share. While willing to consult, Ron was also comfortable with making his own mind up. In other words, Ron would gather intelligence and reflect upon it, but he did not necessarily feel obliged to comply with what colleagues wished or preferred. Information did not always determine the decision he took, but it helped him to anticipate the implications and ramifications of the decisions made.

Confidential information

Being in the middle of an active communications network it was not surprising that he heard things he chose not to pass on to others. Individually staff would say things to him which he would not repeat elsewhere. Ron also shared some material with me which he regarded as confidential. On one occasion Ron said, 'There were a lot of things I would talk to you about last year that I wouldn't have talked to anybody else about' (interview).

In part, Ron's revelations can be accounted for by his willingness to aid the research through granting me access to his personal feelings and professional observations. Yet it could also be the case that he enjoyed having an audience and/or appreciated the opportunity to unburden himself by talking about private and confidential matters.

Ron also acknowledged that there were some things he did not grant me access to, nor anyone else:

Ron:　Some [information] I will share with nobody. Some I will share with somebody else if it's necessary, I think. It is the most dangerous area of all, I think. Very dangerous.

GS:　Why dangerous?

Ron:　Well, I think people tell you information, tell you things which are very personal and private to them. They are not just telling you in confidence, they are also somehow passing over some form of control to you; they are giving a part of themselves to you, they probably wouldn't give to other people on trust. I think it's a strange dilemma that people probably need to do that, yet could well regret it afterwards [pause]. Yes, I think so.

GS: What about another kind of information then. Since there are also professional matters about an individual's performance.

Ron: That's equally as dangerous as the first actually.

GS: Why do you say that?

Ron: Because it is easy to let it slip unintentionally. Very easy to do that. The conversations and situations you have with people and about people, sometimes other people will need to know that, and other times not necessarily need to know that. You can be put in a situation of trying to explain to somebody else who doesn't know the information, why people have acted in a particular way. I mean, it is very easy to illustrate it by giving them a piece of information.

(Interview)

Ron's notion of dangerous material perhaps explains why he tried to keep to one principle of procedure when dealing with conflicts between staff. When Ken and Marie were finding working together difficult in September, Ron saw each teacher individually, but he made it clear to both he would not act as a go-between. He was prepared to be involved so long as whatever was said to him was also said to the third party (based on Fieldnote).

Another aspect of what was secret was what Ron thought of his colleagues. Headteachers, of course, write and read references on staff (and in Ron's LEA these remained confidential) and, sometimes, engage in off-the-record contacts, although in Ron's case I have no evidence of the latter. Moreover, Ron evaluated the staff — as some of his comments concerning the acting deputy head appointment demonstrate. These judgments could be both appraisals of teacher quality and expressions of expectation about teachers' careers. He was, privately, a talent spotter and career forecaster:

Ron: One should be able to identify within your unit leaders people who are likely to be leaving in the next couple of years for deputy headships. You should be able to identify people who are not unit leaders, who could be in that position in another three years, that's a general pattern.

GS: Is that the way it's been in the past?

Ron: Yes, most of the time.

GS: Is that the way it is now?

Ron: Not quite. I can only see a couple of potential heads.

(Interview)

In forming career judgments on the staff Ron was not simply conducting covert teacher appraisals. He was thinking about teachers' and the school's development, since it was recognized that the school had previously thrived upon a throughput of teachers who, having worked hard and contributed to curriculum developments were promoted either internally or elsewhere. Anticipating which staff might move on was also an attempt to gauge what opportunities might exist for enlisting new recruits who would make fresh contributions to the school.

Ron's confidential appraisals were formative judgments, and helped him to decide on courses of action. For example, during the winter period Ron noted that Dave was a little less consistent than formerly:

[Dave's] presence wasn't around this morning, first thing, particularly in terms of supervision and in checking that the school was running smoothly by the clock.

(Interview)

Over a three month period Ron felt he had detected a drop in Dave's enthusiasm and support for colleagues. Ron attributed this pattern in Dave's work to his disappointment after a number of unsuccessful applications for headship in the autumn term. While recognizing the cause of Dave's reduced effort, Ron nevertheless felt 'the pattern has to change' and decided to take action to encourage and support Dave (based on Fieldnote).

Being centrally located in the school's communication network and being an active networker meant Ron knew a lot, either from what he saw, heard or was told. Also, some of what he learned was confidential, being sensitive information he would not share with others. Moreover, Ron formed his personal judgments of the staff and these he largely kept to himself. The combination of public, private and personal intelligence which he held placed him, like other primary heads, in a privileged position (Laws and Dennison 1991:55). Ron not only knew a lot, he knew some of the school's secrets.

In closing this section, there are ten points to make about Ron's work as headteacher of Orchard school. First, Ron was not a remote figure. He was approachable and accessible to his staff and visitors. He was at the centre of an extensive and active network of contacts inside the school and beyond.

Second, Ron often dealt with visitors to the school. The arrival of visitors could be expected or unannounced. In the case of the latter, Ron was dealing with unplanned encounters which required him to be spontaneous. Ron also dealt with a high number of problems which he and/or others wanted resolved.

Third, Ron's work was a mix of planned and unplanned activities. He dealt with routine tasks, and unplanned occurrences. Some tasks were of short duration and simple, others were stories, unfolding over time and complex. Activities also overlapped, and impinged upon other aspects of the school. Nor should it be overlooked that there was a dramatic quality to some events since they were dynamic and had an emotional content (Acker 1988:7). Although some of Ron's work was new, there was also a pattern to his work since the annual cycle of schooling provided some predictability to his tasks and encounters.

Fourth, Ron worked with a diverse number of individuals and groups, before and especially during and after school. He worked long hours, often late into the evening and during some weekends. Much of his work was face-to-face, but he also dealt with the school's paperwork. There were some signs that the amount of time he devoted to documentation was increasing as information from the DfE and SEAC began to arrive in school. Ron also felt he was spending more time than formerly off site during the school day, as a result of briefings concerning the requirements of the 1988 Education Act.

Fifth, although Ron gave time to all who contacted him, and while he expressed concern about the contribution of the school's governors, he placed greatest importance on his work within the school and with the teaching staff. He took a strong interest in the teaching and learning that was taking place in the school. He placed a high premium on trying to develop the teachers.

Sixth, although he no longer taught children on a regular basis, he regarded headship as a hands-on experience. He felt he needed to be in school, watching the action, joining in. Through his questions, attention and praise he exemplified what he expected and wanted. He also made it fairly obvious what he was not keen on. Ron's monitoring influenced the staff. When he toured the school and visited staff he not only collected information, he also promoted his preferences.

Seventh, Ron thought deeply about what was happening in the school. It was characteristic of him to deliberate before responding to others and he gave himself and others time to think about ideas and proposals. He was neither hasty in decision-making himself nor did he expect it of others. As such, Ron projected to the staff the image of a reflective practitioner. Ron regarded reflection as a key element in good teachers:

> [good teaching involves] the ability to think carefully, deeply and constructively about what you're doing and why. . .[teachers] often say they haven't got time and think life is too busy to think. . .The best teachers do both, they're very active but they're also very reflective in and out of the classroom.
>
> (Interview)

By being reflective himself Ron was not only being judicious, he was implicitly modelling how teachers should behave.

Eighth, in gathering information from a range of sources Ron had an extensive knowledge base. Moreover, his capacity and willingness to reflect on what he learned meant he was processing the information (Leithwood and Montgomery 1986:115); he was refining what he knew and making sense of it. Ron not only knew a lot he placed his own meanings upon the knowledge. And the distinction between knowledge and meaning is important. Heads who make meaning 'successfully achieve mastery over the noisy, incessant environment — rather than simply react, throw up their hands and live in a perpetual state of "present shock"' (Bennis 1984:65–6).

Furthermore, Ron's long standing knowledge of the school meant he held the institution's memory. When his knowledge of the past was coupled with his extensive awareness of what was presently happening in and around the school and his capacity to make sense of all he knew, Ron can be seen as the leading meaning-maker (Hultman 1989:148; see also Bennis and Nanus 1985; Bates 1986; Schon 1986).

When these nine points are added together they create a tenth. The information Ron gathered and processed provided him with a considerable amount of intelligence about the school. Indeed, when all the different kinds of information at Ron's disposal are amassed they show that Ron knew not just a lot, but a powerful amount. Ron's knowledge base was his power base.

Section 3: Power, Development and Change

From studying what Ron did I began to understand that underpinning many of his actions was a wish to control what happened in the school. This understanding grew when I considered the nature of power in the school, looked at how the school's curriculum was developing and focused upon Ron's response to externally generated changes. These three topics interrelate and together they show that Ron was powerful and wanted to direct developments in the school.

Power

My examination of the nature of power in Orchard school draws upon Hoyle's (1986) interpretation of Bacharach and Lawler's (1980) work. Hoyle starts from the Weberian definition that:

> Power is the probability that one actor within a social relationship will be in a position to carry out his own will, despite resistance, and regardless of the basis on which this probability rests.
>
> (Weber 1947, cited in Hoyle 1986:73)

While this definition is generally useful, the concept of power 'gains precision only as its inherent complexities are unpacked and given specific form' (Hoyle 1986:74). Hoyle agrees with Bacharach and Lawler that there are four sources of power, two types of power and four bases of power. The four sources of power are:

structural:	power as a property of a person's office or structural position;
personality:	power as a function of personal characteristics, such as charisma or leadership qualities;
expertise:	power as a function of specialized knowledge or skill or access to information;
opportunity:	power as a function of the occupancy of roles which provide the opportunity to exert power through the control of information or key organizational tasks.

> (Hoyle 1986:74)

The two types of power are authority and influence:

> Authority is that form of power which stems from the legal right to make decisions governing others. Influence is that form of power which stems from the capacity to shape decisions by informal and non-authoritative means.
>
> (1986:74)

Authority is the static, structural and formal aspect of power in organizations. It bestows upon an individual the right to make decisions. Authority flows downwards and is unidirectional. Yet it is circumscribed, since the scope of an individual's authority is defined by position. Influence, by contrast, is the dynamic, informal and tactical element of power. Influence is not sanctioned by the organization and can flow upward, downward and horizontally. Moreover, influence is not necessarily related to position in the organization, the source of influence may be personality, expertise or opportunity. Nor is influence clearly defined, its scope and legitimacy is ambiguous (1986:74–5).

The four bases of power are:

coercive:	the ability to apply the threat of physical sanctions;
renumerative:	the control of material resources and favours;
normative:	the control of symbolic rewards;
knowledge:	access to information as a basis of power

(Hoyle 1986:75)

The idea that there are different sources, types and bases of power can be applied to Orchard school. In this section I will especially concentrate upon the two types of power, beginning with Ron's authority, and then consider how he sought to influence his colleagues. At a number of points I will also note his sources and bases of power.

Ron's authority sprang from his position as headteacher of the school. A headteacher's legal responsibilities are fully described by the Education (No.2) Act, 1986, which defines the responsibility of a head in relation to those of the school governors and the LEA. Further responsibilities are laid down in The Education (Teachers' Pay and Conditions of Employment) Order, 1987, while the Education Reform Act, 1988, lays a duty upon the head to secure the statutory requirements for the school curriculum. Under the 1987 order:

> the head, subject to the statutory limitations and to the Articles is 'responsible for the internal organization, management and control of the school'.
> It is important to note that there is also an obligation upon the head to consult, 'where this is appropriate', with the LEA, the governors, parents and staff of the school.
>
> (The Head's Legal Guide 1992:1.39)

These are extensive responsibilities which create a general assumption that a head has considerable authority in his/her school (ILEA 1985:66). Moreover, this assumption was shared by staff at Orchard school.

At no time during fieldwork did I detect any sense that the staff were questioning the position of headteachers in schools. There was a taken-for-grantedness about the position. Nor did I discover any resistance to Ron being the headteacher of Orchard school. For sure, there were grumbles and complaints about specific things (some staff felt he let meetings go on too long, that he was a poor chair of meetings, could appear indecisive and vague, others said that he favoured some staff more than others), but no one suggested Ron lacked the authority expected of a headteacher. The staff of Orchard school, in common with those in other schools, did not believe they could dispense with their headteacher (Nias *et al.* 1989:148).

Ron himself acknowledged his authority. He saw a section of his work as relatively free from staff involvements. In some matters he felt he had the authority to make decisions alone, although this was not always the case (see also Mortimore *et al.* 1988:281):

There are a lot of things which the staff will just expect me to make a decision on. There are other things which obviously they would feel, rightly, that they should be consulted about.

(Interview)

Ron admitted that he sometimes determined the agenda of curriculum meetings in order to respond to 'priority documents' that arrived in school from the LEA, or to incorporate his, and sometimes others' wishes (Dave, Marie). He was not afraid to exert his authority. At one staff meeting he devoted the first part of the meeting to restating his views on marking children's work. He made it clear these were the school's policies. Having issued the school's marking policy to all at the meeting and spoken about consistency amongst teachers, Ron said,

There are, therefore, two principles I want to establish. First, the need to mark only with the child present. Second, the principle of planning activities in appropriate sizes of groups so that marking can be done intensively, while children continue.

The staff sat very quietly through this. Marie made a few notes. At 4.27 (sixteen minutes after he started) Ron said: 'Perhaps, we can go through this document.' Everyone picked up the marking policy document and began to look at the aims.

(Fieldnote)

On another occasion, when Helen's classroom performance and control of children while on duty became a concern, Ron exerted his authority by intervening directly. During a unit meeting, arranged ostensibly to discuss curricular plans, Ron explicitly stated his dissatisfaction to her. Fortuitously, later that day, I met Ron at another venue:

He told me he'd just had his meeting with Helen and Marion that day at 3.30. 'How did it go?'
'OK,' said Ron, with a small shrug of the shoulders. 'Bit of a shock to Helen, I think,' he said. 'No, perhaps shock's too strong a word; more of a surprise perhaps, less of a shock.' I waited for him to say more. 'Essentially, I told her that she needs to improve her planning, increase it in detail by several notches. There's too much of a discrepancy between the two classes. That needs to be ironed out,' said Ron. He pulled on his cigarette before continuing, 'I suppose, she's really got to stop driving the Robin Reliant down the motorway, change the Robin Reliant for something that will go a bit faster.' He laughed at his own metaphor. 'She's got to produce some clearer plans in greater detail for Monday, and show them to me. We also talked about the support she's been offered when we've got the plans.' He went on to say it had been a long time since he had been so direct and specific with a teacher, most recently it had been with students.

(Fieldnote)

Later, the teacher concerned said:

The help I've had is through criticism. Ron's once or twice criticized the way I've done things, or perhaps asked me to tighten up the way things are done in my unit, but not exactly said how you can do it, he's more

or less left it to me to decide. Perhaps that's the way it should be, I don't
know.

(Interview)

Although a great deal of Ron's authority arose from a structural source, he
gained further authority from his expertise and personality. Ron possessed expertise because amongst the staff he was the oldest practitioner and the longest serving professional.

Teacher: I think he's the best headteacher I've worked for. . .he knows
his stuff!

(Interview)

Additionally, he was, as the latter part of section two showed, an expert
because he had access to information. Ron also had authority because he was
personally respected. He was regarded by the staff as being interpersonally skilled
and a sensitive person.

Teacher: I think he makes it very clear that everybody's views shall be
respected and valued.

(Interview)

While Ron had authority and was prepared to use it, he also relied upon his
influence a great deal. However, it was difficult, sometimes, to separate the two.
The head's authority and influence and the influence of the teachers and other staff
were blurred and overlapped. For example, the decision to have an anniversary
exhibition was overtly taken by the staff, although they soon disliked the form
and timescale of it. Nevertheless, the exhibition was mounted because, in part,
Ron did not relax the pressure for it. When he and I were putting up part of the
exhibition he spoke about the staff being 'sandwiched' between the invitation to
parents to visit the exhibition and the need for teachers to put up the exhibition
on time. He spoke of this being a high demand week and how this created a bit
of tension which he regarded as healthy. He sometimes felt that if things in school
needed a push, 'then I'm capable of giving it a push' (interview).

Later, Ron acknowledged deriving satisfaction from having such influence:

. . .'It's to do with power.'
'In what sense?' I asked.
He thought for a moment. 'About making it happen. Knowing you
have still got the power to make something like this [the Anniversary
Project] happen may be the best way of describing my reaction to it'.

(Fieldnote)

Although it was difficult sometimes to distinguish between authority and influence, Ron himself was aware of his ability to influence the staff, as his previous
remarks and those to follow demonstrate.

Ron: I can sit down and say nothing, but I am still exerting an influence
by the fact that I am saying nothing.

(Interview)

Ron also told me that some years ago an analysis had been conducted into meetings in the school and it appeared that he tended to act as summarizer for meetings, thereby often projecting his interpretation of what was being said onto others:

> *Ron:* My major contributions came in the last twenty minutes of the meeting which were, in many ways, a form of summarizing and bringing the thing together.
>
> (Interview)

He also exerted considerable influence through normative control. Being the school's only headteacher he was clearly regarded as its founder. He had, from the outset, established the school's structures and procedures. Although over the years these had developed, they were developed only by staff appointed by Ron, along with the governors. In other words, Ron exercised a strong influence upon who else might play a part.

Normative control was also exercised by others on Ron's behalf. The use of unit leaders ensured that each new, less experienced teacher worked with a more experienced teacher. In particular, the unit leader was familiar with the school, had been selected by Ron as being someone whose practice was acceptable and approved and was expected to give a lead and keep Ron informed if anxious about a partner (interview). The unit system was a tacit apprenticeship model.

Transcripts of interviews with staff bear testimony to the presence of normative control within the staff group. Each of the following extracts comes from a different teacher.

> *Teacher:* Perhaps I shouldn't say what Ron expects, it's almost what other members of staff said I should be doing.
>
> *Teacher:* No-one's actually said to me, 'You should be doing this. . .' You just sort of go with the flow to some extent. . .
>
> At the end of the first term, me and Dave sat down and he asked me, 'How's it going?'
>
> And I said, 'Well, I'm going to change all this.' He asked why and I said, 'Because it's not working.'
>
> He half smiled and asked, 'What are you going to do about it?' I explained I was going to do some more practically oriented things and he just smiled and said, 'Fine!' So I think he was going to tell me that, but perhaps I was aware in that instance that something was wrong.
>
> *Teacher:* I do now think about things far more deeply. In that way I found coming here a tremendous stimulus. And I've really enjoyed it. I think that does go back to Ron's way with the school.
>
> *Teacher:* I think the biggest advantage of working in a school like this is that whoever you're working with or near, you pick up a tremendous amount from them.
>
> *Teacher:* Here you are expected that if your displays are not very good, then a term later they will get a bit better and perhaps the next term better still.
>
> (Interviews)

Consequently, Ron could appear, sometimes, to be relatively uninvolved in shaping the work of individuals. Through the unit leaders' example; use of positive reinforcement and support; the work of the deputy as another intelligence gatherer; and, staffroom socialization; newcomers learned about, or were told, how to teach at Orchard school. The unit leaders were Ron's trusted lieutenants — surrogates of his authority, agents of his influence.

Yet Ron did not rely too heavily upon the normative control exercised by others. He also believed in what Fullan (1991:132) calls ' the primacy of personal contact' for effecting change in teachers. Section 2 shows how Ron toured the school and displayed close interest in the teachers' and children's work. He knew a great deal about what was happening in the school, and staff appreciated that he was monitoring their work. Although much of this interaction was apparently relaxed and good humoured, thus being similar to Ball's (1987:93) notion of 'benevolent surveillance', staff recognized he was engaged in quality assurance and control. They knew he was judging them because of what he said, and did not say.

Teacher: I think people feel he's the ultimate 'yea or nay' as to whether they take a trip, do a project, order equipment. I don't know whether he would admit to that but he is. If he doesn't like what you're doing he can make it quite difficult for you, I think. He can ask very searching questions. He doesn't make pleasantries about something he disagrees with or doesn't like. He's quite straight I think, and you know if he doesn't like something that you do, or if he does. I think he's quite good at managing people in a sense.

I think he has quite a pervading. . .in a funny sort of way he imposes his own atmosphere on people, on staff and children, but it's nothing you can say specifically that he does, but I think he does quite a lot. Do you know what I mean?. . .It's as much what he doesn't say as what he does say. . .He can be quite unnerving as a newcomer, when you don't read the signals. He still manages to make you feel uncomfortable if you're blurbing your way through something or doing something that's, you know, not right. I think his signals can be quite frosty and I think that's easy to interpret. I think lots of people feel that very early on. He's got quite a reputation from other people, from other staff in different schools, of being quite frosty.

GS: Has he?

Teacher: Yeah, I think so. They're all quite scared of him — quite intimidated I think. Even though he's ostensibly very jolly and bright and relaxed. . .I think he likes being fairly enigmatic actually and I think enigmas and mysteries are quite powerful forces of, not control, but they pervade.

(Interview)

Ron's influence was pervasive because Ron made frequent and consistent use of his conversations with members of staff. As Gronn has shown, in a detailed case study of a headteacher, talk is his/her *work*, insofar as it consumes most of the head's time and energy, and is central to the head's achievement of control (1988:289–91):

> Words do the work because each participant has a subjective understanding of school life that is made manifest in speech. If some degree of intersubjectivity is to be attained, they must to some extent share meaning and engage in sense making (Ball 1972). Talk becomes necessary and is powerful in two senses: first, talk does things for the speaker, making known his or her version of something to others that must be attended to: second, talk gets others to do things, not only to take note or account of what is said, but to be influenced by what is said.
>
> (Gronn 1988:308)

This interpretation of talk suggests two things. First, Ron's visits to teachers enabled him to reap information and to sow seeds. He found out what teachers were doing and why and, in turn, suggested other things they might try or think about. Personal contact with colleagues was a conduit for his professional influence. Furthermore, because his influence 'was worked at linguistically and worked at never-endingly as an on-going, everyday activity' (Gronn 1988:311), Ron's influence was pervasive and persistent. Talk was simultaneously central to his work and his power to control the work of others.

Second, unlike authority, influence is not unidirectional; it is interactive. Therefore, at the same time as Ron was influencing others, he was exposing himself to their influence. To what degree this occurred cannot be measured, but it should not be discounted. Consequently, although Ron exerted authority and influence, staff were not powerless. At the very least staff possessed negative power (Handy 1981, 2nd. ed.:120), that is, they could refuse to follow instructions or remain impervious to his influence. Certainly there were instances when staff disagreed with him and challenged him, as both Sarah and Ken did in staff meetings. Members of the teaching staff also overlooked collective decisions such as the one taken to implement a revised marking code (fieldnote).

Teachers felt at liberty to interpret agreed decisions in their individual ways, which Ron described as a looseness in the structure and something he tolerated:

> Ron and I were talking about the structure in the school, 'it's sometimes a loose structure. It's got to be loose, not too tight. The looseness enables people, who might otherwise be too rigidly and tightly tied together, to work together in different ways,' said Ron. 'The looseness also means that by not being tied, we sometimes create a semblance of unity. There's enough space for us then all to get along, because if we had a tight structure, differences in approach, teaching style, planning, could make it rather difficult.'
>
> (Fieldnote)

His tolerance of looseness may also account, in part, for why he was not perceived as authoritarian. Indeed, Ron's notion of structural looseness, his tolerance of individual differences and awareness of his own influence upon the staff suggest that he was sensitive to the dynamics of power inside the school (Coulson 1986:86). At the same time, his shrewdness about his own influence, and his awareness of other individuals' views and positions suggests he was involved in bargaining and coalition building. Taken together, all of these points disclose that there was a micropolitical dimension to his work and that Ron was very much aware of this in his encounters with members of staff.

Certainly I witnessed Ron dealing with individuals and making allowances for some, for example, when Graham decided not to submit work for the Anniversary Exhibition (fieldnote). Ron also exercised personal influence which could be interpreted as being

> based on the exploitation of some kind of special relationship. A social and personal relationship or a relationship of power or exchange. Influence is normally exercised in private regions, backstage, behind the scenes. It is known about, hinted, used but not observed.
>
> (Ball 1987:131)

Certainly it was not always clear to me as an observer what exactly was occurring when Ron was dealing with staff members. Nor can I discount the possibility that Ron was manipulative. In previous comments concerning his reflections he said he was deliberative rather than spontaneous and that he always had a game plan. No member of staff explicitly suggested he was manipulative, but some of their comments came close to it:

> *Teacher*: I'm sure that he knows the way, I think he's very skilful when we have our staff meetings, sometimes he walks out if we start to discuss things, he'll walk out, he'll come back in again and that's a deliberate ploy to let people chat when he's not there, and then he'll come in again. Underneath I feel as though he is still very in charge and very controlled and although it may seem to be democratic I don't really think it is. I think he knows what he wants and he goes to get it, that's my feeling.
>
> (Interview)

The charge of manipulation does sit easily with someone previously described as kind and considerate. Yet, the two may nevertheless be sides of the same coin since Ron had to deal with competing demands (such as a teacher's domestic concerns and an after-school commitment) and needed to balance the needs of individuals with his desires for the institution. The latter was particularly strong since he wished to create a sense of *whole school*. By whole school he meant the development of a sense of unity amongst the teaching staff, in terms of both shared educational beliefs and the classroom practices which were an enactment of those beliefs. To secure such unity Ron needed to foster staff participation on the one hand (to develop unity, shared beliefs) and retain control on the other (to ensure the beliefs matched what he saw as educationally sound and right — his vision (interview).

Participation and control are a dilemma for headteachers (Ball 1987:157), but Ron sought to reconcile them by negotiating with individuals, in ways similar to those described by Nias *et al.* (1989:160–1). He made accommodations to colleagues' 'interests-at-hand' and worked assiduously to develop and sustain a working consensus (Pollard 1985a:158–61; Nias *et al.* 1989:168) or 'negotiated order' (Ball 1987:30). Some of the negotiations were open, others were conducted in private, for example, acting-deputy headship decisions. Sometimes decisions were tacitly reached, or remained opaque, since not all staff knew when decisions were taken. Speaking of staff meetings one teacher said,

They're just so confusing. . .any decision that's made somehow gets lost in the process of making that decision. So we have staff meetings and we go through this show of meeting, but we don't seem to get a lot out of them.

(Interview)

Undoubtedly there was an organizational underworld (Hoyle 1986:125) at Orchard. Although I did not consciously venture far into it, Ron knew his way through this labyrinth, was a shrewd negotiator and was able, through a judicious blend of authority and influence, to sustain or further his interests-at-hand (to develop staff alignment on the school's espoused aims; to stimulate staff to put the aims into practice; for staff to participate in school processes and events; for staff to work together).

From this account of Ron's authority and influence four points can be made. First, Ron possessed authority because of his position. Both he and the teaching staff accepted the prerogative of those in promoted positions in the school's hierarchy to exercise authority over subordinates. Authority was invested in positions — hence unit leaders could exercise normative influence over colleagues as well as Ron. Indeed, the position of the head was unquestioned in the school. Staff at Orchard, in common with other primary teachers, were deferential towards the office of headship (Hoyle 1986:76) and were authority-dependent (Nias 1989a:28–30). Moreover, Ron's authority was further enhanced by the staff's regard for his professional expertise and their respect for him as a person.

Second, the particular circumstances of Ron and the school increased his authority. His longevity and founding role in the school, coupled with the fact he had appointed all the staff and was the most senior person in terms of age and professional experience meant he was regarded as a mature and wise colleague who knew the school, its context and the community it served.

Third, Ron was sensitive to his exercise of authority and influence. Occasionally he exerted his authority overtly, spelling out to colleagues what he believed in or thought was needed. Often his authority was latent and indistinguishable from his influence which he exercised through normative control, frequent personal contact and verbal interaction with staff.

Fourth, he was an active participant in the micropolitics of the school. He listened to others, canvassed their opinions and sought out their concerns. Throughout much of his interaction with staff he negotiated staff members' commitment to the school's and his educational beliefs and their participation in translating shared beliefs into action in classrooms. To encourage staff participation he tolerated some differences between himself and members of staff, accepted challenge and debate in meetings and allowed individuals some latitude in their work. Such participation helped to prevent the school from becoming an authoritarian organization. Thus, although he was invested with authority, power was sometimes contested (Ball 1987:85).

Together these four points support Hoyle's view that each school 'is a complex configuration of authority and influence' and 'the specific configuration of a particular school will turn on formal procedures' for decision-making and less formal uses of influence, including micropolitics (1986:79).

At Orchard there was an asymmetrical distribution of power. As Ball (1987:85) says, the dice were loaded in the head's favour. Two factors explain this imbalance.

First, while teachers possess professional influence, such as subject expertise and teaching experience, heads, by contrast, have legal authority and (usually) they also have professional influence (see Hoyle 1986:83). Certainly, Ron enjoyed both and the combination of the two was sufficient to outweigh the teachers' influence. Second, Ron was an active participant in the school's power play. Moreover, (as noted in previous sections) being free from teaching duties, Ron was able to pursue information and devote time to thinking about what was happening in the school. He not only knew what individuals and groups in the school thought and felt, he had also reflected upon it and made some sense of it. Thus he knew a lot and knew what it meant for himself, his colleagues and the school. Cumulatively Ron's ways of exercising authority and influence gave him tactical superiority. Although Ron did not always get his own way (a revised marking code, for example, was never fully implemented), he nevertheless was the predominant figure in the school.

There is one further point. Behind Ron's predominance in the school lay a particular motive for exercising power. Ron did not seek power for the sake of possessing it, rather it was to have some control over his work. He was not a 'jungle fighter' (Blumberg and Greenfield 1986:159), an organizational manager whose goal is to compete for power in a kind of win–lose game, nor did he have a concern for self-aggrandizement. Rather, Ron had a notion of the kind of school he wanted to develop, and he needed to have the power to do it (Blumberg and Greenfield 1986:158–9). He had a sense of purpose (Viall 1984:85–104), or vision (Greenfield 1987a:56) which he saw as the school's mission. Being powerful meant he simultaneously had the energy to develop the mission and a need to control it. Ron sought power to be purposeful.

I recognized that there was purpose behind his power when I focused upon Ron's interest in curriculum development in the school and Ron's comments and response to externally imposed changes. It is to these I now turn.

Curriculum Development

This sub-section and the next are organized around a distinction between change and development. I shall take change to mean initiatives, both organizational and curricular, devised and required by agents external to the school. By development I mean ongoing, evolutionary revisions by the staff to the school's organization and its curriculum. This distinction is based upon the way Ron referred to change and development, the ideas of Handy (1989:3–10) and definitions offered by the Shorter Oxford English Dictionary.

I have already suggested that Ron and his colleagues worked in a dynamic as opposed to a static setting. One reason for the occurrence of alterations within the school was the staff's apparent willingness to generate modifications to their practice since they were constantly revising and developing the curriculum.

Curriculum development was a strong feature of the school as I learned from talking to the staff, attending staff meetings and looking through the staff's curriculum folders and Ron's files. The following fieldnote was made after studying the latter two:

> [they] show that the school has in the past, undertaken a considerable amount of curriculum review, discussion and development. Indeed, in

Ron's filing cabinet one can see this in another way, since all the documents from the past are included in there, with the updates. Moreover, during this term the school's language documents are being revised because a new reading record is being developed, by Marion and Marie. One can also see curriculum development has gone on through discussion, presentations, workshops and in-service education and that this has been a continuous process.

(Fieldnote)

One particular sheet caught my eye since it recorded which areas of the curriculum the staff had looked at over a period of years and how staff had reviewed and/or developed each particular area. Curriculum issues were regularly discussed in the weekly staff meetings:

Ron talked about the sheet that was on the wall which Dave had written up, having sent a paper round to everyone, asking for individual preferences about curricular areas staff would like to see reviewed. Ron thought that quite soon people would indicate their priorities. He talked about the need for us to share expertise. Ron mentioned the need to be aware of newcomers on the staff, that there had been a good staff turnover this year and last year, and that he was aware he, Dave, and Sarah were the only members of staff who knew the origins and processes by which particular curriculum documents, now filed in his office and in staff folders, had come into being. . .

He also said that we need to think about curriculum review not just in the sense of sharing expertise and of sharing insights and observations on existing documents, but also to consider what the outcomes of any curriculum review might be. The outcomes could be seen in a variety of ways. For example, outcomes could be seen as in-service for individuals; the increasing of skills and competencies. Outcomes could also be developmental sequences across the whole school, in terms of the kinds of things children should be doing at particular ages or stages. A third potential outcome was that of guidelines; people might want some guidance, and that could be published. Or there could be a policy decision, so that after agreement on a particular aspect of curriculum we all go on and do it, he said.

Ron then invited Marie to talk about in-service. Marie's thesis was the need to think through how much external imposition by the LEA the school wanted to go along with. She talked about the imposition, this term, of a mandatory requirement [from the LEA] that each school presents to its new governing body a discussion document on science. Marie saw this as an imposition and reflected on the extent to which the school had choices, if any, about that requirement. 'Do we have a choice?' asked Sarah. Marie believed they did. Ken, on the other hand, said that his experience in Newham was that he thought it was sensible for an authority to make certain requirements of schools and he thought it was sensible, too, that a school which had experienced and was still experiencing a fairly high turnover of staff, should have a set of documents to which newcomers could turn.

(Fieldnote)

This meeting revealed that Ron believed curriculum review and development was part and parcel of being a teacher at Orchard school. As one of the teachers once said, 'We design our own curriculum here' (fieldnote). Given this strong emphasis on internally generated review and development, which was wholly consistent with Ron's use of Schiller's writings (fieldnote), it was not surprising that Marie should raise concerns about externally imposed requirements. Certainly, congruence between developments inside and outside the school was a concern of Ron's. At the initial meeting for this study I asked him how he viewed the coming year.

> I think there are two levels — there are things that are within your collective control, as a staff, and there are things that are not within your control that you will be expected to respond to. In some ways, the pattern over the last two or three years has been that the things we wish to respond to, and, perhaps more significantly, the way we want to deal with those, are sometimes increasingly incompatible with the way we are expected to respond to them. In terms of curriculum development work there is some outstanding work left over from this year that we want to pursue and that's particularly in terms of continuing the review of the language policy throughout the school.
>
> There are two pieces of work from the Authority, one is a science statement and the other one involves computers which we are expected to respond to by December.
>
> (Interview)

While Ron believed that development arose first and foremost from inside school, he also knew that, in the late 1980s, initiatives from outside the school had to be taken into account. Innovation had to be managed in the school, but some of the changes sprang from sources beyond the school's boundaries. Consequently he saw his work as blending developments arising from inside the school and changes created from outside the school.

> If you ask me where I would put my enthusiasms and efforts, I will be putting effort into the governing body to try and get them to work effectively. I will be listening carefully to what is said from the National Curriculum, what is expected of us, and what the Authority will expect of us in terms of replying and responding to their own curriculum development statement that will come forth. The enthusiasm and effort, I think, will be directed towards individual staff and the children they will be teaching next year. I think that's the greatest long-term satisfaction. I think it would be flippant to say that it's going to extend one's ingenuity to avoid the excesses and expectations from outside the school, but there's an element of truth in that. I think we have a group of staff who have firm convictions about how children should learn and I think that is developing all the time, within themselves, both individually and also within the staff group.
>
> (Interview)

Ron's awareness of innovation and initiatives emanating from inside and outside the school shows that he was monitoring how the school altered. Earlier

Ron was depicted as monitoring teacher and pupil performance. Now, it is possible to see his monitoring in two other ways. First, while Ron accepted curriculum development as essential to his work with the staff, such developments had to be closely watched. Developments, in Ron's terms, had to be positive, they had to improve quality. Second, in wanting to avoid the excesses of external expectations, and in listening carefully to the National Curriculum, Ron inferred he wanted to retain control over curriculum initiatives. Changes and developments might occur, whether generated externally or internally, but they needed to be compatible with the staff's firm convictions — which were, of course, congruent with his educational beliefs. Thus Ron's wish to retain control suggests some measure of proprietary interest. Developments and change could take place, but they should not alter the school's and *his* guiding principles and beliefs.

Ron also suggested that he saw external change as a bigger threat than internal developments. One reason for this was the probability that internally generated developments were domesticated ones, that is, developments proposed by colleagues who subscribed to the school's and Ron's beliefs and who, while altering some practices (e.g. reading records), would simultaneously ensure continuity at the level of beliefs. External change was associated with the 1988 Education Reform Act, its very title suggesting major change.

The Shock of the New — External Change

Ron was concerned to find out what the 1988 Education Act had in store for him and for the school. While the broad outlines of the reforms were known (National Curriculum, testing and assessment, local management of schools, open enrolment) specific details only emerged during the course of the school year. Ron became acquainted with the details of the change either by attending increasingly frequent LEA briefing meetings for headteachers or from documents mailed to him by the DES. I noted in my fieldnotes his attendance at the briefings and tried, in our conversations, to ascertain his responses to the changes:

> In the staffroom Ron began telling Dave about the previous day's area headteacher's meeting. The agenda had included: a welcome by the senior area education officer; the introduction of new colleagues; and the implications of aspects of the Education Reform Act for the County Education Service Plan. There were also workshops led by the LEA advisers to discuss implementation of the National Curriculum.
>
> (Fieldnote)

> I asked Ron how he felt about the National Curriculum and the need to begin implementation work. Really he felt there was no option, there were no choices now left, and he said: 'I just can't help but feel that all these changes that are coming are flawed, badly flawed.' And despite his vivacity today he said it with considerable melancholy; it was perhaps the one point in the day when he seemed less than optimistic.
>
> (Fieldnote)

Ron said to the chair of governors that they both needed to go to an LMS meeting soon, together. Wendy said he'd have to give her apologies, she couldn't make it.

(Fieldnote)

During the afternoon, Ron was working at his desk looking through the files that the DES had sent to school immediately prior to Easter. These files contain the statutory orders for the National Curriculum in respect of mathematics and science. As I entered the office to ask him something, he said, 'We will have to start using these sometime this term, certainly when we are planning.' Then he showed me a new set of folders he had started himself. One folder was entitled, Charges for School Activities, another was entitled School Responses to the National Curriculum, others were called Administration of Pupils and Registration of Pupils; Teacher Appraisal, Qualified Teaching Status, Licensed Teachers; Religious Education; LMS; DES Circulars re: National Curriculum, Sex Education, Animals, Plants in Schools, Complaints Procedures. Ron said: 'Quite a lot of information in these folders is necessary, because it is the mechanical things that come first. Some of the current practices will have to change, such as charges for school activities. In that sense it is useful to have some of this information, the wording one should use in letters and so on, which is shown in some of the County Policy stuff. Much of it is nuts and bolts stuff. I've not really read it all. I take it home to read because I think I ought to read it, but quite often I don't even understand it all then. I have the feeling that there is an awful lot I should have done by now that we are not actually doing.

'Is Dave up on all this material?' I asked.

'No', said Ron.

I asked, 'What about the National Curriculum and things to be done this term with the staff?'

'I am thinking about planning project work and especially science, we will need to think about that,' said Ron. 'Essentially, what it does mean and what we do need to do is comply with it.'

(Fieldnotes)

Watching and listening to Ron I noted three points. First, Ron was in some ways shielding the school from the full force of the changes. He sometimes held back from sharing with the staff all he knew in order to insulate them, at least a little, from the impact of initiatives external to the school. Second, Ron felt he needed to understand the changes in a working manner (fieldnote), but he lacked such know-how because the changes were not yet implemented and operating. Lacking first hand experience he did not feel in full control.

I don't feel that you are on top of it and understand it completely until you have actually used it. Then it becomes second nature to you and to other people who are using it.

(Interview)

Third, part of not being in full control could also be attributed to feeling he had to comply on certain matters, as he amplified when I explored his notion of compliance:

Ron: I think there has been an increasing feeling of a loss of autonomy, probably over a period of years. It may hinge upon a sense of licence that probably they [heads] have enjoyed in the past. I think it's rather like being in one of these rooms where the ceiling and the walls start moving in on people and if you happen to have created a large room for yourself to start with then you still have an element of freedom around you, that you are aware of the constraints — the ceiling coming down — I think.

(Interview)

While Ron was concerned about all the changes he faced, the introduction of Local Management of Schools (LMS) especially troubled him. As with the other changes Ron felt he had to comply with the LMS initiative and lacked experience of it. However, Ron's discomfort with LMS was that it threatened his conception of headship.

Back in Ron's office I noted a brand new, rather attractive, looseleaf folder from a project called The LMS Initiative: Local Management in Schools — a Practical Guide. It was quite a thick document. 'It seems to be the thing that's giving heads some concern,' I said.

'Well,' he said, 'it's the one thing which is additional to our job. Everything else is a revision of what we're doing, but LMS is brand new.'

I asked, 'Is it frightening a lot of heads?'

'I suppose so,' said Ron. 'It'll please some others too. Those who keep catalogues in a top left-hand drawer, those who have Dymo labels stuck all over the car telling them their tyre pressures and which indicator does what in their car.' And he giggled. 'I don't think I'm suited for LMS,' he said. He also said that his worry was that LMS might take over the whole of headship.

(Fieldnote)

Another time Ron said,

I am very anxious about LMS. I am aware it is going to take up an awful lot of time. I also wonder, if we look at the type of people who might want to become headteachers then I suspect that, more and more we are going to see people whose first love, as it were, is actually teaching and who may have been happy to extend that role as deputy heads, but may not [now] be so enthusiastic about the prospect of moving from the deputy head's role to the head's role with that [LMS] type of responsibility. Maybe I'm wrong, I don't know.

(Interview)

Ron saw LMS as creating a fork in the path heads took.

Ron: I don't think I do have an optimistic outlook. I think there is a nucleus of headteachers and teachers who are going to continue to be excited and enthusiastic and get pleasure from the job they do with the children; which probably is the reason they came into the job in the first place. But I think there may also be those, who were originally in that category, finding that they cannot translate that type of enthusiasm and excitement into completing curriculum audits or LMS.

GS: Out of those two which group do you think you would most likely. . .

Ron: I think I would feel myself happily sitting in the first group, which is probably one of the reasons why I feel not very satisfied about my own role in that area, in the way people are teaching and what they are teaching and how children are learning. I don't think I've done a good job in that direction at all this year, in supporting people and I think there are some extreme examples of that in the school which could have done a lot more support, which I should have given them and haven't.

(Interview)

And on another occasion he said,

[National Curriculum, and LMS are] going to change the way I do my job because the job is changing. I don't happen to believe that it's a particularly good way, I don't happen to believe that it equates easily with the type of learning and teaching I would like to see happen in the school. I don't feel that there are many occasions when I can view the demands with enthusiasm, knowing that it's going to be clearly beneficial to teachers and children.

(Interview)

Ron did not enjoy the prospect of headship becoming, as he saw it, preoccupied with administration and accountancy. Moreover, he found many of the changes frustrating because they were, to him, a distraction. They ate into his time when he was in school, preventing him from doing other tasks and they caused him to be out of school attending briefing meetings.

Ron: I have been pulled in other directions. I mean normally until this year, I would have expected to see the students on two or three occasions each. I would have expected to have seen them teaching and to talk with them afterwards, and to look through their files. Now I can give you an overview of how those students performed this term, but [I had] only one meeting with two of them. I didn't have any planned meeting and that has not been the pattern in the past and that is a sadness. I'm aware that I haven't pursued [with the staff] discussions on schemes of work this term, not in a formal way, and that again has always been a regular fixed feature. I think I've personally found it a frustrating year. I think I've felt this year, more than any other year, that I haven't been able to give enough continuity of time to what is happening in the school. There are times when I begin to feel out of touch with the day-to-day life and work of the units, definitely.

GS: What has got in the way. What's stopped you feeling. . .?

Ron: I suppose the amount of time I've been required to be out of the school, but it is more than that. . .[it's] how you think about the job.

GS: So you see the work of the head changing?

Ron: Yes, I do, I think I see it in the future as more of a challenge within a set framework rather than [pause] working out a personal vision.

(Interview)

And why he saw it that way might be explained by something he had said some months earlier.

GS: What about the unrewarding aspects of headship?

Ron: I think they're almost always concerned with frustration. Frustrations I think are in looking at — particularly now — looking at what is likely to change then feeling quite often that what underpins that change is itself suspect when weighed against your personal beliefs in primary education.

(Interview)

Eventually Ron came to the conclusion that headship was changing into a new pattern that he could neither accept nor adopt:

Ron: It would have been interesting to talk to Dave, who has just recently had an interview for a headship and see the type of questions that are perhaps being asked now. There maybe a lot of questions, I suspect, about management, about implementation and assessment, teacher appraisal, LMS. Now those almost have a standard answer. If you read the textbooks the answers are there. . .I don't think you can create your own rules as you were able to do in the past. . .I don't think I can do it [headship] any other way — I don't think you can somehow pour the agenda into a series of pots called headteachers and see them cooked and boiled and come out as identical plates of rice. I don't think you can do that.

(Interview)

Ron's feelings of frustration and his anxieties about the way he saw headship altering reveal that he felt strongly about his work. External change helped to show the affective side of his work. Blumberg and Greenfield (1986, 2nd ed.) suggest that American school principals operate under constraints on their behaviour, that is,

the managerial role carries with it a mythology that managers are supposed to be rational at all times, be able to separate their feelings from their thoughts and to keep themselves under control at all times. . .Principals are expected to behave with. . .decorum. . .they are 'professionals' and so must behave in a professional manner. It is not clear, of course, what that means precisely but, for sure, it excludes the free expression of emotions. . .

(Blumberg and Greenfield 1986:159)

Ron worked with similar constraints, as his wife's earlier comments support. Consequently, identifying the feelings he experienced as headteacher was difficult; he usually kept them well hidden. Yet the threat to his identity of the National Curriculum and LMS brought his feelings closer to the surface, as one of the staff recognized:

> I think sometimes he lets his own feelings about the educational system, his emotional feelings, rule his management skills. I think he has a gut reaction, like I do, a lot of us do, about all the impositions we've had put upon us through the National Curriculum, and I think we've just got to get on with it really now and do it and make the most of it. In some respects he's quite good at that in that he doesn't make us change, he doesn't say, 'Right, got to stop doing all that, do this.' But, on the other hand, he doesn't seem to have reconciled himself with this problem and resolved it in his own mind. So you know that sometimes some of the things he says are really just him having an awful moan about it because he doesn't like it. Which he's got to do I suppose and I think he kind of lets his feelings. . .they're still in there fighting him. . .
>
> (Interview)

Certainly Ron experienced happiness and delight, such as after particularly impressive showing assemblies. Yet, as the year drew on and he learned more and more about the impending changes, he experienced feelings of growing power-lessness, an increasing sense of impotence.

Taken together Ron's reactions to the external changes suggest three points. First, Ron was less in control of his work and the school than he was accustomed to. He was unfamiliar with the new curricular and administrative procedures and so lacked operational understanding of some aspects of his work. In learning about the specific nature of the changes Ron was out of school more than usual. Also, when he was in school, he was kept busy by the arrival of new documents and instructions. While he was undoubtedly busy dealing with all the new information, Ron nevertheless did not feel he was working at the heart of the school. He was spending less time with the teachers and children than he wanted to. He felt he was no longer providing the support and attention to staff and their teaching. Dealing with the changes gave him more to attend to while simultaneously giving him less time to deal with everything else. As a result, Ron felt frustrated since he believed he was distracted from his principle task of monitoring and developing the work of his staff. In short, the external changes diminished his capacity to influence his colleagues. The changes reduced his power within the school.

Second, by limiting his power to influence others the changes threatened his occupational identity.

> Occupational identity represents the accumulated wisdom of how to handle the job, derived from their own experience and the experience of all who have had the job before or share it with them. Change threatens to in-validate this experience robbing them of the skills they have learned and confusing their purposes, upsetting the subtle rationalization and compen-sations by which they reconciled the different aspects of their situation.
>
> (Marris 1975:2)

Ron saw headship as being concerned with the possession and projection of an educational vision. Being a headteacher meant transmitting one's educational beliefs to others, especially teaching colleagues so that they would join in with, and add impetus to the work of the school — the education of children according to agreed beliefs. Ron's interest in teacher development, the unit structure which exposed individual teachers to their partner's practice and the relatively high turn-over of staff were all connected with the transmission of beliefs. The Orchard school was something of a greenhouse school, a place where teachers were nurtured, developed and growing. Ron was an educative leader (Duigan and MacPherson 1987; Nias *et al.* 1989:109–11), that is, he was actively teaching his colleagues, educating them about his educational ideas and beliefs.

In terms of his respected Schiller, Ron was a pioneer — patiently pulling his school along. With reference to his first day's address to the staff (fieldnote), Ron was a pied piper, leading the staff, dancing in step and singing in harmony to what was his, but also their, tune. Yet, as he acknowledged in that same address, it was not easy to respond to a distant drummer. And Ron feared that the external changes would turn him into a distant drummer by keeping him away from the teaching and the learning in the school. If so, he could no longer educate his staff, no longer nurture and sustain his vision for the school. Ron saw the changes as invalidating his whole approach to headship. Crucially, he could no longer be the head he was nor lead the school he had created and infected with his beliefs.

Third, in letting go of one professional identity and contemplating or learn-ing another, the individual passes through a zone of uncertainty (Schon 1971:12) and experiences a sense of loss, struggle and anxiety (Marris 1975:2). The relin-quishing of one social script for another results in cognitive and affective re-sponses by individuals (Bredeson 1991:6). Moreover, as Ron struggled to come to terms with the changes and their impact upon his work and passed through his zone of uncertainty, his comments and rationalizations suggested that headship was an intensively personal task. Headship was not merely a job, rather, it was the articulation and implementation of his educational beliefs. Headship was the op-portunity to put one's own educational philosophy into action; it was, to use Ron's own term a licence, a form of self-expression. Being a headteacher was personally empowering.

Section 4: Portrait of Ron Lacey, Headteacher: Professional and Personal Dimensions

This section is split into two related sections. In the first I will draw together the insights I have developed from the previous three sections. I will present the main characteristics of Ron's work in an attempt to create a portrait of him as a head. A key finding will be that Ron's headship is made up of both professional and per-sonal dimensions. In the second section I will use the case of Ron to explore further the personal dimension of headship because little work has previously been con-ducted into it and because the exploration casts new light on the nature of headship.

Portrait of Ron Lacey as Headteacher

On a number of occasions I asked Ron to say how he saw primary headship (to describe what it was like; to talk about leading a school; to encapsulate the key characteristics). On each occasion I was unsuccessful in eliciting a pithy, succinct statement. Initially I found his replies frustrating and I secretly blamed him for being non-committal and evasive. Later I held myself responsible, believing my questions to be too direct and narrow. The very question suggested there was an answer and perhaps Ron was only trying to avoid being wrong. However, during our penultimate interview, I again revised my position. Ron would not say what headship was because he would not reduce it to a formula. He told me he did not believe the job could be described in recipe terms (interview).

For Ron, then, headship could not be captured in a single snapshot. To portray headship an album of pictures is needed with a series of shots showing the subject in different settings and performing different tasks. I would not claim to have a full set of pictures, even less all the perspectives needed. Nevertheless, from this study of Ron it is possible to develop a portrait of his headship. The portrait is a composite picture being made up of a series of characteristics.

Ron worked long hours. His school day was from around 8.30 a.m. until 6.00 p.m., if he had no evening commitments. When he had evening meetings he could be in school until after 10 p.m. I never logged Ron's weekly hours, but I estimate, based on an average of two evening meetings a week, a 60-hour working week was normal. I include lunch and coffee breaks within that figure because he used those times to talk to colleagues, supervise the children's lunchtime behaviour, answer the telephone, meet with staff and socially mingle in the staffroom. He was always on call, on duty. While the greater part of his working days were spent on the school premises, work sometimes took him outside the school.

He met, face-to-face, lots of people. When he was in school he was frequently encountering individuals — staff, children, parents, other visitors. Often his encounters were informal or unplanned and of short duration, taking less than five minutes. Over the course of the school year he was involved in a range of planned, formal meetings both in and out of school. In school he regularly held staff meetings. He met with all the teaching staff at least once a week. Once or twice a term he formally met with the deputy and INSET co-ordinator together. Ron also tried to meet formally with the unit teaching pairs each term. He met with the caretaker and CDO, or her assistant, once a week. After school he formally met, once a term, with the school's governors. He also met informally with the chair of governors several times each week. Ron attended LEA meetings for headteachers out of school, and PTA and community group meetings after school.

Ron's work involved using the telephone and receiving and preparing documents. He wrote letters, but often only when he could not contact individuals by phone. He drafted reports to the governors and provided written information to the LEA. He received from the staff their teaching plans. He also dealt with incoming messages, either written or by telephone, and the mail. As part of the mail he received advice and instructions from the LEA and central government. During the latter part of the year there were signs that the amount of reading he needed to do increased.

While he dealt with a range of different individuals, groups and agencies, he was most actively concerned with what the teachers and pupils were doing. Even in the context of being head of a community school, with all the potential distractions that created (room lettings; conflict between school and community usage; additional meetings to attend; organizing play schemes; annual village festival, parish pump politics), Ron sustained his interest in teaching and learning.

A great deal of his attention was devoted to observing what was happening in the teaching units of the school. He visited the units during the school day. While some of his visits were prompted by other reasons, Ron nevertheless used his visits to note what the children were working on and how they and their teachers were conducting themselves. Additionally, Ron used the weekly showing assembly as an opportunity to learn about the pupils' work and he informally met with teachers, after school and conversed with them about individual children, classroom organization and teaching plans. Ron persistently monitored what was occurring in the school.

As part of his monitoring role Ron was a critical friend to the teachers. He questioned their teaching intentions, probed their thinking and suggested alternatives. He did this most often when he met staff individually, after school, on a seemingly casual basis. Ron also, occasionally, challenged teachers' views in staff meetings — and some of them challenged his. He watched how teachers and teachers and pupils related to one another and how the school's curriculum was developing. Ron often spoke about the quality of the children's work. Without doubt he evaluated teacher and pupil performance, sometimes adopting an inspectorial stance. He was the school's quality controller.

In addition to monitoring, Ron reflected upon what he saw and knew. He reflected in order to make sense of what he believed was happening. He also reflected to determine possible courses of action he and others could take and to resolve problems he faced. Possibly the greatest single problem Ron dealt with was the appointment of an acting-deputy head for the autumn term 1989. This problem illustrated that Ron was not hasty in making decisions and preferred to give himself and others time to think things through. The event showed that some problems took a long time to unfold and could not be immediately resolved. Ron also regarded reflection as a key component of effective teaching and he modelled to the staff the virtue of reflection.

Ron regarded himself as a developer of the teaching staff. He had established an organizational structure which helped staff to learn with and from one another. Newcomers and less experienced teachers were supported and advised by their unit leaders. Showing assemblies enabled staff to learn what they were each teaching. Staff meetings aimed to encourage sharing and professional development. Ron's informal, after-school conversations with staff enabled him to tacitly coach members of staff. In all of these ways Ron encouraged teachers. As a developer of staff he was facilitator, enabler and teacher. His intention was to be educative (Nias *et al.* 1989:127). While he no longer taught children regularly, he coached teachers and this was something he saw as at the heart of his work and gave him a sense of satisfaction.

Ron was keenly interested in developing the school's curriculum. There was a tradition of reviewing and refining school policies and practices. During the year of fieldwork this tradition continued. At the same time, subject frameworks from the NCC were also examined by Ron and the staff to see how easily they could be adopted and translated into practice.

The combination of Ron's interest in teaching and learning, his monitoring and evaluation of classroom practice, and his wish to develop the staff and the school's curriculum meant that he saw himself as the school's instructional leader (Beare *et al.* 1989:155), or as Hughes says, the leading professional (1985: 218).

Ron's leadership was a blend of influence and authority. He used his contacts with staff as opportunities when he could influence them. During his encounters with staff he promoted his educational, social and moral beliefs. He used positive reinforcement to foster the implementation of his ideas about quality teaching in all the units. He also withheld praise by avoiding being effusive. Staff acknowledged he set high standards and learned to read his signals and pick up the cues. Those staff who most closely matched his ideals were promoted within the school and became unit leaders.

Another aspect of Ron's influence was his involvement in the micropolitics of the school. He was engaged in a constant process of negotiation which helped create the social order of the school as an organization and provided a working consensus within which individual's interests were reconciled. He dealt with interpersonal tensions amongst staff. He also claimed he usually had a game plan for what he wanted to do.

A further source of Ron's influence was his extensive knowledge of the school. He was in receipt of a great deal of information because he was at the centre of an extensive communication network. Like other heads, he was the 'spider in the information web' (Hultman 1989:149). He held some of the institution's secrets, including his career judgments on individual members of staff and information individuals had shared with him about themselves or third parties.

As well as being influential Ron exercised authority as headteacher. Staff recognized and deferred to his positional authority. He was their leader who knew what he wanted. He had appointed them all to the school and promoted some of them within it. Staff also believed he was an able headteacher. Staff appreciated that he possessed educational and managerial expertise. They also understood that he was knowledgeable, had founded the school and was the school's historian. Staff were aware Ron knew a lot about what was happening in the school and also outside it. Ron's intimate knowledge of the local community was valued, and staff felt he knew what the school's governors wanted. Moreover, Ron was personally respected for his sensitivity to staff. No one on the staff challenged his authority as headteacher.

Ron's approach to headship corresponds to Ball's (1987:88–95) interpersonal style of head. The characteristics of the interpersonal style are:

- personal interaction and face-to-face contact between head and staff with problems and grievances sorted out on a one-to-one basis with the head;
- informality in relationships, use of informal networks for communication and consultation;
- the head is the focus of communications and dispenser of patronage, the school is the person;
- the head is visible around the school, in the staffroom at break;
- the head's open-door policy encourages the head to feel s/he has his/her finger on the pulse beat of staff concerns and opinions;
- in a number of respects the head is a part of the staff of the school, regarding him/herself as still a teacher;
- the head has an authenticity and facility in social interaction;
- a great deal is done through talk, paperwork is accorded much less importance.

(Ball 1987:88–92)

In addition to these characteristics Ball says:

> It is tempting to introduce an imagery of feudalism. The stress upon personal relationships and individual favours from the head to staff members sets up a sense of mutual obligation. By the granting of 'boons' the head ties his or her teachers in a bond of fealty. . .[Yet there] lies an intriguing contradiction between the highly visible role of the headteacher him or herself and the private and relatively invisible operation of power in the organization. The mechanisms of decision-making and policy-making are not set within the public arenas, as for instance. . .working parties and staff meetings. . .The head will tend to consult quietly and unobtrusively. Staff meetings will be used to 'air' opinions rather than arrive at decisions. . .The sinews of power remain invisible. . .just the person and power of the head. If staff sometimes feel that they do not know what is going on, the head certainly does feel s/he knows what is going on.
>
> (Ball 1987:89, 92)

Ball's description fits how Ron often operated and suggests that Ron was not wholly unique. Also, Ron's approach to exercising influence and authority meant that at Orchard school there was an assymetrical balance of power between him and the staff. Given the particular circumstances at the school — his longevity, foundational role and the fact he had appointed all the staff — the balance of power was heavily weighted in Ron's favour. He was the predominant figure in the school.

Although Ron was the central figure in the school he was not sure he would be able to continue to be so influential in the future. Impending changes from central government, particularly the introduction of a National Curriculum and LMS, prompted him to speculate about how headship might alter. At the same time, the threat of changes to his work helped to reveal his views on headship. Ron regarded headship as essentially individualistic. He valued the latitude he had to make choices about how he used his time, organized the school and selected priorities for curricular development. In Ron's terms headship was an individual licence.

Furthermore, Ron saw headship as a personal activity. It entailed the projection and enactment of *his* educational beliefs. He wanted to see his school embody his educational vision. He saw himself as a member of the pioneer corps, in the vanguard of development. As staff acknowledged, Orchard was his school because he had made it. Ron was the principal creator and maintainer of the school, as well as its developer, and he understood this close association between himself and the school. Speaking of autonomy he said:

> Probably one aspect of a sense of autonomy is the way that schools are known by their headteachers. I think the very first comment about a school is related to the person who is the headteacher of that school; so you will hear things like 'Roger runs a good school'. I don't think it happens to secondary schools. I've never heard that happen. . .it certainly doesn't have the personal element as in the primary school. Because of that, I think the choices that are available to headteachers to make their mark in a school, to feel that they have actually achieved something for

themselves through other people and by other people has been related to how autonomous those people have been. Certainly if you go back to say the 60s, the changes that were happening then in the schools and were probably happening in the education system, were school led and headteacher led, so that in the vanguard of open plan, or progressive [education], were people apparently able to create a great deal of freedom for what they did. They were able in individual schools to teach in a way that hadn't been thought of or tried before. There was a feeling of a vanguard movement. Now, looking ahead, I find it difficult to see where that school-based vanguard is going to come from or, even, if it can come.

(Interview)

When I asked Kate what observations she could make about headship she said:

I think he got a kick out of it, an incredible kick out of it because you are your own person, very much, and you can run that organization the way you want to and you can develop things as quickly and as slowly as you want to. A lot of control there.

(Interview)

It was, moreover, control which relied upon the combination of professional expertise and personal beliefs. His stated attraction to those who could work so that their personal and professional beliefs were fused (Schiller, Tanner) (interview), and his efforts to do likewise, made it inevitable that headship should be an intensely personal experience for him. He said,

I think I do have a very strong personal determination to try and achieve, through these people [the staff], what is right, what I believe is right for these children.

(Interview)

Ron's sense of authority and his wish for the school to follow what he personally believed was educationally right relates to Coulson's (1976; 1986) work on primary heads. Coulson (1976) argues that heads are given great latitude to administer and organize the schools according to their own convictions. Building on the work of Donaldson (1970) and Cook and Mack (1972), Coulson describes a traditional approach to headship. To paraphrase Coulson (1976), this approach aims to develop a close correspondence between the head's preoccupations and personality and the character of the school. In particular, the head expects to influence teachers by his/her own example and to persuade them to identify themselves with his/her aims and methods. The traditional concept of headship is characterized as a blend of personal control and moral authority. At its root lies the head's ego-identification with his/her school. A head thinks of the school as his or hers in a very special way and feels a deep sense of personal responsibility for everything and everyone in it. S/he places priority on providing a recognizable direction and philosophy for the school and one which is conveyed by personal precept and example rather than explicitly stated (Coulson 1976:275–86). And:

British primary heads and teachers believe that the head's managerial behaviour should be integrated with, and serve the realization of, his particular educational and organizational vision.

(Coulson 1986:84)

This latter observation is also supported by empirical work conducted by Nias *et al.* (1989:98–9). While Coulson's work, and that of others (Donaldson 1970; Southworth 1987; Nias *et al.* 1989) acknowledges the personal dimension to headship, there has not been any further exploration of it. The personal side of headship remains, by comparison to the professional aspects, relatively underexplored.

When I was studying Ron, from time to time, I collected data which related to the personal side of being a headteacher. Sifting through this material I came to the view that it helped to illuminate not only what it personally meant for Ron to be a headteacher, but also the nature of headteachering. In the next section I will explore this material.

The Personal Dimension of Headship

There are three main points I will consider in this section. First, Ron's conception of headship inferred a strong sense of his own identity. Second, Ron believed he had developed as a head. Third, the nature of his headship was personally demanding.

Ron's view that he was pursuing a personal vision is consistent with the long standing tradition in this country of teachers who see themselves as crusaders or missionaries (Nias 1989a:33). Indeed, Cohen (1976:51) argues that 'for some of us, a key portion of our identity is our claim to be among the vanguard of some movement.' In turn, such identification with one's work has been shown (Woods 1984; Pollard 1985a; Nias 1989a) to be related to teachers' self-image and self-esteem. Earlier I argued that change threatened Ron's professional identity. Now I want to suggest that, given Ron's blurring of the distinction between professional and personal, being a headteacher relates to one's sense of *self*.

Speaking about feeling a sense of achievement Ron once said that a lot of his self-esteem had 'to be self-generated' because few others, outside the school, knew what he was doing in the school (interview). As Lortie (1975:161) notes, the career line of teaching gives the occupation an unusual quality; once tenured a person can work for years without public recognition for his/her greater mastery of core tasks. In the absence of public recognition and contact with other heads, there was a risk Ron could be left alone and isolated. Perhaps the potential loneliness of being a head made him value visitors, especially LEA advisers. Visitors who know the school 'give you some form of personal recognition that you are doing a good job' (interview, 17.7.89). Although Ron was not isolated, he nevertheless was often thrown back upon his own resources and relied heavily upon himself to resolve the problems and challenges he faced. Headship encouraged him to be self-referential.

Yet Ron's sense of achievement could be shaken despite his strong self-belief in his convictions. I once raised with him the notion of confidence, saying that by conventional measures he might regard himself as a successful head. He was in his third headship, had not encountered any major calamities, the school was seen as healthy, insofar as people were brought to the school (for example, during 1988–89 new inspectors wanting to see *good* primary practice came to the school, there were overseas visitors, and heads from other LEAs on courses concerned with primary practice also visited) and, at the time of this interview, he had recently gained promotion to the advisory service. Ron agreed that all contributed to his confidence, but he also admitted his confidence could be disturbed:

> I mean, a parent you know wants to come and talk about moving (his/her child) to private school, it makes you think twice. It's a reflection on the school, a dissatisfaction. . .[it affects] professional confidence, and personal confidence as well.
>
> (Interview)

On the one hand, Ron was personally convinced of the rightness of what he was trying to achieve. He pursued his vision, was empowered by his sense of mission and was powerful in the school. On the other hand, his confidence could be shaken and his self-image disturbed. As King (1983:86) says: 'Headteachers are often judged by the success of their school; its failure is their failure.' Ron may have been a missionary, but he could also have been a martyr.

The second point, Ron's development as a head, is related to the first. When Ron reflected on his three headships he told me he believed he had worked differently in each school (interview). He also felt he had changed as a head while at Orchard, becoming 'more relaxed than I was in the earlier stages of the school' (interview). Further, he believed he was now more patient as a result of being older and maturer (interview).

Ron felt he had altered the way he influenced teachers. In his first headship he had tried to be an exemplary teacher to his colleagues. Later, and especially during his time at Orchard, he saw himself no longer as an exemplary teacher, but as trying to work through the teachers by influencing them.

> I think if you can do that, through other people, and can still retain a great delight in children, even though it's in many cases secondhand, then you can move into some form of second, third, fourth phase of headship. . .The practice [in the school] now does not reflect my personal teaching practice of ten years ago. But what it does reflect, I think, is my thinking about practice that has changed and developed over the period of time and I think is still doing so in conjunction with other people.
>
> (Interview)

Underneath Ron's different approaches to influencing staff were changes in his own thinking. When he talked about his teaching career he mentioned teaching with his wife. I once asked if they had the same philosophy. He replied:

> I don't think we really had a philosophy at all then actually. I think you just did the job and learnt things about the job and how you teach a bit and talked about it and it grew from there. It's forming unconsciously at that point, I think.
>
> (Interview)

On another occasion he told me his philosophy formed through practice as a teacher and through talking with other teachers (interview). The same influences had affected his thinking as a head:

> Working with the type of people you have been lucky enough to work with, has meant that you thought a lot more about what's happening and how things are going than before. The school has changed very considerably, it's a totally different school than it was nine years ago.
>
> (Interview)

And, in some ways, Ron felt he was different. Lots of people he felt had influenced his thinking and:

> [They] help to push your thinking and therefore you change. It was interesting I was listening to the radio in the car last night and there was somebody, it was an American writer talking about his beliefs. . .and he said something like, 'When I was younger I wrote about things being in black and white, but as I got older I tend to write now about things that I think are the truth and the truths for me.' I thought that was quite an interesting idea.
> GS: Can you say what you think it means for you?
> *Ron*: No, not really, just sounded good to me [laughter]! I think there is something there, I think in terms of first/second headship there was a black and whiteness about it. There was a way you wanted things done. . .and by and large you got them done that way. . .It was still very close to your personal practice.
>
> (Interview)

Two points can be highlighted from Ron's comments. First, although Ron had a strong sense of conviction, his educational ideas were still developing. Further evidence for this claim can be found from Ron's claim that the Len Marsh course had influenced his thinking, along with his reading of Schiller and Tanner who he felt articulated what he believed in. In other words, Ron had a vision, but it was not necessarily inflexible since his beliefs had altered over time.

Second, Ron's approach to headship had altered. In believing he had changed the way he influenced teachers and had moved into a different phase of headship, Ron implied that he was embarked on a process of growth and development. His comments about feeling more relaxed and patient suggested he associated these feelings to being older. Hence his development was linked to maturation. Moreover, given the connection between the professional and personal dimensions of his work, Ron's development was very likely a professional and personal process. Also, while in-service courses and study played a part in his growth, for the most part his development was stimulated by first-hand experience of other schools and teachers and the lessons he drew form these experiences. Development relied, in part, upon Ron's personal growth and his capacity to teach himself. In large measure Ron's development as a head appeared to be a process of self development.

Moving onto the demanding nature of headship there are three points to make. First, while Ron recognized that fundamentally his job was about people and that the great bulk of his job satisfaction ought to come from within the

school (fieldnote), he was simultaneously aware that dealing with people sometimes brought frustrations. Early in the school year a conflict arose between a pair
of teachers in the same unit. Ron called it a mini crisis since he received a phone
call at home from one teacher and felt he had to bring the two together the next
day. His reaction, he confided to me, was to say 'Oh shit!' (fieldnote), partly
because he was tired at that point and partly because the episode rather distracted
him from other pressing concerns at the start of the school year. In short, dealing
with so many issues was not necessarily satisfying. There were frustrations and
competing priorities.

Second, dealing with people sometimes was painful for him. Speaking about
his criticism of Helen's work he said:

> I told Helen that this was professional and not personal, it was a profes-
> sional issue which was why we were talking about it, but I don't think
> that's true. [he said to me]. It's bound to hurt her, she's bound to take
> it personally. I think that's one of the things we say to each other.
>
> (Fieldnote)

I added to this fieldnote the following observation:

> He gave me·the impression that he had found the meeting difficult, in-
> sofar as it had created its own disturbances in him, as well as in Helen,
> and that having been frank with her this had given him some cause for
> concern.
>
> (Fieldnote)

Despite Ron's placid exterior he sometimes worried about his work and found the
job emotionally taxing. When I asked him what his worst memory of headship was
he said spending two days with the parents of a pupil who had died (interview).

Third, Ron worked long hours and devoted a lot of physical, mental and
emotional energy to the job, sometimes at a cost to himself. Early on in the study
I was impressed by his willingness to give time to others, including myself, to
stay in school late into the evening, or return on Sundays for a couple of hours
to catch up on the paperwork. Working so hard sometimes took its toll. At the
end of the autumn term he was for a few days unwell, but still attended school.
'Ron looked quite ill, he was pale and when I asked how he was, he said he was
ill with headache, flu, upset stomach' (fieldnote).

The only time I witnessed him being irritable coincided with the most demanding sequence of afterschool meetings, when over fifteen weekdays he was at
home for just two evenings. He also told me when we met once after and away
of school,

> 'Maybe it's me being tired, but I had one of those days of basically telling
> children off all day. One ran home this afternoon as well!' But he didn't
> elaborate on what happened. 'I was teaching in the third years too. . .And
> after I had growled and spoken sharply to one or two, they all got the
> message,' he said, 'and quietened down. But again,' he said, 'it was
> probably me being tired.'
>
> (Fieldnote)

When I made that note I also added:

> Ron doesn't readily acknowledge tiredness, I took that to mean he must be quite fatigued. Although he expressed only tiredness he seemed to be somewhat low in spirit and I wondered what this might indicate for his feelings and emotions.
>
> (Fieldnote)

Furthermore, his response to the demands and pressures was to extend his working day in order to accommodate his work. Speaking about the particularly heavy load of evening work he experienced in the spring term he said, '. . .the school day just sort of extends in the time you're involved in school' (interview). Nor did he have a strong sense of differentiating between work and home.

> It's just life. It's just one. . .The organization of social, domestic things is just one of those things that has to be fitted in, in the same way as other things in the week. The only thing I'm conscious of is changing from one to the other, but part of it [work] never goes away.
>
> You don't think about it as working. No, I don't think I do.
>
> (Interviews)

In short, headship was always with him. It filled his head so that the school resided, in a sense, inside the head's head! Something Kate knew more than most —

> It's [headship] extremely demanding, totally consuming of the person. . . it's time consuming. . .it's a way of life. . .It looks like someone really not doing anything other than things pertaining to headship. It's a hobby, everything. You get up in the morning and go to work and you think about it all day and you come home, perhaps, for supper, and you're still thinking about it and you go back and spend the whole evening there and you come back and you're still thinking about it. You try and shed it a little bit before you go to bed and then you get up and start the whole day again and that goes on and you just don't shed it, not *ever*!
>
> (Interview)

Headship was not a job, it was a way of life. It was the integration of professional and personal beliefs and experience which were not so much worked out as *lived out* in the school. The school was an extension of him. Thinking about the school filled much of his day and was forever with him. And he carried headship with him because it was him. He had become a head and, in some senses, headship had become him.

Chapter 4

Reflections on the Case Study and Conclusions

This chapter is split into two sections of unequal length. The first section, reflections on the case study, opens with Ron's response to the study. Thereafter I present my observations on five topics which the case study touches upon: deputy heads, schools as settings for heads' work, micropolitics, phases of headship, and gender. In the second section I present the main conclusions I draw from the case study and briefly discuss them.

I have adopted this structure since, by discussing my reflections first and conclusions second, I replicate the processes of analysis and deduction which I followed. Having written the case study I continued the search for its meaning by looking at some of the issues which emerged from it. These issues, in turn, helped me to perceive more clearly the main conclusions I now hold about Ron's headship.

In one sense, the portrait of Ron is less important for its representational accuracy than for what it revealed to me as I attempted to create a likeness. As Berger says of the act of drawing, 'For the artist drawing is discovery. . .A line, an area of tone is not really important because it records what you have seen but because of what it will lead you onto see' (Berger 1960:23). The tones and lines of the case study have led me on to see and reflect upon a number of topics and, in turn, these contributed to the formulation of the conclusions I drew from the research.

Reflections on the Case Study

Ron's Response to the Study

I wanted to share my interpretation of Ron's work with him not only for ethical reasons, but also because

> one must be ready to handle the criticisms of those who actually live this life. The closer they think you come to describing it, the better you can feel about your data gathering, your organization and your analysis.
>
> (Wise 1974, cited in Coulson 1986:8)

Because of the Whole School Curriculum Development (WSCD) project Ron had already seen and cleared the case study I had constructed for that project (Southworth 1989). Some of the data were common to both projects so having seen the WSCD case study meant Ron was somewhat prepared for the more detailed portrait of himself, as he appreciated when I interviewed him to discover his response to it. He said,

[the case study] didn't come as a surprise because I'd seen some of the background information for the first project. In that sense there was nothing surprising. No [pause]. . .I thought it was a very perceptive mirror of the year in many ways.

(Interview)

Ron's response to the case study was positive. His first comment, in the idiom of a football manager, was, 'The lad done good really! Great!' [laughter] (interview). Generally he thought the picture of his headship was representative:

I thought it was very accurate, I didn't feel there were any dimensions that were missing. . .I didn't feel there was anything in the interpretations that I felt were askew somehow (interview).

Moreover, when questioned directly about the view of him as central and powerful he thought that was accurate. Similarly, he accepted the staff's views of himself. I raised these points with him because the case study of him for this research is markedly different to that in the WSCD project study. The portrait of Ron focuses strongly upon his power and the personal side of headship. It was important that these differences were checked out with him. In fact, Ron raised no objections to the case study at all. He brought to my attention two small factual errors which I promised to correct.

Finding his acceptance of the study reassuring I elected, as part of the interview, to share with him some of my concerns. I did so for two reasons. First by modelling critical reflection I hoped to draw out of him any reservations he might hold, but which he was not prepared to disclose otherwise. Second, I genuinely wanted him to be a dialogue partner since the topics I raised were ones I was then puzzling over.

I first raised with him the idea that some parts of his work were perhaps too lightly touched upon. He accepted that I had not covered his out-of-school activities in as much depth as some other aspects of his work, but did not regard that as a serious flaw in the study. He also said that he felt he was an *overt* leader in many of the groups he worked with after school (Community Association, Festival Committee). When I put it to him that I felt he was quite a leader in the governors meetings, he agreed with that impression (interview).

Next, I asked him about his partnership with Dave and how I had represented it. He felt the account was accurate and said, 'I think it was a senior and junior partnership. . .I was the senior partner. . .'

'Was it always like that?'
'With Dave? Yes' (interview).

With prompting, Ron was prepared to be critical of the portrait, but not in any major way. I could lead him to make minor criticisms, but his demeanour suggested that he was well disposed to the study. Both then and on several subsequent occasions (since he continued to take an interest in the research and liked to hear how the work was progressing), he appeared to have been in full agreement with it. While the case study did not generate any major critical comment, it did provoke Ron to reflect on some of the tensions that existed between members of staff, on the conflicts which arose from time to time and how he dealt with them. Ron felt these tensions were only hinted at in the case study. Ron felt there were three 'instances of conflict' during the period of fieldwork:

> One was the exhibition, [another] was the relationship between the two fourth year teachers, and the other was the question of the acting deputy headship. I think they surfaced in the study but I don't think they were connected [and related to one another]. I think there is a connection in some form of control there. . .
>
> (Interview)

Ron went on to say that he believed he tried to pre-empt conflict situations by 'making contact with individual people on a very regular basis' and channelling the disagreements towards curriculum issues 'rather than the personal stuff'. He recognized that some of the tensions were interpersonal, but tried to defuse the disputes that might arise between staff. Yet Ron was unclear whether he did this for professional or personal reasons.

> Whether you alleviate it because its nice to have a quiet life and people getting on well together I don't know. But its an element of [the head's] control, its another dimension of power.
>
> (Interview)

When I asked him to say more he added,

> I think [its] appearing to be able to resolve those myriad interpersonal relationships that are there the whole time. I don't think you do it because it sort of gives you any personal satisfaction of power or control, but I think it just helps to channel the school together. But that's just a thought. . .its just a reflection. . .
>
> (Interview)

Ron's reflection suggests he was trying to understand his part in the micropolitics of the school. He did not use the term micropolitics, but I am reasonably confident that he was thinking about how he operated in this domain. I believe Ron was trying to make sense of his role in terms of uniting the staff and creating a negotiated order in the school (see Nias *et al.* 1989:160–170).

The process of clearing the case study provided further opportunities to collect more data (Yeomans 1987:90). Throughout the interview I had to discipline myself because there was a temptation to continue searching for more data rather than check out Ron's reactions to the study. In clearing the case study Ron acknowledged he was powerful in the school. He also spoke about his partnership with Dave and touched upon micropolitics in the school. These were two topics I was then reflecting upon, along with three others: schools as settings for the work of heads; phases in headship; gender. I was reflecting upon these five issues because the case study appeared to throw some light on each of them and I was concerned to note what I could about them for further analysis and research. I shall now look at each of these.

The Partnership of the Head and Deputy

When the case study was completed it intrigued me that Dave should figure in such a pale form because he and Ron appeared, on the surface, to work as partners. They spoke to each other, kept in touch and appeared to enjoy one another's company. Dave covered for Ron in his absence and kept him informed of developments amongst the staff. Yet, when Ron spoke about headship, he tended to talk about it in an individualized, as against shared, way. Ron focused upon what *he* did, or was thinking and planning. Dave barely figured in Ron's analyses. Nor was Dave regularly consulted about what actions to take. Ron tended to determine courses of action about which Dave was, at most, informed. In other words, the partnership of Ron and Dave was relatively shallow. Ron largely worked independent of Dave.

I puzzled away at why Dave did not feature as a planning partner with Ron and can offer six possible interpretations. First, there is a widespread belief that deputy heads in primary schools occupy a position which lacks explicit definition (Coulson 1974:2; Bush 1981:75–6) and so they suffer uncertainty about their role. For example, deputies are seen as filling a difficult position (Kent 1989:81), which requires Janus-like qualities (ILEA 1985:67) because they stand between the headteacher and the staff, being both a classteacher (in the great majority of primary schools) and a senior member of staff who is close to the head in positional terms. The combination of uncertainty and ambiguity concerning their role caused Bush (1981) to conclude that the 'position of deputy head in primary schools has little substance or meaning' (p. 84). Moreover, Reay and Dennison suggest:

> The deputy is a teacher whose main function is to deputise for the head during any absence. The main duties are as a 'go-between' (keeping the head and staff informed of what the other side is thinking), as a counsellor of staff and as an organiser, doing those jobs no-one else thinks are part of their responsibilities.
>
> (1990:44)

Following this line of argument, one would say Dave is a slight presence in the case study because, like many other deputies, he lacked a substantial definition of his role.

A second interpretation centres upon Ron's attitude towards headship, and by association, deputy headship. It seems to me that Ron held a traditional, paternalistic view of headship (Coulson 1976:276). Such an outlook locates the head at the centre of the school and places the deputy in not only a subordinate role, but also in a less than central one, perhaps even in a peripheral role. The unequal nature of the head and deputy's role is reflected in the literature concerned with primary school leadership and management. In numerous texts overwhelming attention is devoted to headship while deputy headship is given only a brief mention (see Waters 1979; Whitaker 1983; ILEA 1985; Coulson 1986; Dean 1987; Bell 1988; Hill 1989; Kent 1989). In all of these texts the impression gained is of the school revolving around the headteacher, with the deputy performing a relatively minor and supportive function. Such a pattern can also be seen in DES documents. Descriptors of headteachers' conditions of employment, general functions and professional duties run to over three pages, while those for deputy heads take up just one third of a page (DES 1989:20–4). Furthermore, Ron himself regarded Dave as a junior partner and himself as senior (see previous section). Dave's presence in the case study was relatively weak because Ron was such a strong figure in the school and this particular imbalance reflects wider assumptions about primary school head and deputy partnerships.

To this second interpretation can be added a third, based upon Nias' analysis of a head and deputy's partnership in a nursery and infant school (Nias 1987b:30–53). This, the only published ethnographic account of a head and deputy's partnership, supports the idea that partnerships are characterized by an asymmetrical relationship (p. 49). Yet Nias also suggests that while the deputy's work was unspecified, she influenced staff and the head through her intense involvement in the school's communication systems, personal contact with the staff and expressive leadership (p. 50). To some extent Dave corresponds with this picture. He was always listening in the staffroom (interview); and he claimed he spent much of his time dealing with interpersonal tensions and problems (interview). Dave, too, was sensitive to others and his apparent lack of institutional weight may only be a superficial interpretation because he was simply unobtrusive in his influence. Moreover, he sometimes acted as Ron's eyes and ears, a role suggested by some (Paisey and Paisey 1987:149–50), as appropriate for deputy heads to adopt. In gathering intelligence for Ron it may not have been politic for him to share his knowledge with Ron on the occasions when I was around. Therefore, his manifest behaviour might have disguised a discreet and covert presence within the school.

Fourth, it is possible that my presence adversely affected the relationship between Ron and Dave. As Ron became comfortable about sharing his observations with me, I unwittingly usurped Dave's position. Over the course of the year I became a surrogate deputy head, insofar as Ron confided in me and came, to some extent, to enjoy using me as a sounding board, a role to which many deputies, in my experience, aspire.

A fifth possibility is that during the year of the fieldwork, Dave's motivation temporarily dipped. His morale was lowered by his failure to secure promotion, and his enthusiasm for education in general decreased for a period. Furthermore, given the tensions which existed between some staff, he felt unhappy at being unable to resolve them.

Arising from each of these single strand interpretations is a multi-stranded one which I have come to favour. Dave was a relatively weak figure in the school because Ron regarded the headteacher as the most important person in a school. Hence there was an in-built asymmetry to any partnership between himself and his deputy. Additionally, Ron also saw headship as involving deliberate and sustained reflection about the school. While he encouraged others to join him in his ruminations, their contribution was either to act as an audience or to provide extra material on which he would further reflect. Ron saw the process of reflection as evaluatory and his sole task; reflection was essentially a solitary task. Therefore, not only was Ron the most significant person, but also a proportion of his work involved working alone; there were things he would not share with others. Hence Dave was cast in a supporting role.

Alongside Ron's ideas about what he should do was the fact that much of what Dave did was subordinate to Ron. Dave supervised the entrance and exit of children to the school hall for showing assemblies and he kept the children in order until Ron arrived and literally took command. Dave usually dealt with minor acts of indiscipline, but serious crimes were referred to Ron. Also, it was unusual for Dave to lead staff meetings in Ron's presence. Typically, when they attended meetings together Dave played the supporting role. Dave's actions, like those of other deputies, demonstrated subordination rather than interdependence (see Reay and Dennison 1990:45).

Dave's main work was dealing with colleagues' feelings and teacher morale. In this respect he was an expressive leader. While Ron placed an emphasis on looking after individuals' needs, he regarded the development of teaching and learning as the most important part of his work. Ron was both an expressive and an instrumental leader, but the latter took priority over the former. Dave complemented and supplemented Ron's expressive leadership, but was not a prominent instrumental leader. Moreover, because expressive leadership is less visible than instrumental leadership, Dave's work was less noticeable. In other words, Dave did not make an overtly obvious contribution to the professional developments in the school.

Furthermore, for a period of the fieldwork, Dave did become less enthusiastic and committed. Promotional disappointments affected his morale and interpersonal tensions in the school further frustrated him. Unable to resolve the latter, he became unhappy, if not dissatisfied with himself and his colleagues. His reaction to not being appointed to a headship made Dave introspective, and he withdrew into himself and away from Ron. Also, around this time Ron was out of school a lot more and sometimes, when he returned to school, Dave had gone home. Thus Ron began to feel more alone. Lastly, as the two temporarily drifted apart, I was unwittingly drawn closer to Ron who, to some extent, perhaps, used me as he might otherwise have used Dave.

If this multi-strand interpretation is valid, it probably tells us more about Ron than it does about Dave. It shows that deputy heads are heavily reliant upon their headteachers (Reay and Dennison 1990:45). Deputies cannot be assistant heads, a new role emerging in the 1990s (see Southworth 1994), unless their headteachers facilitate such a partnership. As Whitaker (1983:87) says, the vital factor in determining a deputy head's role is the attitude of the head. However, it is not just a question of attitude. The foremost influence in framing Dave's role was Ron's conception of what he should do as a head. Ron did not relinquish any of his authority to Dave. Hence Dave was able only to exercise influence. Looked at in this light, Ron and Dave's partnership further supports the idea that heads are controlling figures in their schools. Moreover, my analysis and interpretation suggests that studies of headteachers might be conducted by examining what deputy heads do and why. Deputy headship can reflect headteachers' conceptions of headship.

The School as a Setting for the Work of the Head

It is clear from much that Ron said that he was acutely aware of the school as his context; it was his theatre of operation. For example, Ron appreciated that the design of the building affected the organizational structure of the school, as did the school's size, location and community school status. Ron also drew comparisons between the three schools where he had been headteacher. He acknowledged that the individual circumstances of each school had a bearing upon his work as headteacher.

In contrasting his work in other schools, and in being mindful of the constraints and opportunities provided by the present school's circumstances, Ron shows that Fiedler's (1967) contingency theory of leadership is pertinent to primary headship. This theory stemmed from an unease about approaches to leadership which sought to identify a style or combination of styles appropriate under all circumstances (Hughes 1985:266). Contingency theory has for sometime been regarded as useful (Handy 1981:96), yet there has been little application of it to primary school headteachers. Small (1984) has suggested that headship, across a range of school types (infant, first, middle, senior high, and comprehensive schools) is a 'scandal of particularity' because the five heads in his study were 'very dependent upon the circumstances of their school' (Small 1984:ii). Also, Southworth notes that what headteachers do in task terms is dependent upon where they are 1988b:41–2). A number of contextual factors affect a head's work. They are: school size; the age, fabric, design and layout of the school buildings; the curricular strengths and weaknesses of the staff; and the type of school (denominational, county, community, as well as infant, junior, primary, etc.) (Southworth 1988a:42).

It does not need belabouring that Ron's work was determined, in part, by the fact that he was head of a group four (pre-1990 regroupings) junior school and that this was a community school. The study indicates that his work was affected by contextual factors both internal and external to the school. Boyd-Barrett (1981:6) argues that issues of external and internal school management are generally closely connected and he demonstrates how external agencies and socio-ecological factors, (such as school's catchment area, neighbourhood schools, social composition, local history and traditions, demography, population mobility) create a set of physical, social and economic constraints specific to each school (pp. 10–21). However, more information and analysis is needed to discover precisely how these, and other factors, combine and affect individual headteachers. Our understanding of the topic would benefit from multi-site, comparative studies which focused upon headteachers in similar sized schools, of the same type and at the same period in time, but in different environmental settings (urban, suburban, rural, etc.).

Similarly, there is a need to examine a headteacher's contribution to and effect upon the school as a setting. As Coulson has said, the reciprocal nature of the relationship between school and head needs to be seen more clearly (Coulson 1988a:8). In the case of Ron, the school was his context not least because he had been instrumental in making it so. His impact upon the school was perceived to be so strong that, in common with other primary heads (Coulson 1976:285; Nias *et al.* 1989:99–101), it was referred to as his: he was the proprietor of the school. While such a phenomenon is recognized in the literature, it has not been researched in any depth.

It might, for example, be worthwhile for future studies to investigate the difference between being headteacher in a school which the head has opened and one where the head has inherited a school. Research into headteacher succession should throw light upon this particular topic. However, in Britain there is a dearth of such investigations despite interest in the topic in North America (see Miskel and Cosgrove 1985:87–105) and recognition in Britain that succession is a topic of some importance (Lloyd, A. 1985; Coulson 1986; Weindling and Earley 1987; Ball 1987; Nias *et al.* 1989). Little can be said other than that the range of options available to a head is constrained both by established notions of the practices appropriate to headship and by the customs and expectations resulting from previous regimes in each particular school.

(Coulson 1988a:8–9)

The notion of reciprocity mentioned above, also needs to be developed. While Ron was aware of his context he was not an interested bystander, watching from the sidelines. He intervened and was part of the action. Expressed another way, the episodes, events and stories which formed his context were, in part, shaped by him. There was a dynamic interplay between himself and his context. His close association with the school arose not only because of his proprietorial feelings and because he identified *with* it, but also because he was engrossed by it and pro-foundly *absorbed into it.* This last observation also relates to headteachers and organizational culture. A study by Nias *et al.* (1989) showed that the work of a primary headteacher can be understood in terms of the school's culture (or cultures). Organizational culture is an order created by members of the organization through interaction with one another, it is a deeply internalized sense of 'the way we do things around here' (Nias *et al.* 1989:10).

Organizational culture has become an area of considerable interest in school management (see Sarason 1982; Deal and Kennedy 1983; Sergiovanni and Corbally 1984; Westoby 1988; Beare *et al.* 1989; Holly and Southworth 1989; Nias *et al.* 1989; Bolam *et al.* 1993), with headteachers highlighted as important influences upon it. Nias *et al.* (1989:102), for instance, building on the work of Schein (1985), argue that headteachers are the founders of their school's cultures. This observa-tion is true for Ron. His educational values were broadly accepted by the staff, as were his principles for running the school as an organization of adults — (such values as consideration for others, consultation, individual attention). However, while the culture at Orchard bore some relation to Ron's educational and mana-gerial values, there was not a complete correspondence between them.

These observations suggest that although heads play a part in developing the culture of the school, it is unwise to regard their contribution as direct or neces-sarily causal. At present a managerial view tends to be offered, with heads advised to manipulate the culture (Jenkins 1991:25; Leithwood and Jantzi 1990) as if it was an artefact, rather than as a set of dynamic and mutable processes. Also, there is no acknowledgment of reciprocity. Heads might influence the culture, but the culture might also shape them. Heads may not be independent of their cultural settings, but inextricably caught up in them.

These reflections on schools as settings and cultures have highlighted the idea that there is an interplay between heads and their contexts; each affects the other, although precisely how, and to what degree, is unclear. One reason for this lack of precise understanding is variability. In any single school there are many inter-relating and variable situational factors and processes. These combine in such a way as to make the circumstances of a school context specific. Each head must therefore seek to understand his/her school as a setting and act accordingly. Indeed, heads will experience a sense of 'uniqueness which tends to defeat generalizations about schools for anyone who has a sense of how they live and grow from the in-side' (Winkley 1983:15). Working in unique circumstances might increase a head's sense of solitariness and isolation. Only the individual head knows his or her school, and only he or she can determine the best and most suitable course of action.

Micropolitics

The case study shows that there was a micropolitical dimension to Ron's work in the school. The analysis of the data was guided by the ideas of Ball (1987) and Hoyle (1981; 1986). Indeed, the case study reflects Hoyle's definition of micropolitics: 'the strategies which individuals and groups adopt in order to ensure that their interests are served in the decision-making process' (Hoyle 1981:23). Thus the case study shows that Ron and other members of staff were involved in an active process of negotiation of interests. However, micropolitics is treated in a relatively light way in the case study for two reasons.

First, it was only after the case study was cleared that I began to appreciate the nature of some of the differences which occurred in the school. For example, tension was evident in decisions relating to curriculum development. Yet, it was not until I had read work by Ball and Bowe (1990) and Radnor (1990) that I appreciated that the struggle that was occurring in the school arose from the implementation of the 1988 Education Act. What I originally regarded as a head whose professional identity and career were threatened by the impending changes, I now see as additionally involving a struggle about curricular decision-making in the school. Marie and Ron were conscious that over the preceding two years they had experienced a reduction in their autonomy and that they were becoming curriculum deliverers rather than curriculum initiators (Radnor 1990:27–8). Other staff, most vocally Sarah, but also Dave, felt the time had come to 'just get on with it'. In effect then, there was a tussle between some members of staff over whose will was to prevail. Ron and Marie perhaps believed that by moving slowly they might retain some control over the school's curriculum, while Sarah believed the curriculum was now determined by central government and that their role in school was confined to implementation.

Second, researching micropolitics is not a straightforward task. While it would have been naïve to overlook micropolitics, I also felt uncertain about how far I should and could have researched it. Of course, I sometimes recognized its existence and was occasionally caught up in it, but my involvement was at most, spasmodic and, perhaps, passive. In other words, during the course of fieldwork I became aware that attempts to study micropolitics could be problematic because it is 'oriented to interests rather than goals, coalitions rather than departments, influence rather than authority, strategies rather than procedures' (Hoyle 1986:129). It concerns hidden and disguised behaviour which might best be observed by a fulltime participant observer saturated in the institution's history and norms. In short, research into micropolitics requires a full-time insider's account which also draws upon the accounts of several other insiders.

Possibly the case study is weaker for not including a fuller investigation into micropolitics at Orchard school, or for not focusing more strongly upon it as a theme in the study. Yet I decided that a strong focus might have altered the agreements I had made with the staff, and would have made clearance of the data more difficult.

In addition to these reasons for my light treatment of the topic, there is one other reflection to note. I am sure that competing interests and conflict were a part of the the 'political drama' (Lyman and Scott 1975:114) at Orchard school, but there is a danger in over-emphasizing them. Indeed, the more I thought about micropolitics, the more I became dissatisfied with Hoyle's (1986) understanding of the topic.

Micropolitics is largely grounded in a conflict perspective (Blase 1989:400), but this does not adequately explain Ron's influence. For sure, as the case study shows, Ron had a game plan and could apply pressure in pursuit of his interests. Yet Ron was also courteous, considerate and caring and did not usually resort to conflict. While there is much to learn about the negotiation of interests and the resolution of conflict, the language of micropolitics favours a sense of the sinister; of 'micropolitical skullduggery' (Hoyle 1986:125). Such language needs to set against an emerging feature of primary schools, namely the affective side of schools as organizations (Acker 1988; Nias *et al.* 1989). Although negative emotions such as anger and jealousy exist in schools, so too can positive ones such as trust and respect. Too strong an emphasis upon conflict may ignore the presence of compassion, care and humour (Nias *et al.* 1989:70–2, 85–7). In other words, conflict is only one aspect of the organizational drama, it is not the whole picture.

Blase (1989; 1991) eschews the conflict perspective and argues, on the basis of empirical data, that school principals who are open are perceived by their teacher colleagues to be more effective than closed principals — those who are secretive, uncommunicative, manipulative. Blase (1989) relates how the teachers in his study described open principals as sometimes using threats and intermediaries to get their own ways, yet more commonly their work styles involved seven characteristics. The principals were:

1 honest — straightforward and sincere;
2 communicative — expressing themselves in constructive ways and engaged in face-to-face interaction;
3 participative — soliciting teacher input about a range of curricular and organizational issues and decisions;
4 collegial — actively created relationships that minimized status differences;
5 informal — polite, courteous, relaxed, humourous;
6 supportive — stood behind teachers in confrontations with children and parents and were accessible responding quickly to teachers' professional and personal needs;
7 held high but not unrealistic expectations about teachers' job performance.

(Blase 1989:384–6)

These characteristics broadly correspond to those exhibited by Ron.

Blase has subsequently argued that these characteristics plus praise and visibility can be

> linked to increases in teachers' respect for and trust in principals, which in turn, increases teachers' receptiveness to influence. When principals' goals are viewed as morally appropriate, teachers receptivity to influence is further reinforced.
>
> (Blase 1991:43–4)

Now, Blase's points help to provide a richer understanding of Ron's influence at Orchard.

Ron was an open head insofar as he correlates to Blase's seven characteristics. In addition, his views on children and learning were shared by the teaching staff. He was respected professionally and personally and this increased teachers' receptiveness to Ron's influence. As Acker (1988) says in her study of a primary head, values, emotion and affect influence what happens in schools as much as interests (p. 3). However, whatever the source of influence, it should not be forgotten that the outcome is nevertheless an increase in power of individual headteachers. In other words, the political stance of the open principal includes a control dimension. That is, heads do not necessarily need to resort to conflict to gain teacher compliance with policies and personal expectations (Blase 1991:46). Heads can also influence through personal relations and private persuasion (Blase 1989:399).

Perhaps, then, there is a need for research studies focusing on micropolitics to be undertaken in primary schools. Also, such studies need to examine whether a conflict perspective accounts for all that occurs, whether Blase's notion of open interactions provides a more valid explanation, or if open heads also engage in conflicts.

Phases of Headship

The idea that there are phases in headship arises from Ron's belief that his approach to headship had altered over time. While initially as a head he relied upon his exemplary teaching to influence staff, latterly this had ceased and he had become a developer of teachers. He was less a player and more a coach.

Others have considered the idea of heads changing their approaches over time. For example, Hellawell's (1991) study of twenty-four primary heads showed that nearly all stated that over the years they had reduced the amount of time they devoted to teaching. Lloyd (1985) notes primary heads becoming more relaxed in their approach to leadership as time goes by. Lloyd also cites Craig-Wilson (1978), who saw headship as involving 'a personally creative initial stage, a shared planning stage and a third "position" stage which is accompanied by an "inert maturity characterised by a sense of security, complacency and confirmity" ' (Lloyd 1985:303). Winkley (1983:15–26) has also hypothesized that there are three stages in headship (as noted in Chapter 1). Winkley sees each stage as distinct from the previous one, thereby suggesting discontinuity between them. However, the case of Ron suggests continuity. He was the central leader in his first school and continued to be central in his third school; yet his approach to headship had nevertheless altered. What Ron's study may disclose is that while some aspects of headship change, the whole of headship does not necessarily alter.

Two other pieces of work relate to this topic. Nias *et al.* (1989) suggest that length of time in post affects a head's work in terms of the school's organizational culture. Three heads, out of the five project schools which were studied, had been in post in the same school for at least 10 years. The other two heads had been in post for five years and one-and-a-half years. The three longest serving heads felt their schools were congruent with their individual aspirations, whereas the other two heads felt there was some way to go. The former three heads saw their work as sustaining the schools' cultures, while the latter two felt they needed to develop their schools towards their respective visions. These heads were either sustainers or developers of their schools' cultures because of their perceptions in relation to their visions and schools' phases of development (Nias *et al.* 1989:97–8).

The work of Nias *et al.* needs to be set alongside Mortimore *et al.* (1988) study of effective junior schools. This suggests that a headteacher's time in post had a complex relationship with the school's effectiveness.

Where the head was new [having been in post for less than three years] pupils' progress and developments tended to be poorer than expected. In contrast schools with mid-term heads [in post for between three and seven years] tended to have a positive effect on their pupils' progress. The data suggest that having established themselves, the mid-term heads may have been in a position to implement more effective management strategies and/or the results of earlier efforts may have been coming to fruition after several years in post. Where heads had been in their present post for eleven years or more, school effects, on a number of areas, tended to be negative.

(Mortimore *et al.* 1988:222)

What Mortimore's work, other studies and the case of Ron support is the claim that there is a process of headteacher maturation, as others have hypothesized (Lortie 1990). However, it remains unclear as to whether maturation occurs as a result of time in post in a single school or time as a headteacher in a number of schools; nor is it possible to discern a relationship between these two. Equally, it remains obscure whether changes in headteachers are due to greater professional knowledge, closer acquaintance with a school's circumstances, experience of different schools and their environments, personal development and life circumstances. Neither is it possible to say which of these factors, or some combination of them, contributes to making a head more effective in her or his school. Headteacher maturation looks to be a complex issue and one which warrants deeper investigation.

Gender

I noted in Chapter 1 that gender is an issue in primary headship because the role is largely a male conception. Moreover, the majority of studies of primary heads have been conducted by male researchers and writers. The case study of Ron shows that his view of headship was gendered. That is, he held a masculine view of headship; he viewed the world through a male lens (Shakeshaft 1991:3). For example, Ron's career path was described as vertical and staged, a pattern which others have associated with male rather than female workers (Smith *et al.* 1986:29), while all of Ron's headteacher role models were men.

The case study of Ron is broadly in line with two existing observations on teachers' careers. First, in teaching women tend to be found in some roles more than in others (Grant 1989:36). Women constitute a majority of teachers and a minority of managers and administrators in schools in the Western world. In England fewer women than men hold managerial posts in school, particularly senior ones (Riches 1990:142; Grant 1989:36–7).

Second, although it is relatively easy to identify the phenomenon by which 'women teach and men manage' the reasons for it are complex and varied (Jones 1990:110). For example, Burgess (1989) in common with others (see Spender 1981; Connell 1985a; Arnot and Weiner 1987; Acker 1989; Shakeshaft 1989), argues:

the organization of primary schooling suggests that there are clearly defined roles for male and female teachers, equating the classrooms with domesticity and school management with leadership and power which traditionally had a male connotation.

(Burgess 1989:81)

In other words, Ron held a paternalistic view of headship, which can be explained, in part, by cultural assumptions about different roles for men and women. Ron was a product of the social conditioning which has tended to sustain male seniority, if not dominance in some schools.

While this observation is supported by previous studies into headship (see Chapter 1), apart from recognizing the part gender can play in defining roles, it does not increase our understanding about headship and gender. Rather, it suggests that more work is needed to further understand the similarities and differences between male and female conceptions of headship. For example, Eisenstein (1987) argues that there are two clusters of attributes assigned respectively to men and women in Western societies. Men are expected to adopt instrumental traits (tenacity, aggression, ambition, responsibility, competitiveness). Women are expected to develop expressive traits (affection, obedience, kindliness, friendliness, responsiveness to sympathy and approval) (p. 37). These two clusters of attributes form stereotypes of how males and females are expected to behave, which, in turn, can affect the way male and female heads perform their roles (Gray 1987:297; Fullan and Hargreaves 1991:60–1).

The small amount of work that has been undertaken in primary schools suggests that teachers prefer male heads to be co-ordinators and female heads to be facilitators (Johnston 1986:222). However, Johnston also says:

> it is clear that 'directing' is an important aspect of the ideal head's leadership. This suggests that, irrespective of whether the head is male or female, teachers primarily prefer the head to be someone who can plan and allocate the tasks to be done, who can orchestrate the use of facilities and who assumes responsibility for directing the activities of the staff.
>
> (Johnston 1986:222)

Johnston's work acts as a warning about becoming fixated with stereotypes and differences to such an extent that we overlook some of the similarities between men and women. Neither should it be assumed that individuals are by necessity of their biology predetermined to act in a particular way, nor trapped in a role so that they are forced to act in only one way. Ron, for example, displayed at different times attributes associated both with male (ambition, competitiveness) and female (empathy consideration) leaders (see Gray 1987).

At this juncture it seems reasonably simple to say that gender is an issue which lies both on the surface of the case study and beneath it. While the study points towards the need for further investigations, by itself it does little more than support some of the existing ideas and observations about gender and primary schooling and management.

Conclusions to the Case Study

The case study depicts Ron as being the centre of the school, personally involved and closely associated with almost every aspect of the school. In short, he was pivotal and powerful. The portait shows Ron to be powerful because of a combination of five factors. He was the school's founder. He was the most experienced professional in the school. The staff perceived him to be a successful headteacher. He had authority by virtue of his position in the organization. He had political guile and was active in the micropolitics of the school.

Although Ron was powerful he was not inconsiderate towards others. He cared for the staff, children and their parents. He was generally supportive to staff, sympathetic to their personal needs and domestic ties and made allowances for individuals.

Moreover, he consulted staff and sought to involve them in policy decisions. Yet such participation did not mean that power was necessarily devolved from him to them. Blase (1991) argues that there is both a control and a collaborative–collegial dimension to headship (p. 46). While both dimensions were apparent in Ron's case they were not equal. He was willing to consult, but not at the expense of his control.

Indeed, his control pervaded the school. For one thing he was always, in the eyes of the staff and himself, pre-eminent. For another, he was the founder and owner of the school, and directed developments within it. As the proprietor of the school, he implied that developments were individually approved by him, rather than collectively determined. As Hargreaves (1991:12–13) says, what appears to be collaboration can, on closer inspection, be only co-option (Hargreaves 1991:12–13).

According to Ball (1987:278), heads need to simultaneously control staff and encourage their participation which ultimately means for heads, that the control for school organization is significantly concerned with domination — the elimination or pre-emption of conflict. This conception of domination is consistent with culturally oriented anthropologists' understanding of the term: they regard dominance as the 'behavioural expression of social inequality and socio-culturally structured power relationships' (Seymour-Smith 1986:82).

The case study, then, shows that Ron was powerful to the point of dominating the school. The ethnographic portrait of Ron corresponds to the theme, identified in Chapter 1, that primary heads are powerful figures inside the schools they lead. In this sense, the study verifies existing theories about heads. Moreover, in recognizing that the study's main findings are supported by other analysts and researchers (Coulson 1976, 1986; Alexander 1984; Ball 1987; Nias *et al.* 1989; Bolam *et al.* 1993) it becomes likely that Ron is not wholly unique as a headteacher. For example, Coulson (1976) speaks about the hegemony of the primary school headteacher (p. 278), while Campbell (1985) refers to the dominance of primary heads (p. 155) and to their monopoly on decisions (p. 157).

While a headteacher's capacity to dominate the school has long been recognized, it has often been analysed and explained as a matter of leadership style (see Nias 1980; Whitaker 1983; Lloyd 1985; Paisey and Paisey 1987). In the case study, by contrast, I did not attempt to classify Ron's leadership style for two reasons.

First, style is a problematical notion, as Ball (1987:87) acknowledges in his cautious preface to using the term. Style 'does not go very far in recognising the dynamic complexity of leadership behaviour in real life' (Hughes 1985:265). Discussions about style usually rely upon abstract categories and typologies (see Nias 1980; Lloyd 1985; Dean 1987), whereas reality is never so discrete or neat.

Second, analyses of style emphasize how a head does things and so are primarily concerned with behaviour. Yet, to adopt the typologies of Lewin *et al.* (1939), for example, the difference between an autocratic leader and a democractic one is not simply behaviour. Style is an *expression* of underlying beliefs (Sergiovanni and Elliott 1975:116). To understand an individual's leadership one needs to appreciate that style is not the determining factor (Viall 1984:102), rather, it is the individual's beliefs about power and leadership which are important because these underpin the style.

Another way of stating this idea is to say that an individual's beliefs (in this case about leadership) mediate his or her actions (Scheffler 1985:18). Moreover,

> Human beings formulate rules or laws for themselves by which they monitor their own conduct and create ideals to which they try to conform. Such functions go beyond the mere having of beliefs and purposes; here the effect is reflexive; the agent strives to meet a standard. . .What emerges here is implicit self-reference, awareness of how one is acting, whether one has lived up to one's ideal. Such self-reference implies that the agent has, as G.H. Mead put it, 'become an object to himself', has swept himself into the sphere of his own reference.
>
> (Scheffler 1985:24–5)

What Scheffler points to here is the concept for self and identity. As the case study makes plain at a number of points Ron's beliefs about his work and the nature of headship are indicators of a set of standards and ideals about his *occupational self*. From the authority structures of the schools he had worked in and from his colleagues and others he had learned the occupational norms of teaching and headship. Together these helped to form his professional identity, his beliefs about headship and how he should lead the school. Ron's conception of headship is not so much a matter of style as of professional identity.

This claim, that Ron's approach to headship is an occupational identity, is similar to the one that Nias (1989) makes about teachers. According to Nias, what is of central importance to some teachers is their sense of *self* (p. 202).

> It matters to teachers themselves, as well as their pupils, who and what they are. Their self-image is more important to them as practitioners than is the case in occupations where the person can be separated from the craft.
>
> (1989:203)

Given that Ron, like all other primary heads, was promoted from the ranks of teacher, it follows that he should continue, implicitly, to regard his work as an occupational identity. In other words, Ron, being a teacher himself saw his work not as an externalized role, but as part of his professional self.

I have now made two assertions based upon the case study. First, Ron dominated the school. Second, his conception of headship is an identity and not a role. Although I have presented them as separate I believe they are tied together. Indeed, it is their fusion which leads me to the major findings of the case study:

The conclusions to draw from the case study's portrait of Ron's headship are that he was dominant in the school and that dominance was part of his professional identity.

Until the mid-1970s educational management followed models of theory and research associated with traditional science (Evers and Lakomski 1991:1). Traditional science sustained a spirit of rationalism which was reinforced by theories of bureaucracy provided by Fayol and Weber and by behaviourism and logical positivism (Hodgkinson 1983:97–8). Rationalism, bureaucracy, behaviourism and positivism meant, until around 1975, that educational management theory was seen as part of a single paradigm called the theory movement (see Beare *et al.* 1989:24; Walker 1991:13–14; Evers and Lakomski 1991:46–75).

While the theory movement is described by a number of terms, such as systems theory, behaviourism, positivism, functionalism, instrumental rationality, managerialism, bureaucracy, bureaucratic rationality, and although there are differences between them, they have in common four assumptions (Riffel 1986:157). First, educational organizations are, potentially at least, socially useful and 'become instruments of public policy and social progress, however these are defined at various times and in different places' (Riffel 1986:156). Second, educational management is a social science and, like other social sciences, has been 'shaped by the belief in our capacity to control our environments through observation, reason and rational government' (p. 156). Third, influenced by positivists, the study of educational management is guided 'by an interest in formal, verifiable hypotheses derived from theory; and theory is regarded as detached from personal commitment, objectified, highly rationalised and restricted in scope' (p. 156).

These three assumptions are mutually reinforcing and lead to a fourth:

> a particular view of educational organizations and of how social and educational progress are to be achieved. Goal-directedness, efficiency, effectiveness, functional behaviour and directive leadership are primary virtues, to be given theoretical support and empirical bases.
>
> (Riffel 1986:156-7)

Preferring the umbrella term of *formal models*, as against theory movement, Bush (1986:22–47) says that formal models assume hierarchical organization in which 'heads possess authority legitimized by their formal positions within the organization' and 'use rational means to pursue agreed goals' (p. 22). In other words, formal models of school management translate the assumptions of the theory movement into school organization. Together the four assumptions of the theory movement and formal models of school management create and sustain a bureaucratic rationality.

It follows from these assumptions and formal models that 'leadership is ascribed to the person at the apex of the hierarchy' (p. 38). As Bush (1986) goes on to say, 'this individual sets the tone of the organization and establishes the major official objectives' (p. 38). Indeed

> The leader is seen as the hero who stands at the top of a complex pyramid of power. The hero's job is to assess the problems, consider alternatives and make rational choices. Much of the organization's power is held by the hero and great expectations are raised because people trust him to solve problems and fend off threats from the environment.
>
> (Baldridge *et al.* 1978:44)

However, there are four criticisms to raise concerning the bureaucratic rationale. First, there are the moral objections rehearsed in Chapter 5. Bureaucracy creates what Hodgkinson (1983) calls neo-feudalism (p. 15). We are 'all incarcerated within an organizational world [and] whilst we may not live in total institutions, the institutional organization of lives is total' (Burrell 1988:232).

Hence, we are all, more or less, reliant upon organizations in post-Industrial society and so we become conditioned, through the pervasive influence of hierarchical organization, to obedience and submissive to authority.

> Indeed, our entire culture and civilization rests upon a presumption of legitimacy in our institutions (which induces in all functionaries of formal organizations) from meter maids to kings. . .a spontaneous reflex of subservience.
>
> (Hodgkinson 1983:66–7)

Bureaucracy creates organizational oppression.

A second line of criticism centres on the emphasis placed upon structure, control, authority and goals. These are legitimized by appeals for objective, rational decision-making and underpinned by a belief that it is possible 'to produce a hypothetico-deductive structure of law-like generalizations for administrative phenomena' (Evers and Lakomski 1991:48). The objective and the rational supersede subjectivity and affect.

Third, in the pursuit of efficient organization, fact is divorced from value (Rivzi 1990:1–2). Bates, a stern critic of bureaucratic rationality, makes this point in detail:

> Though misconceived and misdirected, the quest for a behavioural science of educational administration continues. Despite the revolution brought about in natural science by Heisenberg's uncertainty principle and by relativity and quantum theory, the scientific model propagated by mainstream theorists of educational administration is still firmly rooted in Newtonian physics. Despite the acknowledgement of philosophers of the impossibility of eliminating evaluative judgements from the interpretive frameworks within which facts are both sought and understood, mainstream theorists of educational administration continue to declare the incommensurability of fact and value. Despite the social theorists' large-scale abandonment of the quest for a value-free science of society, the mainstream theorists of educational administration still pursue positivistic attempts to develop generalisable laws and principles which will explain the structure and dynamics of organizations.
>
> (Bates 1982:1–2)

By divorcing fact from value the positivists present leadership as a matter of making organizations efficient and effective. Such a view ignores the reality that leadership is also a deeply ethical concern.

The fourth criticism concerns the gendered nature of educational management theorizing. This criticism is not peculiar to the theory movement — the great majority of organization and management theorizing suffers from being located within a patriarchal paradigm (Spender 1981:143). As Shakeshaft (1989:94) says, there is bias in educational management because the world is viewed and shaped by a male lens. Studying males is not in itself a problem, but it becomes a problem when the results of studying male behaviour are assumed appropriate for understanding all behaviour (Shakeshaft 1991:3).

According to feminist writers and others (see Gray 1987; Beare *et al.* 1989:115; Jayne 1989; Fullan and Hargreaves 1991:60–1), not only is our knowledge about management a 'cup half full' (Shakeshaft 1991:1), but our theorizing is biased in favour of males (Blackmore 1989; Shakeshaft 1989, 1991) and male-defined measures of leadership (Shakeshaft 1989:160–1). The male view of leadership 'is premised on particular interpretations of rationality, morality, organization and individualism' (Blackmore 1989:99). Such gender blindness (p. 93) has led a number of writers to examine the way organizational leadership is cast and to argue that the theoretical paradigm dominant in administrative theory should be undermined because it marginalizes women (p. 106).

Together, these four sets of criticisms show that the tenets of the theory movement (bureaucracy, asymmetrical power, primacy of efficiency over ethics and objectivity over subjectivity), along with its patriarchal bias, have come under attack from a number of individuals and theoretical perspectives. It is to these I now turn to examine whether any of them offer a basis for reconceptualizing school leadership.

Alternative Theoretical Perspectives

In looking for an alternative to the theory movement I have chosen to review four sets of criticisms of the theory movement to see which is the most appropriate in terms of my concerns about domination. The first two are the work of individuals, Greenfield and Hodgkinson, the third is the cultural perspective on educational management and the fourth focuses on the critical perspective on educational leadership provided by critical theorists.

I have chosen these four because they are the most commonly cited critiques of the theory movement, each offers a distinctive analysis of the limitations of the theory movement and, separately and together, they provide further support for the four criticisms noted at the end of the previous section. Greenfield attacks the primacy of objectivity over subjectivity in the theory movement since his critique is based upon a view of social reality as a human invention (Evers and Lakomski 1991:76). Hodgkinson similarly challenges the behavioural assumptions of the theory movement, but he has also attempted to rethink leadership. The cultural perspective draws upon anthropology and interpretive social science and is antithetical to the positivist assumptions of the theory movement. Critical theorists, on the other hand, adopt neither a purely positivistic, nor wholly interpretive perspective (Evers and Lakomski 1991:148). They pursue an emancipatory intent which is opposed to organizational domination.

In the next four sections I will present, in turn a brief summary of each of these critiques. I will also note the strengths and weaknesses of the criticisms in order, at the end of the fourth section, to identify the one which offers the most appealing basis for reconceptualizing school leadership in line with the moral and ethical concerns noted in Chapter 5.

Greenfield's Critique of the Theory Movement

Greenfield, in his own words, 'challenged system theory's ideological hegemony in the study of organizations' (1978:1) by raising such questions as: What is organizational reality? How should people construe it? What truths about organizations can research discover if its theory and procedures rule out the possibility of alternative interpretations of social reality (p. 6)? These questions challenged the assumptions underlying not just systems theory, but the theory movement as a whole.

There are four points to highlight in Greenfield's work. First, Greenfield was interested in organizations 'not as structures subject to universal laws but as cultural artefacts dependent upon the scientific meaning and intention of people within them' (1975:157). He held this view because he accepted Kant's distinction between the noumenal world (the world as it is) and the phenomenal world (the world as we see it).

> For Kant, a world of reality does indeed exist, but man can never perceive it directly; reality is always glossed over with human interpretations which themselves become realities to which man responds.
>
> (Greenfield 1975:160)

Second, and as a consequence of the first, Greenfield believed that our knowledge of reality, whether natural or social, 'contains an irreducibly subjective component' (Evers and Lakomski 1991:77). Greenfield regards organizations not as things, but as a form of socially constructed reality:

> It is people who are responsible for organizations and people who change them. Organizations have reality only through human action and it is that action (and the human will driving it) that we must come to understand.
>
> (Greenfield 1986:71)

Third, it follows from the above that the study of organizations becomes the study of human intention and meaning.

> The dynamic of organization is made from nothing more substantial than people doing and thinking. . .In their deepest — subjective — reality, they are simply manifestations of mind and will. While this conception of organizations does not make them easy to control or to change, it does locate organizational reality in the concreteness of individual action.
>
> The root problems of organizations thus dissolve into questions about what people do, why they do it and whether what they do is right. Ultimately such questions become the individual's search for identity and for truth.
>
> (Greenfield 1980:27)

Fourth, in arguing against the reification of organizations he demonstrates an emancipatory intent. Organizations should not control people but, rather, people should control them (1980:40). Yet Greenfield's thesis is not explicitly concerned with power. What he sought most was to undermine the assumptions whereby only one kind of reality is permissible and to create a sense of pluralism:

The paradigm I argue for in the exploration of social realities is certainly against overarching (Parsonian) systems of unilateral explanation; it is one that admits the many voices of truth and recognises them as attached to self, to individuals. My chief argument is against those who fit all truth about organizations into a single, objective, non-political, self-less truth called science.

(Greenfield 1980:55)

Greenfield mounts a serious and sustained critique of the theory movement. His argument that organizations are cultural artefacts supports the cultural perspective (see the cultural perspective sub-section in this chapter). By stressing subjectivity Greenfield uproots the positivistic assumptions of the theory movement. Moreover, he hints at the need to understand organizations in the context of an individual's search for an identity. Greenfield also latterly acknowledges that leaders articulate particular values within organizations and that this is essentially a moral task (1986, p. 73).

However, Greenfield's work is weak on three related points. First, in arguing for subjectivity, Greenfield leaves himself open to the charge that subjectivity is all there is and that all knowledge becomes folk theory (Evers and Lakomski 1991:90–1). Second, in emphasizing subjectivity to the extent he does, Greenfield favours unqualified freedom for the agent. As such his argument is inconsistent with structuration theory. In other words, Greenfield's work is weakened by his polarized and exaggerated view of human agency. Third, in his later work Greenfield sees no alternative to behavioural science other than existentialism, mysticism or anarchy (Bates 1989:137). Yet, as Bates goes on to show (pp. 138–40), the work of Giddens suggests other options. It is possible to accept a major portion of Greenfield's argument without adopting his conclusions about the alternatives.

Hodgkinson and the Philosophy of Leadership

There are four points I want to draw out of Hodgkinson's (1983) work. I have chosen these four because they amplify my concerns about and criticisms of the theory movement, bureaucratic organization and leadership. First, Hodgkinson believes that organizations are founded on unexamined assumptions about logic and rationality, derived from the theory movement (Hodgkinson 1983:108). The centrality of values needs to be emphasized, according to Hodgkinson, because rational-legal bureaucracy divorces values from fact, whereas 'the truth is that fact and value are always inextricably intertwined' (Hodgkinson 1983:12).

Second, given the pervasive nature of values, Hodgkinson advocates that organizational leaders be philosophers, by which he means 'the examined life' (p. 57). The unexamined value is not worth holding, nor is unexamined administration worth doing (p. 7). Philosophy as examination is an antidote to the 'agentic state', that is, a condition of ready obedience and willingness to be commanded (p. 66). Philosophical leadership is also offered as a way of overcoming one of the negativities of organizational life, namely executive 'busyness'. This causes managers to be hyperactive, but, because there is no pause for reflection, critical awareness is blunted or stifled. Busyness allows superficiality to blossom (p. 127).

Third, in advocating the centrality of values, Hodgkinson argues for a humanistic view of organizations (Evers and Lakomski 1991:98–110). At the same time, Hodgkinson shows that leadership theory is a sub-branch of the theory movement and argues that leadership should be less narrowly conceived. Moral and ethical issues should be regarded not as a technology, but as part and parcel of leadership. The concerns of leaders are 'affect, motives, attitudes, beliefs, values, ethics, morals, will, commitment, preferences, norms, expectations, responsibilities' (Hodgkinson 1983:202). Leadership is

> practical philosophy, philosophy-in-action. Leadership is intrinsically valuational. Logic may set limits for and parameters within the field of value action but value phenomena determine what occurs within the field. (If leadership is not philosophical) then leadership behaviour could be routinized and, ultimately, computerised.
>
> (Hodgkinson 1983:202)

Fourth, Hodgkinson perceives society as neo-feudal (p. 15) because 'the dominant relationship for the individual within that society is his/her primary organizational affiliation and from this springs the individual's very identity' (p. 15). He is alert to the way power relations impregnate and condition individuals, especially when there is no time or opportunity to reflect upon the agentic state which organizations tend to create and sustain. Hodgkinson is aware of the growth of organization in our society and regards administration as more prepotent and pervasive than ever before (p. 12).

Hodgkinson's work is not without drawbacks. First, the argument he advances is not directed specifically to the management of schools. He works on a larger canvas and is often preoccupied with corporations, executives and their relations with and impact upon society. Second, although he provides an interesting set of propositions, credos and maxims about leadership (pp. 228–9), it is unclear whether any of these are grounded in particular cases. In other words, he prefers ideal types and abstractions. His work has yet to be translated into practice.

Given these two weaknesses, Hodgkinson's work offers further support for the assault upon the theory movement, but little in the way of a concrete, alternative approach to leadership in school.

Cultural Perspective

The cultural perspective is a particular way of conceptualizing organizations and is derived from cultural anthropology, phenomenology and interpretive social science. The framework is concerned with subjectivity: human intention, beliefs and the creation of meaning (Evers and Lakomski 1991:112–3). While the cultural perspective has much in common with Greenfield, who might be described as a forerunner of the cultural perspective in educational management, what is considered most important in the cultural view is the uncovering of some underlying structure of meaning that persists over time and frames people's perception, interpretation and behaviour (Evers and Lakomski 1991:114).

Culture is a fruitful concept for organization theory because in anthropology culture is employed to explain the orderliness and patterning of social life (p. 115). Some writers (see Deal and Kennedy 1982; Peters and Walterman 1982) describe corporate cultures which produce phenomena such as myths, rituals, legends and ceremonies (Evers and Lakomski 1991:115). In this sense 'culture is the social or normative glue that holds organizations together. . .It expresses the values or social ideals and beliefs that organization members come to share' (Smircich 1983:344). As Evers and Lakomski (1991) note, culture provides a sense of communal identity for organizational members, can engender commitment which goes beyond self-interest and acts as a sense-making device (p. 116).

In line with Greenfield and Hodgkinson, the perspective supports the primacy of values. It also extends their work by focusing upon patterns of social interaction amongst organizational members. Cultural theorists consider the perennial issues in the study of organizations of the impact of structures *on* people and the creation of structures *by* people (Hoyle 1986:4). The perspective sees organizations as sites of continuous social interaction, interpersonal negotiation and reality construction, the outcomes of which 'become institutionalised and although continuing to undergo change as a result of individual and group interaction, develop a relative degree of permanence' (Hoyle 1986:10). The perspective does not reduce organizational reality to singular, subjective experience. Rather, its emphasis on values and beliefs brings with it the possibility of organizational members holding conflicting beliefs.

However, to talk about the cultural perspective in educational management is not easy because there is not yet a great deal of writing on the topic (Evers and Lakomski 1991:123). Some studies have been conducted (Nias *et al.* 1989) and a number of commentaries produced (Sergiovanni and Corbally 1984; Westoby 1988; Fullan and Hargreaves 1991). However, underneath some of the interest in culture lies a search for ways to control the organizational culture of schools.

For example, studies of organizational cultures have helped to reveal the part school leaders play in developing and sustaining shared beliefs and a sense of unity (Nias *et al.* 1989; 1992). Some writers (see Sergiovanni 1984; Firestone and Wilson 1989; Jenkins 1991) now advocate that leaders strive to shape the values and norms of the schools they lead (Sergiovanni 1984:105–14). In other words, values and beliefs, although intrinsic to organizational life, should be subordinated to the leader's preferences. Moreover, successful management becomes a matter of getting the culture right (see Beare *et al.* 1989:172–200; Hargreaves and Hopkins 1991:109–23; Fullan 1991:161). Such a view of culture is curiously unproblematic and overrides

> the anthropological concern with culture as a shifting and contested concept which is constantly being constructed and reconstructed and which must be subjectively understood. Instead there is only a managerial concern with the manipulation of and intervention in culture to shape it in ways that enhance the efficiency of the organization.
>
> (Angus 1989:71)

Although the cultural perspective provides an alternative to the assumptions of the theory movement, it has not brought about a reformulation of school leadership. Rather, it has helped some writers to refine school leadership by making school leaders more manipulative, while also remaining fastened to bureaucratic assumptions about power. Some of the ideas emanating from this perspective have been adopted by those who continue to advocate leadership as power over.

Leaders are seen as needing to shape the underlying meanings attributed to the organization as a whole. The cultural perspective has been annexed by the functionalists and instrumentalists. As a result, the cultural perspective provides some interesting descriptions of schools, but offers little in the way of altering power relations in them. Despite the negotiated and contested nature of organizational culture, the perspective has been usurped by those who see culture as a means of control.

Critical Perspectives on School Leadership

Given the focus of my research and the orientation of this chapter I will only attend here to critical theorists' ideas about school leadership. I will especially draw upon the work of Bates (1982; 1983; 1988; 1989) and Watkins (1983; 1989) since they have provided a cogent critique of the theory movement's assumptions about leadership.

There are four summarizing points to which I want to draw attention. First, Bates sees administration as essentially concerned with social control because the preoccupations of managers are with organization, motivation, decision-making, implementation, supervision, evaluation, efficiency, effectiveness, accountability and authority (1983:8). Educational administration is nothing more or less than 'a technology of control' (p. 8) imitating 'the patterns of dominance and submission of the corporate order' (p. 39).

Second, for Bates, school management should not simply be described by a language of technique. Such a language is too narrow. There also needs to be a discourse of ethics (1989:131). School leadership, along with management and organization theory, is not value-free and interested only in rational explanation of behaviour. Such a claim 'has both diminished awareness of the importance of the study of values in human behaviour and focusses upon a limited definition of reality' (Bates 1989:135–6).

Third, Bates draws upon the work of Giddens to avoid too strong a reliance on subjectivity. While Bates accepts Greenfield's thesis that organizations are not things, he parts company with him when he explores how we might 'explain the processes of creation and re-creation of the invented social reality of organizations' and also 'explain the status of the resulting organization and its effects on individuals' (Bates 1989:139). Bates, in line with Giddens' (1979) structuration theory, argues that there is a dialectic between agency and structure. Human agency accounts for a theory of the acting subject, but structure situates individual actions in time and space and allows for social structures to become part of the consciousness of individuals. This position sustains Greenfield's attack on the reification of organizations implicit in the theory movement

> but extends his argument to show not only how the 'invented social reality' of social practice is constituted and reconstituted by individuals, but also how such social practice simultaneously *plays a part in the constitution and reconstitution of individuals.*
>
> (Bates 1989:140, author's emphasis)

Here Bates suggests that the exercise of power over others is not simply a matter of bureaucratic structure, but is also one of professional identity because assumptions about power become a part of the constitution of individuals. As Watkins argues:

> leadership and power should be looked at as relational concepts develop-
> ing over lengthy periods of time. In this sense they should be understood
> as processual in character, in a constant state of flux, where human agents
> both constitute and are constituted by the structures in which they find
> themselves.
>
> (Watkins 1989:30)

Fourth, Bates (1989) draws upon Habermas' work on the traditions of public law to sustain a reconceptualization of leadership. Habermas does not regard the law as permitting only the instrumental interests of the powerful to be imposed upon the powerless (p. 154). Rather

> the law should impose restrictions on the untrammeled deployment of
> power. . .Through the law, power is constrained by cultural and ethical
> 'principles' that lie beyond its reach.
>
> (Bates 1989:154)

Given this belief in the function of the law:

> then the notion of the leader which is implicit in administrative science
> — that of one who discovers and applies the laws of organizational con-
> trol — requires revision. So does the notion of the great man of iron will
> who imposes his moral vision upon his followers by force of presence.
> Neither is an adequate account of the idea of leadership.
>
> (Bates 1989:154)

An adequate account of leadership is one where the practice of school manage-
ment is directed towards an emancipatory interest, rather than used as a technique to control (Watkins 1983:119).

Indeed, critical theory is concerned with emancipation rather than control (Watkins 1983:128–9). Everyone in an organization should have the opportunity to speak out and criticize the arguments of other members. All members of the organization should be able to express their feelings and interests and to require the justification of actions and decisions of others. The goal of critical theory is a life free from domination (pp. 130–1).

This means that school leaders need to seek democratic participation and 'to harbour the growth and support of diverse interest groups who may incorporate a critical element into decision-making processes' (p. 131). In short, critical theory is a way of achieving emancipation through critical self-reflection (pp. 130–1). Furthermore, emancipation of organizational members has important implications for the issues of gender raised earlier in this chapter. Blackmore (1989) argues that men tend to see power as meaning domination while women take a more emancipatory view of it seeing power as a capacity of the community as a whole (p. 122). As Shakeshaft (1989) says, there is evidence that women use power to empower others. Power sharing is based upon the idea that power is not finite, but that it expands as it is shared (p. 206). Instead of power being understood as

privileging the individual, who is often in a position of status, in a co-operative environment power resides in the group. Leadership would be redefined as the ability to act with others; it is a form of empowerment and not of dominance (Blackmore 1989:123). An emancipatory view of leadership is worth pursuing since it addresses both objections to power being understood as power over and the male bias of management theorizing.

Critical theorists offer a coherent critique of the theory movement (or, as they prefer, administrative science). They draw upon Greenfield, yet overcome some of the difficulties noted in his emphasis upon subjectivity. Critical theorists are also broadly in line with Hodgkinson's belief in philosophical leadership since being critical means the examined life. Moreover, Bates and others regard leadership as having an ethical dimension and want to see all members of an organization provided with equal opportunities to voice their concerns. Yet, unlike Hodgkinson, Bates and others (see Foster 1986, 1989; Codd 1989) focus strongly upon leadership in educational organizations and offer alternatives to existing conceptions of leadership which, importantly for this study, are grounded in ethics rather than instrumentality, and begin to take account of those who have often been denied a voice.

While the critical theorists offer an attractive set of theoretical insights they are not immune from criticism and three reservations can be noted. First, there is a failure by the critical theorists to support their work with empirical data (Capper 1991:8). Second, there is a concern that Habermas' dependence on rationality underestimates, or even ignores, the place of subjectivity and affect in theory (p. 9).

The third reservation centres upon critical theorists acceptance of leadership. They challenge the uses of authority in schools, but they do not question the assumption that a leader is necessary in schools. Indeed, and paradoxically, leaders are the persons who will free other members of the organization by transforming them. Moreover, the goal of critical theory is to free organization members from sources of domination, exploitation and repression by empowering others, sharing power with others and transforming society, but this view leans in favour of a bipolar notion of power and powerlessness (Capper 1991:4–5, 15).

These three weaknesses temper enthusiasm for critical theory, but they do not eliminate its strengths. Of the four alternative perspectives to the theory movement reviewed here, critical theory appears to offer the most promise on moral and ethical grounds. Therefore, the critical theorists' prescription for reconceptualizing leadership, namely critical leadership which is transformational and educative, will be considered in greater detail. However, before doing this it is necessary to consider whether these alternative perspectives have undermined the hegemony of the theory movement. If they have, the way will be clear for the introduction of fresh approaches. If, however, the assumptions of the theory movement remain intact this too will have consequences for initiating a change in school leadership.

A Paradigm Shift?

While there has been increasing criticism of bureaucratic rationality and managerialism, this is not to say that at the school level leadership practice has substantially altered, or that there has been a shift towards a new paradigm. Bates, for one, does not believe a paradigm shift has occurred (1988:21) nor do I, for three inter-related reasons.

First, the case study shows how Ron's assumptions about headship were influenced by a bureaucratic rationality. Moreover, since Ron's conception of head-ship was not unique, it appears that the work of other primary heads is influenced by the theory movement's tenets. Second, recent educational management theorizing has generally not impacted upon primary school leadership. For example, no educational management texts apply critical theory to primary schools; interpretive studies in primary schools, such as ethnographies, are relatively scarce; and only Nias *et al.* (1989) have adopted a cultural perspective in respect of primary schools. In short, recent theorizing has generally not been applied to primary schools nor vice versa.

Third, the bureaucratic rationale is not in retreat. Recent developments in local management of schools have introduced the language of accountancy to school management. Teacher and staff development has moved in the direction of training, rather than education, while organizational needs rather than individual ones are in the ascendancy. Indeed, the notion of schools needs (Bradley 1991:15) exemplifies how bureaucracy can swamp subjectivity. These trends are indicators of the metavalues of efficiency and effectiveness to which modern organizations are committed (Hodgkinson 1983:43). And schools, no less than other organizations, are committed to efficiency and effectiveness as the effective schools movement shows. Indeed, to appreciate fully the persistence of the bureaucratic rationale a review of the effective schools research will be useful.

School Effectiveness

During the mid- to late 1970s there emerged a body of research literature:

> on what was variously called exemplary schools, effective schools, school effectiveness and school improvement which argued that individual schools could themselves have major effects upon children and that schools could be changed and improved in ways that would directly benefit their pupils.
>
> (Austin and Reynolds 1990:167)

It is claimed that effective schools research has found that certain internal conditions are typical in schools that achieve higher levels of outcomes for their pupils (Hopkins 1990:185). The effectiveness of a school is defined, sometimes very narrowly, by pupil achievements. Schools in which students achieve good academic results, after controlling for home background factors and ability measures, are termed 'effective' (Weindling 1989:55).

The research is now sufficiently established and ongoing for a first and second wave of studies to be identified (Reynolds 1982) and for the findings to be divided into two sets: organizational characteristics and process characteristics (Purkey and Smith 1983:440; Austin and Reynolds 1990:168). The findings of different studies demonstrate a high degree of consistency with these two sets of characteristics (Purkey and Smith 1983:443–6; Austin and Reynolds 1990:174–5; Shipman 1990:68).

The bulk of the research has taken place in North America, while in Britain two projects have attracted attention; Rutter *et al.* (1979) *Fifteen Thousand Hours*, and Mortimore *et al.* (1988) *School Matters: The Junior Years*. The latter is especially pertinent to this study, as I suggested in Chapter 1.

Effective schools research has attracted much attention with the findings often taken as an incantation of what staff in schools should be striving to attain (see Scottish Education Dept. 1990; Jenkins 1991; Shipman 1990). Indeed, there is a tendency for findings to be taken as a blueprint for school improvement (Austin and Reynolds 1991:175). Such a view reduces both the complexity of the school as a social system and the nature of teaching and learning to a limited number of characteristics.

While there is consistency amongst the characteristics identified in individual research projects this is not to say they have attracted equal attention. Leadership usually comes top of any list of characteristics (Mortimore *et al.* 1988:250; Weindling 1989:59; Shipman 1990:68). Leadership is also prominent in HM Inspectors' writings (DES, 1977; 1987; 1990). Heads of effective schools are frequently described as successful leaders and characterized as:

- setting a strong administrative example;
- recruiting their own staff;
- being fully supportive of teachers;
- providing a structural institutional pattern in which teachers can function effectively;
- achieving a balance between a strong leadership role for themselves and maximum autonomy for teachers;
- providing strong instructional leadership;
- firm disciplinarians providing strong behavioural role models for teachers and pupils alike.

(based on Reid et al. 1987:24)

Such findings have spawned particular interest in effective leaders (see Southworth 1990) with many of the resulting studies echoing the same sentiments as those expressed by Reid *et al.* For example, Rosenholtz (1985:360–1) believes leaders must be strong, purposeful, goal-oriented, communicate certainty and increase their capacity for rational planning. Jenkins (1991:86) advocates instructional leadership, supervision of teachers, resource management and quality control.

With reference to primary heads Coulson says:

> Successful heads are goal oriented insofar as they have a vision of how they would like to see their schools develop. Thus they give the school a sense of direction. . .which has the effect of inducing clarity, consensus and commitment regarding the organization's basic purposes.
>
> (Coulson 1986:85)

The emphasis upon visionary leadership is widely supported (Bennis 1984:67; Achilles 1987:18; Jenkins 1991:86) and conjures up the image of messianic leadership discussed in Chapter 5. As Hargreaves (1991) notes, there is a strong sense that the vision is primarily the headteacher's to which all other staff will conform (p. 12). The crucial question of whose vision is it? is unproblematic: it is the head's vision. Heads are granted a proprietary claim over the school's goals and values

(p. 12). Moreover, this claim infers that visionary heads are more visionary than anyone else (Angus 1989:73). As such they are assumed to be moral paragons (Hodgkinson 1983:59). Ultimately, the idea of vision assumes heads know best.

The emphasis effective schools researchers place upon leadership uncritically associates power with headteachers. Effective schools are

> institutions shaped by powerful and determined administrators [heads] who transform their schools through qualities such as singleness and clarity of purpose; assertiveness, being prepared to confront norms of teacher autonomy and, if necessary, to sacrifice interpersonal relationships for the sake of student achievement; and political and bureaucratic acumen, focussing on purposes which will be endorsed by their superiors and shaping their relationships to promote their interests.
>
> (Riffel 1986:168)

The muscular nature of the head's role is pronounced in the effective schools literature and little attention has been given to the likelihood that strong leadership in one effective school 'may translate directly into "administrative thuggery" in another' (Huberman 1990:24–5).

Effective schools research is effective in creating a 'modern, ritualised hero system' (Watkins 1989:29) which sustains all the assumptions of bureaucratic rationality:

> The imagery which the above view of administration and the use of power in educational organizations evokes persistently, while perhaps benevolent in its concern for student achievement, is limited and ultimately despotic. The biases that it reflects are fundamentally anti-democratic.
>
> (Riffel 1986:168)

Indeed, the researchers' belief in monopolistic leadership undermines their advocacy of collegiality (Southworth 1987:67). While effective schools research identifies the involvement of teachers in school policy-making (Mortimore *et al.* 1988:251), such consultation should not be confused with democracy. Consultation is not prescribed because of any perceived moral merits, rather, the basis for consultation is solely an instrumental one: it makes schools better, more effective (see Rosenholtz 1985:373–5; Austin and Reynolds 1990:172). Consultation and involvement build commitment, ownership, team work and loyalty. Consultation is good only for what it brings to the school as an organization. It may be ethically efficacious, but first it must be efficient.

To summarize then, it seems that the effective schools research sustains and nourishes instrumentality. It supports the metavalues of efficiency and effectiveness. It is not a challenge to bureaucractic rationality, only a modernization of it. Moreover, the effective schools literature associates leadership with formal position in an organization's structure. The leader is a strong and dynamic individual who impresses the staff with his/her vision. The staff are cast as passive recipients of the leader's vision and they are drawn into 'a covenant' of 'shared goals and a common value system that is shaped by the leader's management of the organization's culture' (Angus 1989:75). In turn, this belief in strong leadership has created a myth about managers. This myth has been traced by MacIntyre (1981) who argues that an archetype has developed of the bureaucratic-manager who imposes order, clarity and certainty on a disorderly organizational universe because she or he is an administrative expert, one who knows how to efficiently motivate, control and organize others (Foster 1991:6–7). This sense of expertise also encourages the followers to ascribe power and control to the leader and so increases the follower's dependency upon him/her since they believe there is somebody prescient enough to guide them (Foster 1989:39).

Although there are now alternative paradigms to the theory movement, the effective schools research shows that the bureaucratic rationale continues to underwrite leadership as domination. The alternative paradigms now compete with the theory movement, but they have not overthrown it.

Changing School Leadership

My case for changing leadership is based upon principles of social justice. I have argued that the asymmetrical distribution of power in schools results in the head's domination of the staff group and is antipathetic to democracy. Moreover, because schools socialize children into societal norms, it is unacceptable that a single person holds dominion over all others since children are presented with a model of organization which is anti-democratic.

In this chapter I have criticized the theory movement in educational management for ignoring the moral dimension of leadership, giving pre-eminence to means over ends, assuming leadership to be a function of organizational position (Foster 1989:43), and for making it a subset of power (Watkins 1989:20). School leadership needs to be rethought. At the end of the second section I concluded that the critical theorists offer the most promising ideas for reconceptualizing leadership because they wish to make leadership both ethical and emancipatory. Critical theorists regard educational administration as needing to help staff in school understand:

> how the most 'efficient' and elaborately devised organizational planning often turns out to be a manipulative trap from which organizational members may have difficulty extricating themselves. The traditional school principal with a disproportionate degree of power was often able to create and implement such manipulative traps through the ability to shape much of the language, direct much of the discourse and guide much of the practice within the educational community. By adopting a critical view of leadership within schools, by recognising that all human agents have some degree of knowledge, by unmasking manipulative, deceptive tactics, school administration would be founded on a more equal power basis.
>
> (Watkins 1989:27)

It follows that the ideas of critical theorists on school leadership warrant close inspection. I shall carry out this inspection by considering the work of Foster (1986; 1989; 1990; 1991). There are two reasons for this choice. First, Foster offers the most developed set of ideas about leadership in terms of critical theory. Second, Foster's work covers the ideas of other critical theorists who focus on transformational or educative leadership (see Smyth 1989; Codd 1989; Watkins 1989). There is one other point to make. In reviewing the work of Foster I intend to focus on how his ideas will serve my concern about the need for leadership to be ethical as well as effective.

Foster's Ideas: Critical Leadership

Foster has argued that there are five interrelated dimensions to leadership (transformational; critical; educative; ethical; emancipatory). Foster does not offer a succinct title for his work, so in line with the title of one of his papers (1989), I have decided to subsume his work under the general title of *critical leadership*. In addition to being brief, this title indicates Foster's theoretical orientation. In this section I will summarize the five dimensions and in the next discuss the strengths and weaknesses of his work.

First, Foster adopts the idea of Burns (1978) that leaders *transform* others because leadership is a special form of power (Foster 1986:176) and is oriented toward a vision. Yet, because we all have different visions of the possible, and resources to achieve visions are limited, leadership will involve competition and conflict (p. 178). Leaders do not exist in isolation, apart from followers' ideas and wants, they are inseparable from followers' needs and goals. Followers interact dynamically with leaders. Moreover, at times, followers are leaders and leaders are followers (p. 178).

Foster believes transformational leaders do not just try to meet the goals of followers, they also try to transform them, to raise them to a different and higher level. The leader challenges the followers to meet goals that the followers and sometimes the leader, never even dreamed about. This notion of transformation rests on two other ideas. First, that leadership does not flow from an individual in a position of power. Leaders engage in leader acts at various times in their lives; then they are leaders, but at other times they are followers (pp. 181–2). Second, power need not be *power over*, but may be *power to* (p. 178). Leaders transform followers by offering them new ideas, values and ideals (p. 179) and, because leaders need to negotiate their ideas with others, transformational leadership is political.

Second, Foster regards leadership as critical. He believes leadership can be rescued from the bureaucratic paradigm by developing a critical model which includes critical reflection and analysis, especially of power:

> Power must be a dominant concern of leadership: the modern organization, with its rules and hierarchies, develops a technological mentality that limits autonomy and freedom of action and shackles vision and critical spirit. Leaders who have vision and spirit can share power. In so doing they release the very human potential of the agents in the organization.
> (Foster 1986:183–4)

In addition, leaders should enable others to recognize that organizations are not natural structures, but human constructs which, if we wish, we can change (p. 184). The taken-for-grantedness of organizations is part of our language, as well as our thinking, and so leadership involves the probing of language structures and the unmasking of distortions. In this sense leadership must be *critically educative* (p. 185). Here Foster draws upon the ideas of Fay (1975; 1977), who regards educative as meaning the enlightenment of individuals so that they come to see themselves and their social situation in a new way and can themselves decide to change the conditions they find repressive (Foster 1986:185).

For Foster it follows that leaders do not manipulate a group in order to achieve a preset goal, rather leaders empower others to evaluate what goals are important and what conditions are helpful:

> At its heart, leadership — the search for democratic and rational parti-cipation in social events — is political. It is a political act to educate people; it is a political act to demystify structures and penetrate 'normal' condi-tions; it is a political act to argue for participation in decision-making. Leadership involves the careful interplay of knowledge and action; knowl-edge of organizations and action on behalf of undistorted communica-tion. In this respect we can all exercise leadership.
>
> (Foster 1986:187)

Leaders do not just accept their given organizational conditions they:

> attempt to change the human condition. . .leadership does not reside in systems of management, in grids or formulas. Leadership is conscious of conditions and conscious of change. . .[it] is the process of transforming and empowering.
>
> (Foster 1986:187–8)

Third, in his later work, Foster (1989) has made it explicit that when leaders critique traditions which can be oppressive, and aim for a transformation of such conditions, then they are educative (p. 53). Being educative means presenting 'both an analysis and a vision' (p. 53). For Foster, analysis stems from self-reflection, by the leader and other members of the community, on the structures that orient their working lives and means time is devoted to talking about organizational purpose and power. And vision means having alternative possibilities to address and suggests that change is possible (p. 54).

Fourth, the ethical dimension to leadership focuses upon the danger of power being attached only to an individual's ends which then results in the leader treating people as means to his or her ends. Leadership, however, should be founded on moral relationships (p. 55), offering new possibilities to others in the community. Moreover, leadership must maintain an ethical focus which is oriented toward democratic values within a community (p. 55). Ethical leadership is therefore con-cerned with means (like the exercise of power and relationships) and ends (such as developing or sustaining democratic values in the community).

Fifth, Foster believes leadership needs to occur in communities where leader-ship aims at developing emancipatory types of relations; 'any other type of lead-ership is basically oriented toward the accumulation of power' (p. 49). Emancipation here does not mean total freedom, rather it means the gradual development of freedoms, from racial oppression, ethnic domination, the oppression of women and so on. Furthermore, emancipatory leadership is not the property of enlight-ened individuals, nor a function of position. 'It occurs within a community where leadership is shared and transferred between leaders and followers so that the two become interchangeable' (p. 49).

In his more recent work (1990; 1991) Foster has attempted to synthesize his earlier thinking and further develop the ideas through the notion of 'transformative intellectual':

> By educative leadership, I mean something like the following. Leadership in school settings involves the empowerment of followers through engaging in a mutual vision oriented towards end values, such as freedom and equity (Burns 1978). More than this, it rejects control as its ultimate expression. Leadership resides in the mutuality of needs, and in working out ways to achieve those needs. . .Such a leadership is communally based; it strives to find a communion between members of the institution. In so doing, it rejects a scientistic view of administration, seeing administration more as a co-ordinative effort for achieving a communal peace. In this sense, a realist and critically naturalist view of organization is important, for these help the leader/follower to understand *their* historical and situational placement and to recognize the possibility for transformational action.
>
> Such a leadership is also educative. Leadership and education are, in fact, inseparable, but focusing on the educative dimensions allows us to consider the ways in which the transformation of the school might lead to the provision of both equity and excellence. School leaders must be, in Giroux's (1988) phrase, 'transformative intellectuals', ones who know how to analyse critically modern forms of discourse which disguise power relationships and who can bring to a specific site the ability to inform and educate.
>
> (Foster 1990:16–17)

For Foster, then, leaders are critical of existing traditions and customs. They seek to transform prevailing power relations through analysis. Critical leaders do not command others, they enlighten and educate them and are, in turn, themselves educated by others. Leaders and followers not only interact, they rotate. Power is not the property of an individual but of the group. Power does not disenfranchise, it empowers. Leadership is based upon a moral relationship and is ethical, being concerned with means and ends. Leadership is not about control it is to do with emancipation.

Strengths and Weaknesses of Critical Leadership

I perceive six strengths and four weaknesses in Foster's work. The six strengths are as follows: First, critical leadership is centrally concerned with ethics and morals. It is not governed by a narrow, instrumental quest for efficiency focused only upon means. Rather, it is concerned with both means and ends, where the ends must be moral and consistent with the principles of democracy. In contrast to the positivists, whose views on leadership anaesthetize values (Hodgkinson 1983:9), critical leadership examines values.

Second, Foster regards power as principally power to, rather than power over. Critical leaders are not interested in securing dominion, but in changing the organizations in which they work. Moreover, power is not the property of an individual, but of the group, and power is not finite, it is infinite. The more people that are empowered the greater the power of the community to which they belong.

Third, leaders are not divorced from followers, indeed, leadership cannot occur without followership. Also, leaders and followers are interchangeable. At one time an individual will lead, only later for that person to become a follower. Fourth, since critical leadership is not attached to any single individual, at least not for a protracted period and not on a formalized basis, the problem of individualism is avoided. The personalization of leadership which encourages the cult of the individual and associated notions such as charisma, personal power, discipleship and, ultimately, dependency should not arise. Leadership is the property of the group and members of staff are dependent on one another not on a single person.

Fifth, because Foster is concerned with increasing staff members' awareness of their workplace conditions, critical leadership will raise awareness of non-dominant groups. This will have an important bearing upon the role of women in schools. The present patriarchal bias in school management theorizing has resulted in leadership being largely constructed in masculine terms. If womens' experiences in management are taken into account, the prospect for altering the ways in which leadership and power are conceptualized may be enhanced because women understand these concepts in different ways from men (Shakeshaft 1989:194–210). Critical leadership is essentially concerned with emancipation, and this should enable alternative perspectives to be voiced rather than suppressed.

Sixth, although Foster sees critical leadership as changing the taken-for-granted ways in which organizations function, the process of change is based upon education not dictat. Leaders and followers educate one another and increase their awareness and understandings. Only after, and in the light of dialogue and critical appraisal, will changes occur. Changes to organization arise not because of the whims of individuals, but because of the wishes of the community.

The four weaknesses are as follows: first, like other critical theorists, Foster does not provide any empirical data to support his case. The practical implications of his ideas have not been addressed. Second, Foster does not address the issue of what is to be done with existing formal leaders. Are they to be abolished, as White (1983) makes plain in her thinking? Foster seems rather coy about this point. The impression one gains is that formal leaders such as heads will remain in place. This is an ambiguity which needs to be clarified.

Third, the notion of educative leadership needs to be presented in greater detail than at present. For example, others have written about primary heads being educative (Nias *et al.* 1989; 1992) and I make a similar claim for Ron. These heads are educative insofar as they are professionally developing teacher colleagues. One consequence of this is that the teachers believe they are working in the right way because their work matches the head's expectations (Nias *et al.* 1989:111). Yet, none of these heads could be described as a critical leader because of being dominant figures in their respective schools. Like Ron, none of these heads apparently considered the just use of power, nor was power a topic of formal staff discussion. None could be described as emancipatory.

The same concern extends to the transformational dimension of Foster's ideas about leadership. Foster is aware that others have taken the language of transformational leadership and translated it into the needs of bureaucracy (Foster 1989:45). For example, others have applied it in an instrumental as against an ethical, critical sense. However, in Foster's terms, transformational leadership is concerned with consciousness raising (1991:11). In a sense, Foster has not specified, with sufficient clarity, what he means and does not mean, particularly with reference to school leadership.

In other words, Foster's ideas need to be grounded in schools. Foster fails to recognize that teachers and heads, occupationally disposed towards control, deference to those in authority, and conditioned to exercise power over others, will probably interpret educative and transformational leadership in particular ways. Unless Foster protects his ideas by being more specific, they are likely to be subverted.

The fourth weakness is also my major criticism of it. Foster believes critical leadership will occur because individuals will be rational and intellectually transform themselves. They will emancipate themselves by critically thinking themselves out of the conditions of oppression into which bureaucracy has cast them. Such an outlook ignores the fact that what is at stake here is the identity of individuals. Foster assumes that leaders will readily change themselves. By not addressing the issue of how leaders will themselves become critical he appears to tacitly believe that the transition from domination to critical leadership will occur smoothly.

Yet, the case of Ron suggests that it is primary headteachers' occupational identities which will be the barriers to critical leadership gaining acceptance amongst them. Although heads could increase their understanding of bureaucratic rationality and its associated structures which holds them and their staffs in a relationship of dominance and subordination, knowledge alone may be insufficient to enable some heads to transcend their identities wherein domination is an integral part.

Foster is right to reconceptualize leadership and to attack the theory movement. Yet he has not gone far enough. In this study I have developed the thesis that Ron behaved as he did, not simply because of his position in an organization which embodied bureaucratic structures, but because of his occupational identity which was rooted in teaching as well as headship. Domination will not be overturned simply by addressing the canons of managerialism, authoritarianism and bureaucracy. A bureaucratic rationality merely heightens what was socially sanctioned as a teacher, namely power over. For critical leadership to flourish, occupational identities need to be transformed.

The weakness with Foster's work is that it is incomplete. It focuses too strongly upon leadership. Leadership is not the whole picture, nor is bureaucratic rationality. Foster fails to recognize that headship in primary schools is an occupational identity. Schools as organizations reflect a bureaucratic rationality which structures a particular set of attitudes towards school leadership. Moreover, classroom life conditions teachers' assumptions about power. Domination is thus sedimented into the occupational identity of teachers; upon promotion to headship it assumes an even greater significance. For leaders to become emancipatory they need to let go their existing identities, a process which, at best, is both slow and painful (Nias 1987a:50).

Foster offers some valuable signposts for rethinking leadership. He points in the right direction insofar as he is concerned with social justice and democracy.

However, Foster does not say how leaders are to undertake their journeys, nor does he appreciate that the journey involves a transition from one identity to another. Critical leadership is a worthy alternative to domination, but its implications for headteacher development have yet to be considered.

Summary

In this chapter I have searched for an alternative approach to school leadership which is socially just. In the first section I criticized the theory movement in educational management arguing that it is neo-feudal, prizes objectivity over subjectivity and efficiency over ethics and is biased in favour of males. In the second section I considered four alternative theoretical perspectives: Greenfield's subjectivism, Hodgkinson's philosophy of leadership, the cultural perspective, critical theory. While each attacks the theory movement the critical theorists provide the most cogent challenge to bureaucratic rationality. They seek to equalize the distribution of power in schools, value subjectivity and regard leadership as ethical and emancipatory.

In the third section I argued that while there are competing theoretical perspectives the theory movement has not been defeated. I supported this claim by arguing that effective schools research is a modernization of the tenets of the theory movement. In the fourth section I examined Foster's work on critical leadership. Foster offers the most developed set of ideas about leadership in terms of critical theory and his work covers the ideas of other critical theorists. His ideas were seen as promising. However, Foster does not appreciate that the development of critical leaders will necessitate a change in professional identity.

What emerges from this chapter is the idea that any attempt to alter headship must be recognized as involving changes to heads' occupational identities. Consequently, there is a need to consider the implications of reconceptualizing leadership in terms of headteachers' professional development. Chapter 7 will look at this issue.

Chapter 7

Headteacher Development

The previous chapter has shown that critical theorists provide a basis for reconceptualizing school leadership. Critical leadership in schools is a communal act and an educative process. The wisdom and skills related to the leadership act are not necessarily the monopoly of any single individual, nor are they necessarily hierarchically distributed in the school. Leadership is a reflective activity. All who participate in the school must become more aware of self, task and the context in which they work. Leadership is thus educative since critical enquiry rests upon a desire to increase awareness and learn (Duignan 1988:11). Moreover, leadership is concerned with ethics and morals as well as technical matters because it is not a value free process and schools are value laden institutions.

While critical theorists have produced a cogent critique of bureaucratic rationality and offer a basis for reconstructing school leadership, their work is deficient in two respects. First, they fail to appreciate that headship is an occupational identity. Second, they have not addressed the issue of how dominating heads will become critical leaders. Rather, they appear to assume that it is unproblematic for heads who are central and controlling to divest themselves of their power and become members of an empowered community. In short, they have not considered how powerful heads will themselves be transformed into transformational, ethical, educative and critical leaders.

In this chapter I will focus on this question by looking at how headteacher development might be rethought to support the practice of critical leadership. I shall focus, in turn, upon four related issues. First, I will argue that at present headteacher and management development are grounded in a wholly instrumental rationale. This I suggest needs to change. Headteacher development ought to be regarded as a reflective and educative enterprise and include a moral component. Second, I propose that the most appropriate context for headteacher development is a particular kind of discussion group. Third, I argue that although discussion groups are important, there is also a need to challenge headteachers' assumptions about leadership. Fourth, I acknowledge that headteacher development is only a sub-branch of the changes needed to promote critical leadership. Teachers and their development also need to be considered.

There is one other point to make. I assume throughout the following discussion that the position of headteacher will continue. I do so because there is no concerted call for the position to be abolished. Indeed, only two sources amongst the whole of my reading for this study even contemplate the idea of doing away with heads (Hargreaves, D. 1974; White 1983). Therefore, the argument in this chapter rests upon the belief that it is the nature of headship which needs to be transformed and not that the position needs to be restructured as part of a major reorganization of schools.

Existing Trends in Headteacher Development

The prevailing emphases in headteacher and management development are instrumental and technical ones (Greenfield, W. 1991:28). This should be no surprise given the earlier conclusion that in school management theorizing a bureaucratic rationality remains largely intact. Nevertheless, two reasons can be offered to justify the claim. First, headteacher development has generally been regarded as *training*. As Coulson (1988a) says, the implicit assumption has been that leadership can be trained into people by a person who knows how others should behave and teaches them how to do it (p. 255). Moreover, course participants are defined as recipients: they are the object not the subject of the endeavour (p. 261).

Second, although training courses for heads have recently been given less emphasis than formerly, the underlying instrumental rationale remains undisturbed. The School Management Task Force (SMTF) (DES 1990) sought to broaden the scope of management development by regarding it within a general development model (Styan 1990:18), by making activities school-based and promoting more flexible methods of learning than simply attending INSET courses (Glatter 1990:36). However, SMTF's report is essentially preoccupied with tactics for developing managers in school. It did not reconceptualize the enterprise. Indeed, SMTF actively draws upon the instrumental rationale to justify their proposals for management development. For example, school effectiveness studies are cited in the report as demonstrating the need for enhancing school management performance (pp. 5–6). Also, Styan, a member of the Task Force, has argued that management development is needed to support the implementation of mandated change (1990:17–18). The SMTF Report remains wedded to the metavalues of efficiency and effectiveness.

There are three consequences of this instrumental approach to headteacher development. First, because training has been the overriding concern, management courses have been preoccupied with technical matters at the expense of critical thinking and reflectiveness (Coulson 1988a:255). Second, it has been assumed that a head's management style is an objective, rational and cognitive strategy external to, and detached from, the person (p. 260). By not understanding behaviour as an integral part of an individual's being and as an expression of his/her underlying values, little attention has been paid to the individual's beliefs and feelings (pp. 262–3). Third, management training has not attended to the ethical dimensions of school leadership. Heads and others should, as part of their development, identify and analyse the ethical dimensions of their work. Heads need to be able to apply appropriate principles, rules and ideals since they are moral agents (Greenfield, W. 1991:23, 8) and schools are moral institutions socializing and preparing children for citizenship in society (p. 2).

Instrumentality means that headteacher development is ill-founded and limited. There is a need to consider other approaches. In particular, if critical leadership is the desired goal, attention needs to be given to four characteristics:

1   education rather than training should be the aim;
2   activities should create contexts for personal and professional reflection;
3   the development of critical awareness needs to be fostered;
4   the analysis of the ethical as well as the technical dimensions of school leadership and organization needs to be included;

The following three sections will consider how headteachers can develop in line with these characteristics.

The Place of Group Work

In Chapter 4 I suggested that headteachers mature with greater experience of the job, although precisely in what way and how other factors contribute remains unclear. While primary heads develop experientially, the case of Ron suggests that this process of learning will be largely solitary and *ad hoc*. It will be solitary because, generally speaking, heads make sense of their work experiences by themselves. Heads are offered few opportunities to meet with other headteacher colleagues to share and reflect on work experiences and rarely with the expressed intention to learn from the sharing process. Development is *ad hoc* because experience in a school is contingent upon the circumstances of the school. There may be ample opportunities for a head to learn some things, (such as how to support staff; manage limited funds), but not others, (such as how to appoint staff, induct new staff members) because these procedures do not occur in some schools with stable staff groups. In other words, although heads can develop by themselves the process is limited in scope and in terms of contact with others.

Moreover, the solitary and *ad hoc* nature of school-based experiential learning makes it likely that some heads, apparently, may never encounter a need to examine the ethical dimension of their work, nor challenge their assumptions about organizational power and control. Experiential learning throws an individual back on his/her own resources and confines him/her to his/her own perspective.

By contrast, group work offers a context for learning with and from headteacher colleagues in ways which can help to increase awareness of others, deepen understanding of self and challenge individuals' assumptions about their work. Also, groups can provide a supportive context for the examination of self and occupational identities. In this section, therefore, I shall argue that group work has an essential role to play in headteacher development and I shall draw upon the work of Whitaker, Coulson and Nias to support my case.

Whitaker (1986) notes how his experience of small group work led him to a belief in the power of groups to provide a fertile learning environment for individual's growth (pp. 276–7). He describes an approach to in-service which was person-centred in that course members regarded themselves both as the agenda for the course and the context for learning (p. 276). He concludes that:

> the deep seated and sometimes imprisoned seeds of growth can be activated when a safe psychological climate is created. . .learners have enormous resources for their own development once they have given themselves 'permission' to learn. . .attitudes, assumptions and values can be reworked and reformed in a climate of enquiry and growth.
>
> (Whitaker 1986:281)

Coulson also sees such a climate as necessary for individual growth.

For Coulson (1988a) primary headteacher development, being related to personal development, relies upon the creation of a learning environment of trust and security within which heads will explore through communication and interpersonal interaction their beliefs, values and their ways of being with others (p. 263). A secure context is necessary because of the self-appraisals each member is undertaking and because any consequent professional growth means a redefinition of his/her identity, something which Nias also understood (Nias 1987c:43). Moreover, shifts in identity depend upon the

> modification of people's cognitive structure or organized pattern of thinking and feeling about themselves and their world. This change is difficult and for the mature individual, often disturbing. . .for many the process of 'loosening' existing assumptions and values, essential if change is to occur, evokes defensiveness and resistance.
>
> (Coulson 1988a:264)

What Coulson points to here is the efficacy of certain kinds of groups for simultaneously supporting and transporting alterations to an individual's professional identity.

Nias (1987c) has considered in some detail the nature of such groups. There are five points to highlight from her work which support the case for group work. First, Nias accepts that critical reflection is the central activity for self-transformation and emancipation. Through critical reflection individuals can become aware of the educational and institutional structures which determine their self-understandings. Once individuals understand the beliefs which underpin their actions and treat all situations as problematic, rather than given (Nias 1987c:42), they will begin to see the possibilities which exist for 'self-transformation by altering the structures and institutions which control and condition them' (p. 43; see also Carr and Kemmis 1983:180).

Second, Nias does not regard self-transformation as a solitary exercise. Using the ideas of Foulkes, a psychotherapist, she argues that by regularly bringing together groups of people and fostering open discussion they can learn about their unconscious processes and compare their own perceptions with those of others. Their attitudes and actions will 'encounter' those of other people and 'opposing realities' (1987c:17). In this way an individual's basic assumptions can be uncovered, shared, analysed and discourse take place about the possibility of changing them.

Third, it follows from the second point that communication is of major importance, especially talk. It is through communication that individuals make sense of their world. Communication also enables them to reaffirm and develop the groups of which they are a part. The group depends for its existence upon its members' capacity to speak a common language. The group can only grow by what it can share and only share by what it can communicate (p. 20).

Fourth, communication develops within the group the capacity not only for increased awareness and transformation, but also for support. Personal growth is a difficult and painful process. Positive, constructive and open communication encourages more, rather than less communication and 'helps members face irresolution, anxiety, conflict and reluctance to change' (p. 20).

Fifth, certain conditions are necessary for discussion groups to function productively. No single person should be regarded as more important than any other. No one should be allowed to use any hierarchical power or status in the group. No person or alliance should be entitled to impose their perceptions on the rest of the group (Nias 1987c:17–18). Nias draws particular attention to Foulkes' emphasis on equal status in the group's members and the need for the group to have a conductor rather than a leader. A conductor does not exert authority and never imposes views, or plans the group's strategies. The conductor listens and creates an atmosphere of tolerance and appreciation of individual differences and models facilitative behaviour. Above all, he or she promotes full and free communication within the group and active participation in this by every member (pp. 21–2).

Nias' argument hinges on the individual as a participating member of the group and upon the group as a means of enabling the individual to question and change his or her perspectives and relations (pp. 45–6). The group is a context for 'perspective transformation' (Meizirow 1981, cited in Nias 1987c:27).

My argument, then, is that particular discussion groups are a means of bringing together different perspectives with the aim that individuals share and discuss their underlying beliefs and values. At the same time, critical assessment of group members' values will help reveal the dominant ideology which conditions and shapes their actions, and if members so wish, they can begin to change the way they act. Furthermore, such change is not merely a matter of rationally deciding. Rather, it involves letting go deep-seated beliefs which, being part of the individual's identity, are self defining and therefore difficult and discomforting to change. Yet, because discussion groups can provide a supportive context for individuals, they can be hospitable for identity change.

There are three further reasons why discussion groups are important for the development of headteachers. The first concerns group leadership. Nias' advocacy of conductors, rather than leaders, is well suited to reconceptualizing school leadership. The presence of a person who is facilitative rather than dominating, who works within the group as an equal member, and who is open to hostility and comment from other members (Nias 1987c:24) is consistent with the goal of critical leadership.

Second, in addition to encountering the group conductor's leadership, when headteachers form the membership of the group they will be able to broaden their knowledge of how other heads operate. Grouping together headteachers broadens each head's repertoire of role models and reduces their tendencies towards isolation and self-referencing.

Third, since all members of the group are equals, each will have a voice. Groups might explore the values and distortions of the new managerialism which gives prominence to efficiency, ambition and competition at the expense of caring, nurturing and co-operation (Evetts 1990:183).

Discussion groups which adhere to Nias' specification offer a basis for promoting enlightenment and emancipation. In terms of the four characteristics of developing critical leaders identified in the previous section, such groups create contexts for personal and professional reflection. They are educative and encourage critical awareness. Moreover, the basic rules of the group, namely equality, open communication and facilitative leadership, relate to important ethical issues which group members will encounter in the process of group participation and can also reflect upon in terms of their own leadership in school. Discussion groups are a fruitful way of encouraging headteachers, and others, to analyse school leadership and organization.

The Need for Challenge

Discussion groups embody two important elements for developing critical leadership: personal support and professional challenge. The former arises from the security and trust developed over time in the group. The latter stems from sharing individual perspectives and differences. Nevertheless, it is over optimistic to assume that these groups alone will be sufficient to dissolve headteachers' strongly held role conventions. There are four reasons for this lack of complete faith in discussion groups.

First, the kind of adult learning under consideration here, namely *perspective transformation*, occurs only after headteachers have been subjected to a long period of professional socialization during which they will have expended considerable effort building a workable professional persona for themselves (Coulson 1988a:264). This makes it unlikely that they will readily disassemble something that works, that is, their ways of doing headship.

Second, when heads are grouped together the combined effect is likely to be 'groupthink' (Janis 1972), rather than creative discourse. In my experience, when groups of primary heads gather together there are strong role orthodoxies at work. They bond around their role conventions rather than explore alternatives. Hence, discussion groups can be occupationally parochial and role reinforcing.

Third, the occupational identities of heads rest upon the belief that individuals can make a difference in the lives of children and teachers and that they can affect schools themselves (Goldman 1991:8). The idea of heads being strong leaders translates all too easily into rugged individualism. By definition individualism is hostile and alien to group work.

Fourth, while heads believe in their own importance, seeing themselves as central to the health of the school, they do not always regard it as essential that they review either their role or educational convictions. Earlier I argued that the process of selection to headship bestows upon heads a sense of worth and mission. Yet, many, perhaps the majority of heads, do not undertake any subsequent and formal review of their values and beliefs; nor is there any obligation or requirement for them so to do. For example, an initiative for headteacher mentoring (DES 1991) does not recommend that mentors pay attention to a new head's beliefs about authority and leadership. Yet, in the USA, by contrast, similar initiatives regard such a focus as essential (Daresh and Playko 1989:7). In short, the kinds of critical analysis which critical theorists advocate is something to which heads are unaccustomed.

Together these four reasons make it probable that many heads will be unreceptive both to the processes of group work and the goals of professional reflection and change. A possible remedy to these problems is to suggest that groups are not made up entirely of headteachers. There is some merit in this idea, certainly in terms of establishing in-service groups composed of teachers and heads. However, school-based staff groups, in some ways the most obvious and appropriate constituency, are not especially favourable. The use of staff groups would satisfy White's (1983) appeals for workplace democracy and would simultaneously create a context for demystifying management practices, as staff gained a critical understanding of the processes central to reshaping leadership on a more participatory basis (Watkins 1989:27). However, Nias (1987a) has shown that formal attempts to set up discussion groups within schools are 'unlikely to succeed without drastic changes in educational structures and organisation and in teachers' attitudes' (p. 33). Staff groups do not, in the short term, offer a feasible forum for changing leadership.

Instead, I believe that formal headteacher discussion groups should be established through in-service activities. Moreover, these heads should be offered a parallel programme of study. These programmes would be relatively conventional courses of further and extended study, similar to, for example, existing Advanced Diploma and Masters' programmes. Through regular and formalized seminars participants could study the theory and practice of school leadership. Such opportunities would encourage headteachers to enquire into their own beliefs in a disciplined way and could require a product that could then be carefully examined and refined (Kottkamp 1990:34). Such systematic enquiry would provide heads with knowledge of alternative approaches to leadership and greater awareness of their own and others' assumptions.

One example of just such a course has been provided by Barnett *et al.* (1992) and their description of a programme for leadership development at the University of Northern Colorado. Barnett and his colleagues accept that 'moral and ethical imperatives drive leadership behaviour' (p. 72) and have constructed a curriculum which 'emphasizes the importance of lifelong growth and development' (pp. 72–3) for school leaders. Moreover, participants study five core learning experiences, including using enquiry and, importantly, 'understanding self' which aims to enable 'students to develop an appreciation of their fundamental values and attitudes and how they relate to governance, administration and leadership and curriculum development issues' (p. 72). Interestingly, Barnett and his colleagues also help students to work on their 'educational platforms' as a way of encouraging participants 'to articulate their educational beliefs, values and philosophies' (p. 74). The work of Barnett *et al.* suggests that it is both possible and feasible to devise a study programme which will help school leaders to think deeply and carefully about their work and themselves.

Essentially the study programme would aim, alongside the discussion group, to crack the walls which make us all prisoners of our own perceptions. Like others, I would envisage the study programme as embracing the critical spirit (Grob 1984:36), answering questions about oneself (Hodgkinson 1983:211) and facilitating critical self-awareness (Duignan 1988:5). Programmes of study would help to break the 'tyranny of custom' (Codd 1989:169) which is perpetuated for want of alternatives and in the absence of challenges to traditional approaches.

In turn, the participant heads' widening frames of reference could inform their contributions to group dialogues. This would have the benefit of reducing the potential for the group merely to reinforce role assumptions. The programme of study would feed and nourish group discussion. Moreover, the discussion group could also provide an arena for an individual's developing ideas to be held up for critical scrutiny. There would be no intention that the study programme be seen as a higher status form of learning — merely a different source of stimulus.

In some ways the idea of different kinds of groups has parallels with existing patterns. It is not unusual for primary heads to be members of local support groups and to undertake in-service courses. The former could become discussion groups, the latter, especially where there are higher degree courses, already offer some challenge to participants' assumptions.

Moreover, the case of Ron supports the argument here. His experience of the Len Marsh course for headteachers provided a challenge and stimulus to his educational thinking. It provoked reflection and critical analysis in the context of a group of peers. The case of Ron also suggests that while a head's identity is the product of a long process of occupational socialization, this is not to say the identity is immutable. There was some evidence of Ron modifying his educational vision, which suggests that his beliefs were not intractable.

To sum up then, because of occupational conventions and traditions, heads are not readily or generally disposed to self-scrutiny. For a number of reasons heads can be stubborn learners; yet they are learners nevertheless! Alongside opportunities for discussion and peer group support, heads need to be challenged. As part of this challenge they need opportunities to learn about alternative approaches to leadership. Such a programme of study would be undertaken in a spirit of headteacher self-examination. The resulting insights could be tried out with the discussion group so that both the study programme and the group become mutually supportive. Together, discussion groups and formal study programmes could form a dynamic combination and make a powerful contribution towards critical leadership. However, there remain two other weaknesses in the proposal as the next section makes plain.

Headteacher and Teachers' Development and the Prospects for Change

There are two flaws in the argument advanced thus far. First, by focusing solely upon headteachers, I have sustained a narrow and restrictive view of school leadership. Second, the prevailing political climate continues to favour the bureaucratic and managerial rationale, rather than an ethical and critical one. There are two reasons why the focus on headteachers alone is limited and flawed. First, I have argued in the previous chapter, following Foster and others, that leadership should not be attached to either a single post holder or person. Rather, leadership is something all members of a group exercise. To focus, therefore, upon only heads is too restricted a view. All members of staff should have opportunities to critically appraise leadership. Failure to offer these opportunities will merely preserve the existing inequalities in school between heads and teachers and maintain the domination of the former over the latter.

However, there is one rider to add to this line of reasoning. The change from dominating heads to critical leadership is a radical one. Also, it is a change that cannot be mandated since that would breach the ethical principles of critical leadership. Yet it is justifiable to seek to create the conditions in which critical self-examination occurs and in which all members of staff participate in the processes of enlightenment and emancipation. They can be justified on the grounds that self-examination is educative and participation is ethically just.

Perhaps, then, it is necessary to regard headteacher development as a short-term measure. In the short term, some heads will have particular needs, most obviously in respect of their strong belief in holding a monopoly of power. They will therefore need opportunities specific to themselves — of the kind outlined in the previous section — to offer them the chance to consider other approaches to headship. These may be needed for a limited period of time only. As teachers alter their attitudes towards authority, and, in turn, some become heads themselves, there will be a reducing number of dominating heads. Headteacher development in terms of moral and critical awareness, and in terms of altering power relations in schools, is perhaps best conceived as a supplementary and initial provision.

The second reason why an exclusive focus upon headteacher development is flawed relates to the hypothesis advanced in Chapter 5. The idea that a head's professional identity incorporates domination has influenced much of the discussion thus far. However, I also argued in Chapter 5 that domination in schools occurs as a result of school structures and occupational identities and that both as a head *and* as a teacher the individual exercises control over others. Teachers and heads hold similar assumptions about individualism, hierarchy, authority dependency and control. The roots of a head's use of power reach back into his or her assumptions about teaching and school organization. Domination is not simply a function of headship, it is a working assumption of heads and teachers.

To expect, therefore, a programme of headteacher development to somehow remedy such a widely held belief and to overcome such an extensive process of occupational socialization is unreasonable and unsound. Indeed, it is to deal only with the symptoms and to ignore some of the causes. Teachers too must be encouraged to engage in critical enquiry. Just like their heads, teachers should begin to challenge their own assumptions and to contemplate the likely benefits of more emancipatory forms of leadership and school organization.

Such a conclusion is held by Sarason (1990) who regards altering power relationships in schools as a necessary move if schools, and all who work in them, are to develop. He notes that no one challenges the authority of school administrators to make final decisions (p. 59) and that teachers have no voice in decision-making in school (p. 60). He believes both need to be revised. Furthermore, Sarason recognizes that power relations in classrooms also influence teachers' assumptions about power.

> In the modal classroom the degree of responsibility given to students is minimal. They are responsible only in the sense that they are expected to complete tasks assigned by teachers and in ways the teachers have indicated. They are not responsible to other students. They are solo learners and performers responsible to one adult. They are expected to be rugged individualists. Implicitly and explicitly, the task of the teacher is to foster individualism. When we are told that the overarching aim of schooling is to help each child realise his or her full potential, it engenders the imagery of *a* child and *a* teacher, the latter zealously concentrating on the former. The responsibility of the teacher, a derivative of his or her power, is awesome.
>
> (Sarason 1990:91)

Sarason also says that these assumptions about power are both unrealistic and unjustified. They are unrealistic because it is impossible to do justice to the needs and talents of each child in the classroom. They are unjustified because they rest on the assumption that there are no other ways of structuring the social context for learning (pp. 91–2).

The argument Sarason advances is that schools should exist co-equally for the development of students and staff, and that to accept this challenge is to give up the belief that schools do and should exist primarily for the children (p. 145). Staff need to participate more actively than at present in the management and leadership of their schools. Until power relations alter and become more equable in classrooms and staffrooms schools will not improve.

Teachers then also need opportunities to enlighten and emancipate themselves.

And just as the shift from dominating heads to critical leaders is a large step, so it will be for many teachers to change their ways of working in classrooms. However, as a first step, teachers will need to change their ways of participating in staffrooms. Perhaps once there are more participative and critical encounters amongst members of staff, including the head, there will be changes to classroom practices.

One should not overlook the existing work which is happening in this direction. For example, those who advocate person-centred in-service (see Whitaker 1986), student-centred schooling (see Brandes and Ginnis 1990) and those who advocate a 'poetic approach to teaching' (Bonnett 1991) offer a challenge to existing approaches. There are, then some indications of teaching being conceived in alternative ways, although there does not appear to be an impending wholesale shift away from traditional methods or beliefs about power relations in classrooms and staffrooms.

The latter point, that power relations in schools are not about to significantly alter, relates to the second weakness in my proposals for developing critical leaders. At a number of points in the discussion I have acknowledged that a bureaucratic rationale remains intact and undefeated in respect to school management theorizing. For example, the effective schools research, with its support for strong leadership, sustains a narrow belief in efficiency and effectiveness. Moreover, recent legislation and other initiatives emanating from central government have generally sustained the status quo in schools.

The introduction of LMS has granted to heads increased opportunities to exercise executive control of the school's resources, albeit with the agreement of the school's governors. A recent discussion document published by the DES and despatched to all primary schools in England, reinforces the idea that head is the school's quality controller when it states that:

> Headteachers are uniquely placed to look across that whole school for the purpose of judging its strengths and weaknesses, spotting incipient problems, drawing attention to work of distinction and to aspects of work which call for improvement. Among other things, headship is leadership in quality assessment and assurance and this is a role which will assume even greater importance as the National Curriculum and the Parents' Charter take full effect.
>
> (Alexander, Rose and Woodhead 1992, para. 153:46)

Also, when this report refers to effective headteachers having a 'vision of what their schools should become' (para. 47:47) it maintains both the proprietal norm of primary headship (their schools) and also the assumption that it is the headteacher's vision which counts most. The document sustains the beliefs that heads are all seeing and know best.

Moreover, according to Bottery (1992), most politicians' assumptions about leadership follow the managerial model (p. 178), accepting hierarchy and power as meaning power over. In other words, those aspects of school leadership which I have challenged and the critical theorists attack, continue largely undisturbed in England in the 1990s. Therefore, headteachers continue to work in an environment which supports bureaucracy as I also acknowledged in Chapter 4. Their taken-for-granted assumptions about organizational power are further propped up by the contemporary climate. The environmental conditions are not conducive to rethinking school leadership. On balance, then, the prospects for a dramatic revision to headship appear to be very small.

However, to recognize the problem is the first and most difficult step (Sarason 1990:7). Moreover, it would be inconsistent with notions of ethical leadership and emancipation that anyone should seek to impose critical leadership upon others. The force of the argument should carry the case, not the force of someone's power over others! It seems likely then that, at best, there will be a gradual rather than dramatic increase in critical leadership. But those who begin to try out these ideas in practice will be willing participants and not dragooned submissives.

Summary

I have argued that existing approaches to headteacher development are inappropriate for heads to become critical leaders. Headteacher development is driven by a bureaucratic rationale which values only effectiveness and technical training. Consequently, the development of headteachers, typically through management courses, lacks a critical, educative component, treats the individual as object and fails to address the ethical dimensions of leadership. Instead, the development of heads needs to offer opportunities for personal and professional reflection, to be educative and critical, and to consider the ethical as well as technical issues involved in school management.

These characteristics can be included in discussion group work. Discussion groups, of the kind specified by Nias, and found to be useful by Coulson and Whitaker, bring together individual's perspectives and enable critical discussion in ways which support the person while challenging the professional. They also offer a model of facilitative leadership, broaden individual's knowledge of how other heads work and give an equal voice to all who participate. The rules and processes of such groups are consistent with critical leadership and workplace participation; the medium is the message.

At the same time heads should be offered opportunities to undertake programmes of further study. These programmes seek to overcome the conservative tendencies of heads and the persistence of unexamined role orthodoxies. Study programmes should provide opportunities for reflection while also requiring heads to scrutinize their educational and organizational beliefs and to learn about alternative theories. Programmes of study would complement discussion groups.

In the last section it was noted that both discussion groups and study opportunities should be available to teachers. Otherwise, headteacher development alone would only perpetuate existing inequalities between heads and teachers. Indeed, since the seeds of domination can be found in classrooms, teaching as well as headship needs to be critically analysed. Power relations in staffrooms and classrooms need to change if domination is to be removed from schools and teachers' and heads' occupational identities.

Finally, it needs to be made clear that the scale of change being sought is considerable. To believe that both teaching and headship will be transformed is more hopeful than realistic. Although the case of Ron offers some comfort, insofar as he was reflective and not immune to changing his educational beliefs, overall I am gloomy about the prospects for rapid or wholesale change.

Chapter 8

Conclusions

In this chapter I will draw together the main points of this study, highlight the major outcomes and offer some recommendations both for enabling heads to reflect on their leadership and for future research. Although I have called the chapter 'Conclusions' I should reiterate that the points I highlight are not so much truths as hypotheses I have arrived at in the process of conducting this research. In turn, it also needs to be acknowledged that there is yet more to discover and explore about headship.

The portrait of Ron Lacey shows that he worked long hours, being deeply committed to the school he led. Much of his work, during and after the school day, was devoted to dealing with people. Although he handled documents and wrote letters and reports, most of his work was oral; talk was the work. Ron dealt with a wide range of topics and issues, but he was most strongly interested in teachers and children, teaching and learning. He monitored what was happening in the teaching areas of the school, offered advice and support to teacher colleagues, reflected on what he saw or heard about and evaluated the work taking place in the school. He saw himself as a developer of the staff, the curriculum and the school as an organization.

Ron led through a blend of influence and authority. He was involved in the micropolitics of the institution. He knew, by a variety of means, what was happening in the school and he was at the centre of an information web. He was aware of the interpersonal dramas in the school and sensitive to their implications for the running of the school. Staff accepted his leadership, respecting his experience and knowledge. No-one challenged his authority. Indeed, Ron was the predominant and controlling figure in the school. He regarded headship as individualistic and personal. He promoted his professional and personal beliefs and wanted to see them enacted throughout the school.

Ron did not make a strong distinction between his professional and personal lives, consequently, there was a personal dimension to headship. He had a strong sense of self. His development as a teacher and head was a process of self-development. His professional dealings with staff were sometimes frustrating and occasionally painful for him. Through working long hours and devoting so much of himself to his work, the job consumed him; work was his way of·life. Headship was not a role, it was an identity.

This portrait means that Ron was not only dominant in the school, but also that dominance was part of his professional identity. This conclusion raised three questions. Is domination morally acceptable? What conditions allow headteachers to dominate? Are there alternatives to domination? In addressing the first question I argued that it is unacceptable for headteachers to be so powerful that they dominate their schools. Domination negates participatory democracy, establishes a morally unacceptable distribution of power in the workplace and creates an indefensible authority structure both for teachers and pupils.

In examining the second question I considered organizational power and identity. I defined power as meaning *power over*, a definition which is underwritten by a bureaucratic rationale which sustains hierarchical power structures in organizations. Moreover, so common are bureaucratic organizations in our society that the exercise of power over and submissiveness to authority are taken for granted.

Yet power is also contested as well as invested in organizational positions. Hence power over does not provide a complete explanation for domination. As Giddens (1977; 1979; 1982) argues, individuals can do otherwise. Given, then, that bureaucracy is not an iron cage, I drew upon Giddens' structuration theory. This theory allows agency and identity to be brought into an explanation of dominance and helps to show how individuals who might act otherwise, nevertheless submit to the rules and conditions of bureaucracy.

I argued that identity consists of multiple selves, but recognized that I was qualified only to deal with the occupational self. I argued that the occupational self of some primary headteacher consists of two selves: teacher and head. Although these two selves are different in some respects, they also overlap and are similar. One important similarity is in respect of power. I argued that classrooms are a microcosm of the school in terms of power relations. Primary heads dominate teachers in much the same way as teachers exercise power over pupils. Domination is learned in classrooms and transported into primary headship. Domination is part of a teacher's identity and remains part of a head's identity.

In searching for an alternative approach to school leadership, to answer the third question raised by the portrait of Ron, I criticized the theory movement in school management for being neo-feudal, prizing objectivity over subjectivity and efficiency over ethics, and for its male bias. I argued that although there are a number of counter arguments to the tenets of the theory movement, the critical theorists in school management offer the most convincing challenge to the bureaucratic rationale. Critical theorists seek to equalize the distribution of power in schools and regard leadership as having an ethical component. I also claimed that Foster's (1986; 1989; 1990; 1991) work on critical leadership offers the greatest promise for changing existing conceptualizations of headship.

At the same time, however, I recognized that the bureaucratic rationale remained in place, underscoring much of contemporary school management theorizing. I used the effective schools research to show how durable is the idea of strong, heroic leadership. I also noted that Foster has not considered how presently monopolistic heads will divest themselves of their power and change themselves into transformational, ethical, educative and critical leaders. Crucially, Foster appears to be unaware that changing the nature of school leadership means a shift in occupational identity and his proposal begs questions about the nature of headteacher development.

Turning to headteacher development I argued that to develop reflective, critical and ethical leadership, headteacher development should not be wholly devoted to technical matters. Heads also need to focus upon the ethical dimensions of their work and consider alternative ways of leading.

I suggested that one strategy for fostering critical leadership was a particular kind of group work. The group work I had in mind would nurture critical reflection and help participants see the possibilities which exist for altering the structures and organizations which control and condition them. Moreover, participation in groups enables individuals to encounter the views of others and to uncover and analyse their own values. Discourse is vital to such group work, not only for the way it facilitates an awareness of self and others, but also because sharing creates within the group a capacity for mutual support. I also acknowledged that to achieve all these goals group members need to adopt a certain set of rules or principles of procedure.

Groups are a fertile learning environment for individuals' growth. Groups can help individuals to transform their perspectives. Participants' deep-seated beliefs — their core occupational beliefs which are self-defining and therefore difficult to change — can be examined in a supportive context. At the same time heads should be offered opportunities to undertake programmes of further study. These study programmes would complement and supplement group work by countering the conservative tendencies of heads and the persistence of unexamined role orthodoxies. Part of the study programme would encourage heads to reflect on their leadership and critically examine their educational and organizational beliefs.

However, given that the identity of a headteacher reaches back into their classroom experiences, teachers too need to consider power. Until power relations alter in classrooms and staffrooms, schools will not improve. Schools will not become democratic workplaces, nor models of participative democratic organization for their pupils.

The scale and depth of change needed for critical leadership to blossom is considerable. The scale is extensive because critical leadership rests not only on developing headteachers, but also on altering the assumptions of teachers and deputies. The depth of change in headship is great because deep-seated role conventions must be challenged. The occupational identities of teachers and heads need to be questioned.

Moreover, the assumptions of governors, parents and politicians would no doubt need to be considered. In this research I have not addressed the issue of political power and the way government policies might hold in place existing organizational power structures in schools. I have not dealt with these policies here because I felt they should be part of another and larger study. However, I would not wish to close this book without acknowledging that central government's assumptions about the role of heads play a part in framing the nature of headship. At some point a study of these assumptions should be made.

The likelihood of wholesale change in leadership and power relations is extremely doubtful. Ultimately the conclusion is a gloomy one. The prospects for ethical, critical and transformational leadership are not encouraging. At best, the changes I advocate will occur only gradually and be confined to individuals, not least because critical leadership cannot be enforced, since that would only breach its emancipatory and ethical principles. Nevertheless, I now see more clearly than before that there is considerable merit in developing a particular kind of group work for headteachers.

Although I am not optimistic about the prospects for critical leadership, this study nevertheless shows that, first and foremost, primary heads need to be offered opportunities to reflect on their leadership. One of the findings from the study of Ron was that while he was a reflective practitioner, in terms of thinking about the work of the school, he had not been provided with any formal opportunities to critically examine his approach to headship. He led the school in his accustomed manner. He had not been challenged to explain his approach to headship, nor had he been called upon to justify his way of leading the school. While there are undoubtedly issues of accountability here, my main point is that he had not set out for himself, in some structured and disciplined way, how and why he led in the way he did. Given the considerable powers primary heads possess, it does not seem sensible to allow them to exercise them in a relatively unexamined way. To return to Hodgkinson (1983), if the unexamined life is not worth living (p. 70), then I would add that unexamined leadership is not worth following.

One outcome of this study, therefore, is that I am now convinced that provision should be made for heads, periodically, to articulate, critically reflect on and justify their approach to headship. Such an examination could take place on courses or as part of some supervised study programme. It could also be part of head-teacher appraisal or become a part of school inspections. A headteacher's exercise of power should not be taken for granted or overlooked. It should be examined and challenged so that heads can develop and refine the ways they try to lead their schools.

Along with such a requirement should go the entitlement of every headteacher to at least one term's sabbatical leave every five years. This break from headteaching would enable them to re-examine their leadership along the lines sketched out above. This term out could be used for study, course work, examination of leadership in other contexts and for visits to other schools. At the same time, a term's break would allow heads some relief from the executive busyness noted in Chapter 6. Managerial hyperactivity allows no pause for reflection. Many heads are, in my experience (like lots of teachers too), action men and women. They are on the go most of the day, juggling competing demands for their time and attention — as, on many occasions, was Ron. Consequently, these individuals can become worn down by the demands of the job. Often, especially towards the end of each term, they become almost too tired to think. Yet, as many have said to me, as they sit exhausted, but trying to relax on those evenings they are actually home, they always know there is more they need to do, or worse, there is something they feel they should have done.

One feature of Ron's work is the open-ended nature of headship. There were few tangible mileposts when he felt something had been completed. As he said himself, he never felt there was a time when things come to an end. The work of a head just keeps on going. There is a never-ending feel to headship. Exciting as this work can be, one should not underestimate that it is also a treadmill. The demands of the work are intense and interminable.

In being critical of the existing power relations in some schools, it needs to be said that I am not blaming those heads, much less Ron himself. Rather, I am critical of the *conditions* in which they work. Through this research I have been fortunate to be given the means to spend a little time looking at a single head's work. The opportunity to do so has helped me to understand more clearly and critically that it is the work conditions of heads which often prevent them from being critical, reflective leaders.

Heads are unable to be critical leaders because the process of self-examination is often thwarted by fatigue caused by the open-ended, unceasing demands of the job. Heads need both *time out* in order to learn with and from others and *time off* to temporarily suspend the heavy weight of their work and to reflect critically on their values and beliefs.

A second outcome of this research concerns the hypothesis that domination is part of a headteacher's professional identity. I am sure many will want to argue about domination and will take issue with my discussion of power. There are two points I therefore want to make here. First, as I have already said, I have not in this study conducted an examination of the wider political and ideological context of Ron's headship. I am aware that this study of Ron is, in part, a study of a head coming to terms with the 'market forces' ideology and central government's greater control of schooling. The sub-section in Chapter 3 which is entitled 'The shock of the new : external change', makes it clear that Ron was trying to assimilate and accommodate this new thinking. However, while I only lightly touch upon the macro-political context, what this study does suggest is that schools have a micro-political impact on the pupils. One of the points I would wish readers to consider is how schools create for their pupils model authority structures. For too long, I believe we have underestimated, or underemphasized, the political potency of schools. There is a hidden (or not so hidden) political curriculum in schools. It teaches pupils about: hierarchical organization; super-ordinates exercising authority over subordinates; power and knowledge flowing downwards — from the top; whose voices count and whose are unheard or suppressed. The central issue, and an important outcome, for me, is the need to recognize the moral and political potency of schools and their impact upon young children.

The second point concerns the concept of identity. Whether readers accept the plausibility of the hypothesis offered here is, of course, up to them. What I do think needs to be borne in mind, however, is the dual nature of the hypothesis. I have said that domination is a part of headship (for some heads) and that headship (for some) is not a role but an identity. In now concluding this enquiry I feel it is important to differentiate these two findings because I would not wish the notion of identity to be conflated with what I say about power. It seems to me that if this research has advanced our understanding of primary headship, it is in respect of headship being, for some heads, a professional identity. This idea means that we need to appreciate that for some heads their work is simultaneously a matter of self-definition and self-expression. A head is literally and inextricably caught up in his/her work because the work is his/her *self*.

The idea that headship is an identity leads me to the third outcome. There is a need to explore further, with other studies of heads, especially more recently appointed ones, this idea that a head invests his/her self in his/her work. One reason for suggesting this line of enquiry is to test my findings here. However, another reason is that it seems likely that the topic might help us to understand the motivation of primary heads. At present, we know surprisingly little about this issue. Given that headship is hard work, demanding and unrelenting, one needs to ask what motivates such heads to work as hard as they do? My suspicion is that they believe *they* can make a difference to the schools they lead and have a contribution to make. However, there remains a great deal more to know about why some heads invest so much of themselves into their work.

Indeed, the fourth outcome of this study concerns the need for further research in five areas. All have been raised earlier in the book (see Chapter 4) so I shall only briefly note them here. First, there is a need to examine the work of deputy heads. Little research has been conducted into them and even less into how

In this section I briefly want to discuss four points which need to be raised about the conclusions. The first three are riders I want to add to the conclusions, while the fourth foreshadows the discussion and analysis in Chapters 5 and 6.

The first point is that in showing Ron to be powerful in the school the case study verifies existing theories about primary headteachers. As I have already mentioned in Chapter 2, this finding's correspondence with the prevailing view about heads troubled me for a time because I questioned whether I had been heavily influenced by this knowledge and therefore constructed this portrait because of what I knew, rather than what I witnessed. After much rescrutiny of the data I have eventually reassured myself that the data do themselves support this finding, as, indeed, does Ron himself. Given, then, that one of the study's main findings confirms what others have claimed about primary heads, and that Ron's approach to headship resembles that of other heads, it can be said that Ron is not unique. So saying, however, it should not be presumed that I am claiming that Ron's approach is universal. As I have stated in Chapter 2, this research is not concerned with statistical generalization. Rather, what can be suggested is the likelihood that *some* primary heads appear to work in similar ways to Ron and share similar assumptions about their centrality and exercise of power. As such, it seems safe to assume that the conclusions here may relate to some other primary heads, but by no means all of them.

Second, domination may sound a harsh term and at odds with some aspects of the portrait of Ron. For a period during the analysis I tried to find an alternative to the term, since I initially felt it was somewhat inappropriate as a label for Ron's behaviour and work. However, when I explored its meaning I became satisfied with Ball's (1987) usage of it and now recognize it is the appropriate term. As to the term being at odds with Ron's kindly and caring manner, my reflections here centre on two issues. First, his considerate manner did not mean he was softcentred, only that he was a mixture of both tenderness and toughness, as the staff's comments support. Second, not only can consideration and domination co-exist, but as the work of Blase (1989; 1991) shows, open heads can increase their control of the organization by being concerned about and supportive of their teacher colleagues. It is not a contradiction in terms to see Ron as both kindly and dominating, rather they are complementary.

The third point concerns whether this portrait of Ron is now an historical one. The processes of analysing the data, writing the case study, clearing it with Ron, preparing the thesis and now this book, have all combined to delay publication of the findings. The portrait is thus a retrospective view of a headteacher. Furthermore, the period since the fieldwork has been a time of considerable change in education with multiple changes and initiatives altering much of what goes on in schools. Here one must acknowledge that the advent of LMS, open enrolment, the increase in the role of school governors and the reduced powers of the LEAs have added to the work of heads and altered the balance of their tasks and responsibilities. Therefore, this retrospective account may not only be an ageing study, but a dated one. For sure, there is a sense of that was then and this is now, but I am convinced that in terms of the central findings and conclusions the study remains relevant.

I say this for two reasons. First, as noted in Chapter 1, recent papers and enquiries seem to sustain the view that heads are pre-eminent in their schools. The Alexander, Rose and Woodhead (1992) paper, for example, devotes a whole section to the head's curriculum leadership and thereby suggests a continuing belief in the centrality of the head. Also, the report by Bolam *et al.* (1993) shows that headship may be altering in some, but not all, respects. For example, in discussing leadership and the headteacher they say:

> Although teachers displayed little enthusiasm for the out and out autocrat and management by dictat, nevertheless they seemed to need the reassurance of being able to feel confident their head could be entrusted to keep the vessel safely afloat. Thus, more often than not, the headteacher appeared still to remain the dominant figure.
>
> (Bolam *et al.* 1993:43–4)

What these findings suggest is that some heads have continued to be the paramount individual in their schools because of their own assumptions about leadership and because of the expectations of teachers about how heads should operate. While both of these ideas will be discussed in Chapters 4 and 5, the crucial point here is that some heads have not changed, it terms of their authority and power, but are still the dominant figures in their schools despite school management increasing in complexity and volume.

Second, one of the main features of Ron's work, his monitoring of what was happening in the classrooms and around the school, is now a major emphasis in headship in the 1990s (see Alexander *et al.* 1992:46). Also, quality assurance has become an area of great concern for heads with the introduction of regular school inspections co-ordinated by OFSTED. Therefore, Ron's approach to knowing what was being taught and learned will have some currency for the foreseeable future.

These two reasons, then, account for the study's continuing relevance to primary schools in this decade, as well as the last. Indeed, my fourth point is that the absence in the existing literature of a thorough examination of a head's power and control makes this study both necessary and pertinent. Furthermore, the conclusion that Ron's approach to headship was an occupational identity is a fresh insight, and given further discussion, may add to our understanding of primary headship.

Summary

In the first part of the Chapter I presented Ron's response to the case study and examined five issues in a reflective rather than conclusive way. Ron's response to the case study was positive. He was satisfied with the portrait and validated the interpretation. During the discussion of the five issues raised by the case study I identified where the case study provides some empirical evidence for further research. Throughout the discussion of the five issues there runs a common thread; the centrality of Ron in the school. The relationship of Ron and Dave highlights power and dominance, as do the sections on context and micropolitics. Moreover, the topic of gender suggests a male view of power underpinned Ron's work. In other words, at the very heart of headship lies the issue of power. So saying the first part of the chapter paves the way for the second part.

The second part presents the conclusions I draw from the case study. I argue that Ron was powerful to the point of dominating the school. I also claim that domination was part of his professional identity. As Chapter 2 argues, these conclusions are tentative ones. Indeed, they are working hypotheses based upon a single case. As such they require a more detailed theoretical exegesis to establish if they can be advanced for both the situation in which they were uncovered and for analytical generalization. The next chapter therefore aims to explain, and explore further, the conclusions I have noted here.

Part III

Explanations and Implications

Chapter 5

Theoretical Explanation for the Conclusions

The conclusions that Ron was dominant in the school and that dominance was part of his professional identity raise three questions. First, is an individual's dominance of a group morally acceptable? Second, what conditions allow heads to dominate the schools they lead? Third, if domination is morally unacceptable, are there alternative ways of approaching school leadership?

I will focus on the first two questions in this chapter and address the third in the next chapter. There are three reasons for this decision. First, by looking at these two questions, and in that order, I can develop my argument that headship is a way of life, not a role and that control of others is a major part of headship. Second, there are ethical issues to address when discussing domination and power. By addressing the first question at the start of this chapter I can examine the ethical issues and make my own value position clear. Third, my analysis of the conditions which enable some heads to dominate their schools will provide a theoretical explanation for the conclusions drawn in the previous chapter.

The chapter is divided into two unequal parts. The first section looks at the morality of domination. Drawing upon the work of White (1983) and Rivzi (1989) I will argue that domination is unacceptable because it is inimical to democracy and social justice. The second section considers the circumstances by which domination occurs. It consists of three interrelated sections. In the first section I argue that domination occurs because power is taken to mean *power over* and is legitimized by a bureaucratic rationality. However, this argument is overreliant on structural theory and negates the possibility that individuals could act in different ways. To counter this weakness I draw upon Giddens' (1979) structuration theory which draws attention to human agency as well as the effects of societal and organizational structures. Consideration of agency prompts the second section. Here I attempt to show that the professional identity of a headteacher embodies occupational norms about responsibility for others and exercising control over others. I also argue that these norms are learned as a teacher and as a head. In the third section I attempt to fit together the ideas I have developed in the first two sections. I will suggest that social structures alone do not create the conditions for heads to dominate. Rather, it is these structures in association with occupational norms, which, in turn, become part of the professional identities of heads, which make domination possible. I conclude this second section by proposing a hypothesis about primary headteachers.

There are two other points to note. First, much of the discussion in the second section is speculative and exploratory because the theme of domination has not been explored with reference to identity, nor has the occupational identity of a primary head previously been addressed. Second, and arising from the first, since many of these ideas were suggested by the case of Ron I will, from time to time, use him to illustrate and support the argument I am advancing.

Is an Individual's Domination of a Group Morally Acceptable?

The pre-eminence of the headteacher has been criticized on the grounds that it adversely affects the potency of the school because it hinders the participation of teachers in policy decision-making (see Conway 1978:225). While it is important to consider the difference leaders can make to the effectiveness of the organization, I want to argue that school leadership is not only concerned with the most efficient way to lead a school, but also whether any particular approach is morally acceptable.

In the previous chapter I argued, following Ball (1987) and Blase (1991), that heads, although wanting to involve teachers in the running of the school, also seek to control the staff. Control of school organizations is concerned with domination; that is, the elimination and pre-emption of conflict. Domination 'is intended to achieve and maintain particular definitions of the school over and against alternative' definitions (Ball 1987:278). I also said in Chapter 3 that dominance is the behavioural expression of socio-cultural power relationships.

So saying, I now wish to make it explicit that I believe a headteacher's domination of a staff group is unacceptable because it fundamentally injures democracy:

> a strong notion of democracy implies that to be committed to democratic schooling is to be committed to a more equitable distribution of power relations than that which currently prevails in most schools. . .educational administration should be so structured as to give teachers, pupils and parents some political control over educational decisions. Such a view of democratic governance is justified on a range of moral considerations, including liberty, social justice and respect for persons.
>
> (Rivzi 1989:55)

Rivzi's thesis is shared by White (1983).

White challenges the way power is distributed in society and, in particular, in schools because she regards schools as playing a vitally important role in the political education of children. White argues that since no one can claim to have superior insight into the ends of life, 'the only way to dispose of power in a morally acceptable way is to allow each individual in the community access to an equal share in the exercise, or control, of power' (White 1983:9). Equality in the exercise, or control of power is the basic principle of participatory democracy (p. 13). Furthermore, because individual citizens are responsible moral agents, they should be involved in the making of political decisions themselves rather than have them made for them. Citizens need to be able to make choices and they need the kind of institutions which permit and enrich choices, but do not enforce them. In all the workplace institutions of any society, power needs to be exercized democratically, or be subject to democratic control (p. 17). White argues that a strong sense of democracy involves participation by all citizens, particularly in terms of their work places, rather than the creation of some power elite:

There is no conception of 'consent' to a political elite who are entrusted with political power to make the 'right' decisions and thus shoulder what might be considered to be impossible moral burdens for the ordinary citizen.

(White 1983:65)

For White, democracy means participatory democracy and equality in the exercise of power (p. 13).

Moving on to schools as workplaces White makes three points. First, the formal authority structures in a school need to be organized in ways that can accommodate the idea that people are autonomous citizens (p. 88). Second, the existing power relations in schools, especially the pre-eminence of the headteacher, means that at present schools do not have a 'defensible authority structure' (p. 89),

like workers in any enterprise those working in school should be able to expect that its decision-making arrangements for all internal matters will recognise their autonomy. This means concretely that all those working in the school should participate in decisions which affect their work and be accountable to their colleagues for their delegated responsibilities in the running of the institution.

(White 1983:92)

Third, White argues that in the case of school participation is necessary because of the pupils' political education. In addition to their academic studies pupils also learn:

how their particular school is run. They are developing conceptions of authority, power, what it is to be responsible for something, what are considered appropriate decision-making procedures and so on. . .we have to be sure we can defend our decision-making procedures and the roles and statuses we assign to different members of the institution as the ones most suitable for a school in a democratic society. In this connection we may need radically to revise a common British conception of the school head. Is it appropriate, for instance, for the head of an educational insti-tution to be the [often] unchallengeable determiner of both major educa-tional policies within the school as well as the details of the dress of its members?

(White 1983:93)

As Bottery (1988) asks, what does a hierarchical structure in a school tell the pupils? It tells them that in an age of cultural pluralism there is one person, the headteacher, who is given the final say on matters of value (p. 112).

In common with others (see Hoyle 1969; Coulson 1978; Riffel 1986; Ball 1987; Bottery 1988; Rivzi 1989; Watkins 1989; Clark and Meloy 1990; Jenkins 1991), White believes school leadership needs to change because:

In so far as pupils are getting a picture of an indefensible authoritarianism they are being led into an inconsistency. There is *talk* of democratic ideals, practices, etc., but they *see* that important institutions in society are actually being run on anti-democratic lines. . .It seems to me very important not to underestimate the educative influence of a well-run democratically organized school.

(White 1983:93)

This latter point is supported by Jackson (1989) who suspects that schools and classrooms have 'greater moral potency than is commonly understood' (p. 4). It is also the argument developed by Dewey (1975) whose 'entire political and educational theory centred on the idea of the individual participation of each citizen in political decision-making', because this protects the individual's interests and because the 'central function of participation is an educative one' (Rivzi 1990:5).

It is, then, unacceptable that schools should be led by leaders who are so powerful they dominate the institution. Domination negates participative democracy and creates a morally unacceptable distribution of power within the workplace. Moreover, because dominating heads represent an indefensible authority structure we need to reconceptualize school leadership.

However, before considering alternative approaches to headship it is first necessary to understand more fully the nature of domination and the conditions which enable power relations in school to sustain domination.

What Conditions Allow Headteachers to Dominate?

The answer to this question is divided into three sections. In the first I will focus on power in organizations. In the second I examine the professional identity of heads. In the third section I combine the arguments from both previous sections and formulate a hypothesis about primary heads and domination.

Organizational Power

White's thesis and the case against domination is essentially concerned with the 'just use of power' in organizations (Riffel 1986:167). Different conceptions of power have different implications for their moral acceptability in educational institutions (White 1983:19).

Power is a topic which has generated a large amount of theorizing and debate and which the discussion here can reflect in only a relatively limited way. The study of power may be classified into two broad categories: those based on functionalist theories and those located within pluralist analyses of society (Angus and Rivzi 1989:8). The functionalist literature on power emanates largely from the writings of Parsons (1967) and his concern with the structure of formal authority.

Parsons assumes a fundamental distinction between authority [the legitimate use of influence in a rationally defined formal organization] and power [the illegitimate or unauthorised use of influence] with the idea of power viewed as a degenerate or immature form of authority. . .Authority involves the potential to influence based on an organizational position, whereas power is the actual ability to influence in all kinds of other ways.

(Angus and Rivzi 1989:8)

Parsons views authority as

> a generalized capacity to secure the performance of binding obligations
> by units in a system of collective organization, when the obligations are
> legitimated with reference to their bearing on collective goals and where,
> in the case of recalcitrance, there is presumption of enforcement by nega-
> tive situational sanctions.
>
> (Parsons 1967:308)

Hence,

> Institutional control systems which secure conformity or organizational
> obligations are thus deemed legitimate by reason of their alleged contri-
> butions to collective goals. . .[whilst] the moral legitimacy of the organ-
> ization's formal structure has been taken as given.
>
> (Angus and Rivzi 1989:9)

This presumption occurs because Parsons regards power in terms of its ability
to achieve goals, to get things done. This is to stress power as something positive
rather than negative (Clegg 1989:2). Parson's power was *facilitative*, it

> facilitates the production of binding obligations within organizational set-
> tings. The reality of the power to sanction waits unused but ready, should
> the outcome desired not be secured by the exercise of symbolic power
> over the agent whose outcomes are to be affected.
>
> (Clegg 1989:136)

One weakness with Parson's work is that he takes a strongly consensual view of
power in organizations and disregards conflict (Clegg 1989:137), whereas his critics regard power as 'essentially contested' (Lukes 1974:9).

By contrast, pluralist theories of power (see Dahl 1957) recognize power and
authority as being exercised by individuals or groups in pursuit of sectional interests. Pluralists believe people act for a variety of reasons — there is a great plural-
ity of interests. This belief leads pluralists to focus upon observable conflicts over
policy preferences amongst two or more groups in organizations and to identify:

> who prevails in decision-making in order to determine which individuals
> and groups have 'more' power in social life, because direct conflict be-
> tween actors presents a situation most closely approximating an experi-
> mental test of their capacities to affect outcomes.
>
> (Lukes 1974:13)

Lukes regards this type of pluralist theorizing as a one-dimensional view of power
involving a focus on *behaviour* in the making of *decisions* or *issues* over which there
is an observable *conflict* of [subjective] *interests* (p. 15).

However, one weakness with pluralist theory is shown in the work of
Bacharach and Baratz (1962) who argue that it is insufficient only to consider
overt manifestations of decision-making. As they say, demands for change in
existing benefits and privileges in a community can be suffocated before they are

even voiced, or killed before they gain access to the relevant decision-making arena (Angus and Rivzi 1989:11).

What Bacharach and Baratz show is that the pluralists do not go far enough in their thinking because, as Lukes has argued, implicitly resting upon the underlying mechanism of hegemony (Clegg 1989:2), pluralists ignore:

> the crucial point that the most effective and insidious use of power is to prevent conflict from arising in the first place. . .is it not the supreme and most insidious exercise of power to prevent people, to whatever degree, from having grievances by shaping their perceptions, cognitions and preferences in such a way that they accept their role in the existing order of things, either because they can see or imagine no alternative to it, or because they see it as natural and unchangeable, or because they value it as divinely ordained and beneficial? To assume that the absence of grievance equals genuine consensus is simply to rule out the possibility of false or manipulated consensus by definitional fiat.
>
> (Lukes 1974:23–4)

In other words, those who are powerful can become dominant by creating the circumstances whereby they effectively eliminate conflict.

Although functionalist and pluralist views differ in some respects they nevertheless share a set of common assumptions (Angus and Rivzi 1989:11) since they are bound together by the same basic definition of power, namely *power over* (a relationship) rather than *power to* (a capacity or ability) (White 1983:19). Taking power to mean power over provides the basis for someone, or some group, to exercise dominion over others by making decisions regardless of whether the outcome is in these others' interest or not, and for alternative views, or grievances, to be eliminated by circumstances which prevent them ever arising.

Within educational management theorizing power over is underwritten by a bureaucratic–managerial rationality (Foster 1989:43; Angus 1989:87; Inglis 1989:36). As Rivzi says, educational management theory is embedded within a Weberian view of rationality (1989:58) and

> administrators continue to believe that hierarchical authority is indispensable and to have faith in a rationalist model of organizational thinking which emphasises a fundamental distinction between the conception and implementation of objectives. Most remain committed to the ideas of functional divisions of labour and levels of graded authority.
>
> (Rivzi 1989:61)

Bureaucracy is a special mode of social domination.

> domination arises when one or more persons coerce others through the direct use of threat or force. However, domination also occurs in more subtle ways, as when a ruler can impose his or her will while being *perceived as having a right to do so*. This is the kind of domination that most interested Weber, and much of his effort was devoted to understanding the process through which forms of domination become legitimised as normal, socially acceptable power relations: patterns of formal authority

in which rulers see themselves as having the *right* to rule, and those subject to this rule see it as their *duty* to obey.

(Morgan 1986:276)

As Rivzi (1989:66) warns, bureaucratic administration is always in danger of becoming an instrument of elite hegemony.

The bureaucratic rationale sustains hierarchical power structures in organizations. Authority is invested in organizational positions and those who occupy them can exercise power over others and control the organization. Moreover, the very ubiquity of bureaucratic organizations in our society (government departments, large industrial companies, commercial organizations) as well as within education (DfE, LEAs, schools), means they become so familiar to those who work in them, or have contact within them, that the exercise of power within them is taken-for-granted. Citizens become accustomed to power being wielded over them, and submissiveness to authority is accepted. Hodgkinson (1983:66) regards this as an 'agentic state' into which a subordinate falls when placed in a context of formal organization; it is a condition of ready obedience and willingness to be commanded.

As the case study shows, the distribution of power and authority at Orchard school was taken-for-granted. Staff accepted Ron's power over them, being generally submissive to his authority. Moreover, there was an absence of discussion or dissent about power in the school. The absence of overt concern about power perhaps meant that, in Lukes' terms, there was a supreme exercise of power at Orchard; staff had become so inured to bureaucratic conditions and their domination that, to a large degree they had ceased to perceive alternatives to it and accepted these conditions as normal. Hence, conflicts about power and Ron's authority were effectively prevented from arising in the first place.

Yet, Ron was not omnipotent; occasionally some disputes did arise. Where they arose between staff, these were regarded as pathological. When Ron anticipated, or perceived disputes to affect his interests, he attempted to reconcile the differences by normative control (unit leaders, deputy), or personal interventions (the use of micropolitics). In other words, the existence of micropolitics suggests that a bureaucratic rationale does not entirely explain all manifestations of power and may be distorting in some sense.

Ball (1987:25), for example, argues that the assumption of authority favoured in functionalist and managerial perspectives underestimates power as an active and flexible concept. For Ball, power is not so much invested as *contested* (p. 85). Power is not a monolithic concept, it is not only power over. If it were then there would be no circumstances where micropolitical activity occurred. Yet micropolitics do occur in schools (Hoyle 1986; Ball 1987; Blase 1989), thereby showing that power is also contested, even in situations where the leader is dominant. There are, then, grounds for criticizing the argument that a bureaucratic rationale fully explains the nature of power in organizations.

A bureaucratic rationale is helpful to understanding how domination can occur, but it does not entirely explain the apparent subservience of staff in a primary school. The functionalists and pluralists, in assuming that power means power over, also presume that organizational structures alone will determine that individuals exercise power over others when they attain positions of power. Authority is assumed because of position, and subordinates are assumed not to be deviant because they are 'normatively constrained' (Clegg 1989:132). However, I now want to argue that such an outlook is overly deterministic. It is based upon a belief in structure which is disconnected from human agency (Clegg 1989:138), since there is a presumption that the human agent exercises no individual choice.

My argument for questioning the wholly deterministic thinking of functionalists and structuralists is based upon Giddens' structuration theory (1976; 1977; 1979; 1982; 1984), which shows that social behaviour is neither wholly determined by structure, nor by entirely voluntary action, but by a combination of both. This combination demands

> a theory of human agent, or of the subject; an account of the conditions and consequences of action; and an interpretation of 'structure' as somehow embroiled in both those conditions and consequences.
>
> (Giddens 1979:49)

In simple terms, bureaucracy explains how social organization structures the conditions and consequences of action, but does not account for human agency. Indeed, it ignores it, presenting instead an imagery of the organization as 'a strategic calculus' for those in positions of power (Riffel 1986:165). No account is taken of the possibility that at any time agents could act otherwise (Giddens 1979:56). Bureaucracy is not an 'iron cage' (Morgan 1986:276), since agents can behave in different ways.

Structuration theory admits both a sense of determinism and of freedom (Cohen 1989:25). On the one hand, social organizations are structures with constructed power relations which are asymmetrical with superordinate agents ruling subordinate agents. On the other hand, agency allows for the possibility that agents could act otherwise, implying that all actors, potentially exploit a degree of freedom in their conduct (p. 25). However:

> the proviso that, in principle, agents are always capable of acting otherwise represents only a denial of a thoroughgoing determinism of agency by forces to which the agent must respond automatically.
>
> (Cohen 1989:25)

Giddens is equally opposed to unqualified freedom (Cohen 1989:26). Structuration theory resists the polarities of both determinism and freedom, while preserving all possibilities between them (p. 26).

Structuration theory means that a bureaucratic rationale by itself does not necessarily or entirely explain domination. Account also needs to be taken of the individual's agency. In the case of Ron, he could have acted otherwise as a headteacher. Why then, did he act as he did and in a way which maintained domination?

To provide a more complete answer to this question I shall now consider Ron's professional identity. There are two interrelated reasons for this decision. First, the case study suggests that an acceptance of the right to dominate was part of his professional identity, and the notion of professional identity therefore needs to be examined. Second, by focusing upon identity, agency can be brought into the explanation of dominance. Unless agency figures in the explanation, individuals are in danger of being reduced to mere objects whose behaviour is both predictable and programmed by their position in the organization in which they work. Identity needs to be considered, to explore how agents generally act in accordance with a bureaucratic rationale. I shall argue that the concept of identity helps to explain why agents, who could act otherwise, nevertheless submit to the rules and conditions of bureaucracy.

Identity

The exploration of identity is split into two parts. First, I will examine the concept of identity. Second, I will look at Ron's professional identity.

The Concept of Identity

Although identity is a much used term in educational writing (see Sikes *et al.* 1985; Ball and Goodson 1985; Connell 1985a; Nias 1989a, 1989b; Goodson 1991; Goodson and Walker 1991) it is less commonly defined. In the case study I refer to Marris' (1975) definition of occupational identity to show how change can threaten an individual's sense of self. Now, I want to explore in greater depth the concept of identity as a prelude to looking more closely at Ron's professional identity.

Woods outlines the concept in this way:

> The distinction is often made between personal and social identities. Personal identity is the image one has of oneself — social identity is the image others have. . .Identities have a temporal dimension. Ball (1972) has distinguished between situated and substantial identities. The latter have a more stable and enduring quality. Situated identities are more transient, more dependent upon time, place and situation, though they interact with substantial identities and may affect them.
>
> (Woods 1981:296)

Woods offers an overview of the concept touching upon notions of self, personal and social, and situational and substantial selves. These ideas have been applied to teachers by a number of writers (see Connell 1985a; Sikes *et al.* 1985; Ball and Goodson 1985; Duke 1986), yet none has provided a cogent exposition of identity.

Given that identity has not been more thoroughly defined, at least in terms of its applications to teachers, I shall draw upon the work of Nias (1989a) because she has initiated an exploration of the concept. Although her analysis is limited in some respects, it is nevertheless a pertinent examination since it is consistent with the outline Woods (1981) offers above, develops further some of the notions Woods touches upon and because her work relates directly to primary school teachers.

Nias (1989a) focuses upon the concept of self — which she regards as co-terminous with identity (p. 19). Nias draws attention to three related aspects of self: the self-as-object, the substantial self, and the self-as-subject.

The self-as-object stems from symbolic interactionism. This self is socially constructed by interaction with significant and generalized others (p. 20). Drawing first upon the work of Cooley (1902) Nias argues that 'it is through interaction with people to whose behaviour we attach symbolic meanings we learn to take other people's perspectives and to see ourselves as we think they see us' (1989a:19).

In this way we develop an awareness of ourselves as objects. As a result, ourselves are inescapably social (p. 20).

Nias goes on to say that not all interactions are equally important in determining the way we see ourselves, some are more important to us than others (p. 20). Hence the concept of *significant others* who have a particularly powerful impact upon our self-concept. 'In the presence of one whom we feel to be of importance, there is a tendency to enter into and adopt, by sympathy, his judgement of myself' (Cooley 1902; cited in Nias 1989a:20).

Nias also notes that over time

> and through repeated interactions, we internalise the attitudes not just of particular people, but also of organised and generalised social groups [churches, political parties, community groups, work forces].
>
> (Nias 1989a:20)

This means that our sense of self is conditioned not just in relation to the social context of which we are a part, but also with regard to generalized others, that is, the *reference group* (p. 20) we relate to in any situation. Significant others and reference groups help to explain how we develop situational selves.

However, Nias says that a totally situational view of the self cannot be sustained. She calls upon a number of writers (Katz 1960; Abercrombie 1969) to support the idea that each individual develops an inner self (or core):

> Ball (1972) used the term 'substantial' to distinguish this inner core, which, he argued, is persistently defended and highly resistant to change. It comprises the most highly prized aspects of our self concept and the attitudes and values which are salient to them. . .Rogers (1982) argued, from his experience as a psychotherapist and educationist, that individuals need to maintain consistent self-concepts and will reject new ideas which they do not perceive as compatible with their view of themselves. . .
> There is then support from different disciplines for the idea that we each develop a relatively impervious 'substantial self' which can be distinguished from our 'situational selves' and which incorporates those beliefs, values and attitudes which we feel to be most self-defining.
>
> (Nias 1989:21)

In short, our substantial self is a well defended core of self-defining beliefs. While these core beliefs are strongly held and protected by individuals, they are not necessarily intractable, thus the substantial self is not completely static (p. 21).

Turning to the self-as-subject, Nias says that this notion is even more elusive than that of the self as object 'because "I" turns into "me" as soon as the actor is self-conscious' (p. 22). The self-as-I needs to be considered, according to Nias, because on the one hand many people are intuitively aware of its existence as a deep sense of personal identity (p. 22), while on the other hand, it is that part of the self which is relatively free of social constraints (p. 23).

Nias links the self-as-I to the ego. In so doing, she brings into her discussion other theoretical frameworks. Nias suggests that efforts to explain the social self have failed to come to terms 'with the powerful, instinctual forces of the human personality to which Freud drew attention over a century ago' (p. 23).

In addition to noting the theories of Freud, Nias also touches upon the theories of certain self-psychologists (pp. 24–5). However, rather than rehearse her argument here, I simply want to note two things. First, that different theories yield different interpretations of identity. Second, that what Nias suggests, is that some aspects of the self cannot be uncovered or understood without turning to insights derived from psychoanalysis.

To sum up, Nias argues that our identities are composites of the self-as-object and the self-as-subject. The former consists of situational and substantial selves. Situational selves are developed from interaction with others, especially significant and generalized others. The substantial self is a core of self-defining beliefs which is relatively, but not entirely, impervious to change. The self-as-subject is linked to notions of the ego and is not dependent upon social conditioning for its existence.

Nias's account shows that the self is multiple (Woods 1991:7) and not necessarily unified (Norquay 1990:291). This understanding of self has four implications for the ensuing analysis of Ron's identity. First, it follows from Nias that a thorough investigation of an individual's identity should include consideration of situational, substantial and subjective selves. Lacking the credentials to conduct an examination of the self-as-I, it is necessary, therefore, to make it clear that I will not be exploring the self as subject.

Second, I will discuss only Ron's professional identity. By that I mean those characteristics of his situational selves which can be attributed to his occupation and are identifiable in his comments and actions at work. Third, by focusing upon the occupational aspects of his situational selves I do not deny that there are other facets of his situational self which have been omitted, or can only be a matter of conjecture, for example, parent, spouse, family member, or member of an interest group. Fourth, in saying I am looking at his professional identity I am also saying I am not considering his substantial self.

What follows, therefore, is a partial exploration of Ron's professional identity and is concerned with the occupational self as object. The discussion is an initial and speculative attempt to examine the professional identity of a primary headteacher since there is a paucity of other relevant work concerning headteachers.

Although the study of teachers' identities has been an avenue of interest for some time, much of the work is oriented towards secondary teachers (see Woods 1981; Ball and Goodson 1985; Connell 1985; Sikes *et al.* 1985). Some researchers (Osborn 1985; Acker 1987; Delamont 1987; Pollard 1987; Woods 1987) have ventured into the domain of primary teachers yet, to date, only Nias (1989a) has undertaken a sustained examination of the personal and professional experience of primary school teachers in England and of their occupational identities. Moreover, the limited attention devoted to primary teachers is compounded by a dearth of studies concerned with the identities of primary headteachers. The lack of previous work on the professional identities of primary headteachers therefore means that what follows relies, in part, upon Nias' work on primary teachers.

Ron's Professional Identity

I have suggested that an individual's professional identity is socially constructed from interaction with significant others, generalized others, such as reference groups, as well as from experience in the particular occupation, such as teaching, headship, when individuals are socialized into accepting occupational norms, values and beliefs. In the case of Ron, for example, his significant others appeared to be Schiller, Tanner and Marsh, as well as the headteacher of Ford School. From these individuals, and no doubt others, and from his experience of working in schools over time, he saw headship as an expression of himself and his beliefs about education, as developing members of staff and the curriculum, and as being strongly concerned with the children's learning. He also accepted that headship involved using his authority and influence to control others.

While Ron's approach to headship can be attributed to his experience of headship and knowledge of other heads, there seems to me to be more to his occupational identity than being a head. Indeed, I intend to argue in the next four sections that being a head does not entirely account for a headteacher's occupational identity. Rather, I want to suggest that being a head is superimposed upon his identity as a teacher. Ron has become a head, but he simultaneously remains a teacher.

I will begin this exploration of Ron's professional identity by arguing that he does in part, remain a teacher. Next, I will go on to consider by what means he remains a teacher, while also being a head. Third, I will speculate upon the consequences of retaining the identity of a teacher. I have structured the discussion in this way because it follows the sequence of the development of Ron's professional identity. The fourth element of this discussion, therefore, considers how Ron has become a head.

Ron Remains a Teacher

Here I intend to show only that the case study provides sufficient evidence to support the claim that one of Ron's situational selves was that of a teacher. By utilizing previous work focusing on the identities of primary teachers and matching them against Ron's comments, interests and concerns, it is possible to see that several aspects of his professional identity are the same as those associated with being a teacher. Four elements of a teacher's identity will be discussed, three are taken from Nias (1989a) and one from Lortie (1975); being oneself; being responsible; being in control; and psychic rewards.

According to the teachers in Nias' (1989a) sample, to be a teacher meant being oneself in the classroom (p. 182). A high proportion of the teachers Nias interviewed saw little distinction between their selves at work and outside it and regarded themselves as workaholics (p. 182). Ron also believed in being himself. He saw his work as the combination of personal and professional beliefs, made little distinction between work and home and worked long and hard. Moreover, his justification for having a game plan was to say, 'that's just the way I am.' Indeed, Ron believed in being natural, which is another category Nias generates in her analysis of what it means to feel like a teacher (p. 185).

Second, Nias (1989a) says that feeling like a teacher involves feeling responsible for the children and demonstrating concern for them (pp. 189–91). Nias' interviewees believed that as teachers they must accept the children's dependence on them, appreciate that as a teacher one influences them and also care for the children. These sentiments are echoed in Hargreaves' (1990:18) idea that among elementary teachers there exists an 'ethic of care' and an 'ethic of responsibility'. It seems to me that Ron consistently demonstrated concern and care for the pupils and felt a deep sense of responsibility for them.

Third, Nias' (1989a) research recognizes teachers' need to feel in control (pp. 187–9). For Nias' teachers this meant being able to control children, exercising authority and being organized so that one always retained a sense of direction. These find their correlates in Ron being disturbed by Helen's lack of classroom control, his lunchtime supervision of the children in the hall as they ate and his watchful approach to the children's entrance to school after playtimes. Also, Ron's feelings of not knowing the procedures for dealing with recent initiatives were discomforting for him because he felt less in control.

Elsewhere, Nias (1987a) has argued that teachers are vulnerable to any hint that they may be losing control over themselves, or their circumstances, because they are in *loco parentis* and so need to exercise discipline. Also, pupils and parents reinforce teachers' assumptions that they should be able to control what is going on in the classroom. 'In our culture, it is generally accepted that those responsible for young children's learning will also regulate their behaviour' (p. 12).

Furthermore, Nias (1989a) noted that a number of her interviewees felt that teachers and learners can never be equal, that 'the act of teaching necessarily involves the exercise of power' (p. 188). Ron made no such explicit statement, but his actions demonstrated an implicit belief that teachers exercised power over the children. He expected teachers to discipline pupils and to determine the topics the children should be taught.

Fourth, like the classteachers in Lortie's (1975) study of elementary teachers, Ron's 'psychic rewards' (p. 101) were associated with wanting to 'reach' the children (Lortie 1975:104–6; Huberman 1990:29). For Ron, doing something useful was spending time with the children. His need to spend time with the children was revealed by his feelings of frustration when he was not able to do so. As Sarason says, 'I have never met a teacher who was aware of and not disturbed by the fact that he or she had not the time to give to some children in the class the kind of help they needed' (Sarason 1982:187). Ron's notions of success also parallel those of primary and elementary teachers. He saw success as uncertain (Lortie 1975:142; Nias 1989a:191), but defined it as pupil achievements (see Fullan 1991, 2nd ed.:120; Fullan and Hargreaves 1991:22).

The match between these four elements of a teachers' identity and Ron is sufficiently close to sustain the claim that one of his situational selves was that of a teacher. Ron had internalized the norms we now associate with teachers and these underscored many of his actions. Although Ron was a head he also remained in many ways a teacher.

By what means did he remain a teacher?
There are a number of reasons for explaining how Ron was able to be a head and remain a teacher. First, an individual's situational selves are multiple and not necessarily integrated (Nias 1989a:20; Norquay 1990:292; Wood 1991:7). An individual's situational identity can consist of more than one self, for example, teacher, parent.

Second, there are particular occupational reasons which account for heads being teachers. In England and Wales the law demands that headteachers must be qualified teachers. All headteachers have taught for a period of time, although the length of that period will vary from individual to individual. Upon securing a promotion many primary headteachers continue to teach. In some cases this is because the school's staffing ratio demands it, typically in small schools with less than 100 pupils on roll, as was the case in Ron's first headship. In larger schools and before the introduction of LMS, LEAs required headteachers to cover for absent teachers, usually for the first few days of an absence. The LEA in which Ron worked had just such a policy and required him to teach a registration class for the first three days of a teacher's absence, except when the teacher was attending an in-service course.

In addition to the requirement to be a qualified teacher, there are other expectations placed upon headteachers. For example, headteachers' conditions of employment and general functions (DES 1989:20–3) impute a blend of head of establishment and teaching concerns.

Another occupational reason may be Ron's role models. As one primary head has written, 'I suppose my style of headship is an amalgam from all the different headteachers who have influenced my personal development over the years' (Waterhouse in Mortimore and Mortimore 1991:109). A similar claim is made in the case study and is founded upon the belief that a headteacher's approach to leadership is based upon personal history and the power of modelling, which in teaching is unsurpassed (Mortimore and Mortimore 1991:124). Ron's headteacher role models emphasized a strong connection between teaching and headship and so, prior to headship, Ron became aware of the advantages of maintaining an interest in teaching and learning.

One other factor concerns the nature of career advancement in teaching. Ron's career was staged, that is, he occupied a number of positions. Yet these stages were not hermetically sealed. While separate in terms of time and location they were connected in respect of tasks and focus:

> It is a characteristic of teaching that promotion does not always mean a change of role. Quite often promotion can mean additional responsibilities and another role to play, while also retaining the previous role, namely classteacher.
>
> (Southworth 1990:68)

So it was with Ron. He continued to teach during his first headship because he was a teaching head. In this second headship, although relieved of class teaching responsibilities, he carried on teaching and, according to his account, attempted to be a teaching exemplar to his colleagues. Therefore, his career was staged, but not discontinuous since teaching was always carried forward into the next stage. Having begun as a teacher the implicit message of his career path was that he would continue to be one.

This message is supported by the fact that most heads are promoted straight from the classroom (Kelsall and Kelsall 1969:31) and it is a candidate's perceived teaching abilities and experience which appear to have kudos with selectors (Coulson 1976:282–3; King 1983:88; Southworth 1987:63). Indeed, as Hellawell (1991:322) says, many primary heads see themselves as individuals who were promoted to headship because they were good classteachers. It should not be overlooked that in Ron's case he was indeed promoted straight from the classroom since he had never been a permanent deputy head and had only a limited experience of school management matters. Furthermore, he was promoted from class teaching to a teaching headship thereby sustaining very strong ties between teaching and headship.

Also teachers expect their headteachers to set a good example, to exemplify the educational and organizational values to be adopted by staff and to be fully involved and committed to the school (Nias 1980:262; Coulson 1986:78–9).

> This framework of expectations, which stems from teachers' occupational culture (Hargreaves, 1980), puts pressure upon the head to legitimate his promotion and his superordinate position as head*teacher* by equalling or exceeding his colleagues in the observance of these norms. By so doing he maintains solidarity with his teacher colleagues and builds his credibility as Leading Professional and head*teacher* in their eyes. . .
>
> Primary school teachers in the main deem continued observance by heads of a communion of interest and professional values with themselves as an essential part of successful headship. It is this powerful norm which excludes non-teachers, whatever their managerial ability, from eligibility for headship.
>
> (Coulson 1986:79–81)

This norm also appears to be supported by the scant empirical work conducted into teachers' views on primary heads as leaders (Nias 1980).

Together these occupational requirements, expectations and professional structures create the conditions for those individuals who are appointed to headship to carry with them their teaching knowledge, experience and trade craft, to draw upon it to provide an example and a lead for others, and to continue practising as teachers. Just such a pattern is contained in the reflections of one primary head:

> We all started our careers as classroom teachers, learning a craft, coming to terms with the manner in which young people learn and attempting to understand how and why they experience failure — so often our fault rather than theirs. It is this varied background and experience we bring to our own exercise of headship.
>
> (McDonnell in Mortimore and Mortimore 1991:15)

In other words, there is no disjunction between being a teacher and becoming a head. Rather than being discarded or significantly reduced in importance, teaching is absorbed into headship, as the very title suggests, head*teacher*.

What are the consequences of remaining a teacher?
When Hargreaves (1978) considered what teaching does to teachers he recognized that the work people do leaves its mark on them (Hargreaves 1978:540). In this section I will consider how the hallmarks of being a teacher might influence an individual's approach to headship. The discussion will be speculative since, although it is well known that teachers are promoted to headships, there has been little examination of what this means for them as heads.

The identity of teachers is composed of a number of characteristics (see Nias, 1989a). I have already touched on four of the characteristics in the first sub-section when I demonstrated that there was sufficient evidence in the case of Ron to support my claim that he remained a teacher. Here I want to examine only four characteristics of being and remaining a teacher since these are pertinent to my argument that control is part of the identity of headteacher. The four are: individualism; moralism; acceptance of hierarchy; and control.

Many studies characterize teaching as an individualized activity (Jackson 1968; Lortie 1975; Sarason 1982; Lieberman and Miller 1984; Connell 1985a; Little 1989; Nias 1989a; Hargreaves 1990; Huberman 1990). Furthermore, teachers are led to believe that they are capable of knowing all the children in their care (Alexander 1984:12–13) and that the child-centred ideology which pervades much of primary teaching fosters teacher possessiveness about their children (p. 19):

> Teachers socialised into this tradition tend to identify with their classes, to talk of themselves in relationship to their pupils as 'we'. They tacitly believe that their personal relationship is with the whole class, not just with one child.
>
> (Nias 1989:15)

Teaching is also an individualized activity because of the solitary nature of much of primary teaching. The cellular design of schools often fosters isolation and means teachers struggle with their problems privately (Fullan 1991, 2nd ed.:119). Thus teachers can become self-reliant and self-referencing. Together, these points create a set of ecological conditions which fosters 'autonomous isolation' (Goodlad 1984:186).

The second characteristic concerns the wish of many teachers to inculcate in the children not only academic knowledge, but also personal, social and moral attitudes. Connell (1985:181), for example, says there is a pervasive moralism about the way many teachers talk about their work. Nias presents it thus:

> A sense of autonomy in matters of curriculum and pedagogy is closely related to the ideological freedom which most British primary teachers enjoy. This is particularly important because few of them are satisfied with imparting only knowledge or skills to their pupils. Rather, they have always been chosen, or have selected themselves, in part for their concern with religious, moral, political or social values. . .Lortie (1975); Lacey (1977); Woods (1981; 1984); Connell (1985a); Sikes *et al.* (1985) and Smith *et al.* (1986) have all highlighted the continuing existence within the profession of individuals with strong dedication to religious, political or humanitarian ideals. Kay Shuttleworth's vision of a band of 'intelligent Christian men entering on the instruction of the poor with religious devotion to their work' (quoted in Rich 1933) is still *mutatis mutandis* a recognisable one in many schools.
>
> (Nias 1989a:16–17)

As I argued in the case study, Ron saw himself as a pioneer. Also, his antagonism to prejudice and injustice, his religious background, headship of a C of E school, his attraction to community education and his desire to achieve what he thought of as right indicate he was one of those individuals concerned with religious, social and political values. Furthermore, some of his role models and his significant others exemplified these characteristics. In other words, from his experience of teaching, his role models and significant others, he was encouraged to be an individual, to invest him*self* and to pursue *his* vision.

Third, teachers work in schools which as institutions are inherently hierarchical. Teachers learn that rules, values and norms flow from the headteacher (Coulson 1976:280). Moreover, within schools teaching posts are hierarchically graded; the more responsibility, the higher the post and the greater the status of the individual in the organization — with the pre-eminent position being that of headteacher. Therefore, sedimented into the consciousness of teachers, especially those like Ron, who have little experience of working in non-hierarchical forms of organizations, is a belief in a particular type of power, namely power over. Although structure alone does not necessarily account for an individual's outlook, when the individual has worked inside a particular type of organization for as long as Ron and takes its structure for granted, as Ron did, it seems probable that prolonged exposure to such a structure will leave its imprint upon the individual's assumptions. Teachers and heads are accustomed to hierarchy and learn to accept that power means power over.

Furthermore, acceptance of hierarchy helps to create authority–dependency. Dependency arises not only from hierarchy but also the nature of academic learning, how it is organized and carried out. Knowledge is vested in schools, colleges and universities and:

> As we pass through the educational system we are likely, unconsciously, to acquire the assumption that information comes from above, downwards.
>
> If this assumption is unchallenged, people who become teachers are likely to perpetuate it; the only thing to have changed is their position in the transmission process. The unconscious assumption that learning results from a downward process of instruction continues unchecked.
>
> (Nias 1987a:28–9)

One of the things that schools as organizations teaches those who work in them, pupils and teachers alike, is that teachers know best (Sarason 1982, 2nd ed.:175). Authority–dependency is 'sanctioned and affirmed by the structures within which most teachers work' (Nias 1987a:29). Schools are model authority structures for teachers.

The fourth characteristic is the apparent contradiction of control. I have said that, on the one hand, teachers are autonomous, while, on the other hand, I have argued that teachers are dependent upon their headteachers. These two seemingly opposed positions can be reconciled by regarding them as relative, interacting spheres of influence and control.

A primary school comprises two zones of influence where different and distinguishable types of decisions are devolved to the head and teachers and varied measures of autonomy reside within each zone (Lortie 1969; Hanson 1977). The teacher's zone, the classroom, provides a degree of discretion over teaching style, scheduling of activities on a day-to-day basis and pupil discipline. The head, typically, involves him/herself in every aspect of school life, sees him/herself as a unifying element in the school, is the source of the school's espoused philosophy, formulates overall policy, has executive control over human and material resources and monitors school/community relations (Coulson 1978:78). Teachers exercise control in their zone of influence, namely the classroom, but, in turn, are dependent upon the head in matters of school policy, resources, roles and the like. The teacher's autonomy is not absolute, but governed by the degree of discretion the head allows. Moreover, not only do the two zones interact (as in the implementation of school policies in each classroom), they are complementary. Just as teachers expect children to be submissive to their authority, so, in turn, are teachers willing, generally, to submit to the authority of their headteacher (Alexander 1984:168). Teachers control and exert power over their pupils, while recognizing and accepting that, in turn, they are controlled by their headteacher.

When these four characteristics are added together, they suggest that teachers feel responsible for others and regard themselves as in control of a class of children who, being very young, are dependent upon them. Teachers also expect to work in individual ways and often wish to set the moral standards for their pupils. Given these characteristics of teachers it should not be a surprise that they believe themselves to be predominant and pivotal in the classroom (Alexander 1984:168–72; Campbell 1985:154–6; Pollard 1985a:189–90). Moreover, given teachers' acceptance of authority–dependence and the effects of working in hierarchical institutions, a set of expectations about authority is created. Although teachers may be powerful in their individual classrooms, they are also subordinate to the power of their heads because, generally, they accept that heads should determine school policy and staff should acquiesce. Teachers grant to their heads a similar kind of licence which they believe their pupils give to them in the classroom. Teachers exercise power over children and, in turn, expect their head to exert power over them. Power over is an occupational norm.

Just as power often flows smoothly in the tacitly reproduced practices of day-to-day life (Cohen 1989:153), so too are teachers' assumptions about power readily transported into headship, especially when, as in the case of Ron, he was provided with no opportunity to reflect upon the nature of power in schools, nor to learn about alternative configurations or conceptions of power in other organizations. Power over pervades teaching and percolates into headship.

Ron had become a Headteacher

In the previous sections I have argued that promotion from teacher to head is a continuous process. However, while becoming a head does involve some continuity in occupational identity, I now want to argue that some changes also take place. Being a head is not entirely the same as being a teacher. For example, Ron was responsible for the school, being concerned with its reputation and standing in the community. He dealt with administrative matters, such as monthly salaries, accounts; staffing issues, such as appointments, teachers' responsibilities, allocation of classes, unit pairings; external communications, such as parents, governors, community groups; and demands from other agencies beyond the school's immediate setting, such as LEA initiatives, DES regulations. Moreover, in the eyes of the staff he was the *head*. Staff looked to Ron for a lead on matters of school policy. Therefore the transition from teacher to head involves both continuity and change to an individual's occupational identity. In this section I shall explore six ways in which being a head requires an alteration to, or a change in the individual's situational selves.

First, initial socialization into headship exaggerates the individual's sense of professional isolation. As Weindling and Early (1987) report in their investigation into the first years of secondary headship:

> A new head said, 'It is the loneliness of being the final arbiter upon whose word all sinks or swims. It is this power that isolates and daunts'. . .For many heads, professional isolation and loneliness were part and parcel of the job itself.
>
> (Weindling and Early 1987:122–3)

Whilst corresponding studies into primary school headteacher socialization are lacking, similar sentiments were expressed by recently appointed heads in a small-scale study conducted in Cambridgeshire (Myer 1987:9). Upon taking up the mantle of headship it seems that the individuals feel both more responsible and more alone than when they were teachers.

Second, and related to the first, on becoming a head the individual becomes more self-referential. A teacher's feelings of loneliness and autonomy are engendered in the classroom where the individual adult is faced with a larger number of children than she or he expects to control (Pollard 1985a:33–4). As a headteacher similar but stronger feelings of loneliness are present, only now the head faces larger numbers of adults as well as children. In both roles there is a sense of self confronting a group. Yet, in headship there is the added dimension of the head facing groups of adults (the staff, parents, governors). No investigations appear to have been conducted into this phenomenon. Nevertheless, it seems at least plausible to suggest that, when facing such groups, heads will feel not only alone, but reliant upon themselves as a resource; after all who else can they turn to but them*selves*. In other words, their teacher experiences of self-reliance and self-referencing increase and strengthen as a head.

Third, self-referencing develops into self-belief as a result of the selection process. Promotion to headship can be interpreted as legitimating the successful individual's beliefs. Selection ratifies the new head's educational values and confirms his/her classroom practice, which may account for why heads regard themselves as exemplars (Laws and Dennison 1990:54). Regarding appointment to headship as a vindication of his/her teaching performance and educational values, the newly appointed head may well feel that his/her teaching and professional principles are worthy of emulation by others (Southworth 1987:63). Indeed, Whitaker (1983) says that having been selected from many colleagues in open competition, it will be difficult to submerge the sense of mission that inevitably accompanies the prospect of entry into a new headship (p. 62). In short, selection bestows approval upon the successful candidate and encourages a head to feel licensed (Ball 1987:82) to promote her/his beliefs in the school.

Fourth, a head's self-belief and sense of licence relates to his/her vision. By vision I mean a 'personal picture of a desired future that a leader conveys to members of his or her organization' (Manasse 1985:151). A vision is a set of beliefs about what the ideal state of the organization is, or what ought to be achieved (Bolster 1989:1). Smith *et al.* (1986) noted the existence of deeply held beliefs amongst the members of staff in the school they studied. So strongly held were these beliefs that Smith *et al.* likened them to secular religion (p. 116). The beliefs were zealously held by many key players in the school, including the principal, and 'suggested the label of true believers, men and women of fanatical faith'

(p. 127). One reason for Smith's choice of the religious analogy was his discovery, amongst the staff members' life histories, of the fact that many had experienced an 'intense religious socialisation' (p. 147), rather like Ron.

Now Smith *et al.* analogy resonates with earlier comments about teachers regarding themselves as crusaders, to the moralism of teachers and with Ron's idea that he and the staff were pioneers. In other words, a head's vision is an amplification of some teachers' tendencies to regard their work as a mission. Yet it might also mean a shift from regarding one's work as a vocation, to one of wanting to convert colleagues who hold different views.

A head's vision may be no different from a teacher's. Both are likely to be central to the individual's occupational self, if not substantive self (Rokeach 1960:40–2), since the vision may embody social and moral principles which are so central to the individual that they are self-defining. However, by virtue of promoted position, a head feels empowered to make a vision compelling for his/her colleagues. For example, Nias *et al.* (1989) have shown that primary heads' visions can become the schools' missions (pp. 98–9), something others advocate as a route to institutional effectiveness (see Purkey and Smith 1983; Rosenholtz 1989; Beare *et al.* 1989), since missions are seen as ways of building loyalty and commitment amongst members of staff. Yet, 'If missions develop loyalty among the faithful and confidence among the committed, they also create heresy among those who question, those who differ, those who doubt' (Hargreaves 1990:1).

Visionary leadership pushes headship towards messianic leadership, with staff cast as disciples or, if they disagree, heretics. If this happens, and there are traces of it in Orchard and other primary schools (see Nias *et al.* 1989; 1992), then, for the heads, there is a considerable difference between being a teacher and being a head. As a teacher one needs to enact one's vision in the classroom. As a head one must enact the vision, but also ensure staff are attracted to it and adopt it. A head's vision must somehow become the staff's mission.

Fifth, Lortie (1990) speculates that, as part of the occupational identity change involved in taking on the authority of the principal and internalizing it as one's own, principals, over time, redefine the role from one which is less concerned with instructional supervision and evaluation to one which is more so. Principals gradually learn to accept and, presumably, assert authority over former peers (p. 4). In Ron's case, he actively monitored and evaluated the work of the teachers and had become accustomed to exerting his authority over them. As a class teacher he asserted his authority over pupils, as headteacher he had developed the capacity to supervise and control his colleagues. In terms of change what this means is that those who were formerly his peers were now subordinate to him. His position had markedly altered in relation to them for he is now an overseer and controller of them.

Sixth, Lortie (1990) also suggests beginning principals learn their craft in smaller schools; typically, they then move on to larger ones. Success in smaller schools apparently qualifies a principal to become principal in a larger school (p. 9). Yet, principals who move to large schools need to learn whatever new skills are required to succeed there; this may be a difficult transition for some (p. 9). Again this holds good for Ron. He was initially head of a small school where, because he was a teaching head with a small number of colleagues, he continued to be a classteacher for much of the school day. Yet, as he progressed to larger schools his teaching responsibilities decreased until they ceased to be a regular part of his work. Consequently, as he acknowledges in the case study, he had to develop a different approach to influencing his teacher colleagues since he was no longer able to lead through his teaching example.

Lortie (1990) accepts that, with the passage of time, heads alter, thereby reinforcing the point in Chapter 4 about phases of headship. Moreover, Lortie's work supports the idea that an individual's situational selves adjust even while occupying the same position. Although Ron had been a head for seventeen years, his sense of worth, his conception of his role and his dealings with staff probably altered because his increasing experience of headship was teaching him new things and bolstering existing attitudes. It is likely, for example, that Ron, already endowed with a positive image of himself, following rapid promotion to headship, received further reinforcing signals as he progressed from smaller to larger schools. Moreover, as he appointed staff less experienced than himself, he was increasingly able to play the role of master practitioner, professional sage and educative leader. As he became more experienced and moved from smaller to larger schools, in some respects he changed his way of doing headship. He became less of a teaching exemplar and more of a professional mentor to his staff. Nevertheless, given that a head is also concerned to supervise, appraise and control staff, as well as project on to them his/her vision, the shift from exemplar to mentor marks only a shift in the process of influencing colleagues; it does not connote a change in the need to exert influence upon them. The approach to headship may change but the intention — to control others — remains.

To summarize then, being a head involves both continuity and change in an individual's occupational selves. The identity of teacher is altered in terms of isolation, self-referencing, self-belief and the projection of beliefs. These appear to be inflated on becoming a head. At the same time, a head's wish to change the behaviour of children is supplemented by his/her intention to shape teachers' behaviour. Heads strive to make the staff's aims, values and practices congruent with their own. Heads need to come to terms with influencing, supervising and controlling staff.

To the extent that a single case permits, becoming a headteacher means that the occupational self of teacher is combined with the occupational self of head. Neither is mutually exclusive, indeed, as the very title headteacher signals, the job is inclusive of both selves. And in both selves control of others is a common feature.

Organizational Power and Occupational Identity

In this section I want to put together the ideas advanced in the two previous sections concerning organizational power and identity. I have argued that organizational power, whether defined by functionalists or pluralists, is taken to mean power over. This meaning is underwritten by a bureaucratic rationale which assumes hierarchical authority to be indispensable for organizational efficiency. Moreover, the ubiquity of hierarchical organizations in our society means individuals become accustomed to power being exercised over them. Submissiveness to authority becomes a norm of institutional life.

Although a bureaucratic rationale assumes that authority is invested in organizational positions, power can be contested, as the existence of micropolitics in organizations shows. Therefore, while a bureaucratic rationale accounts for how leaders in organizations might dominate, it does not wholly explain the subordination of staff in schools to their heads. In effect, the idea of bureaucracy is too deterministic. It adopts a structural view of power relations and denies the possibility that individuals might behave otherwise.

By contrast, Giddens' (1979) structuration theory rejects a thoroughgoing determinism of agency, while not accepting unqualified freedom for individuals. Social behaviour needs to be explained as an interpretation of structure, the conditions and consequences of actions and a theory of the human agent. Therefore, to explain how primary heads act in accordance with a bureaucratic rationale, even though they could act otherwise, I explored the concept of identity for two reasons. First, because a consideration of identity takes the discussion into the realm of human agency. Second, because the case study suggests Ron's approach to headship was an occupational identity.

Identity is a slippery concept which is not well defined in educational writing. Using Nias (1989a) I defined identity as the self-as-me and the self-as-I. The latter is especially elusive and, lacking credentials in psychology, I elected not to consider the self-as-I. More specifically, I focused upon occupational identity as one of an individual's situational selves.

Ron's professional identity was shown to be made up of two closely related selves: teacher and head, much of the latter being an outgrowth of the former. The identity of teacher includes being oneself, feeling responsible for others, needing to be in control and defining success as children developing. The continuation of these norms is tacitly encouraged when individuals are promoted to headship because of professional requirements, expectations and structures. Occupational norms of individualism, moralism, acceptance of hierarchy, and control are carried into headship. Also, some of these are heightened and inflated in headship, particularly isolation, self-referencing and self-belief, while others are transformed. The wish to pursue one's vision is changed into making that the school's mission. The hallmarks of being a teacher are not erased, they are thrown into sharper relief. Moreover, these imprints are supplemented by a head's perceived need to control and supervise adults who were formerly his/her peers.

Although the discussion was speculative it suggests three things. First, the very title of the job is apposite. Headteacher accurately labels the admixture of selves that constitute the professional identity of the postholder. Ron was *head*teacher in terms of his position in the organization and invested with power and control. Yet he was also head*teacher*, concerned about the children and his teacher colleagues. He was the leader of his school, rather than his class, judging the school's performance, but still applying the same sentiments and reward criteria associated with teachers.

Second, head and teacher identities are complementary for two reasons. For one thing, role relations in primary schools are based upon the head's dominant power position, both in law and convention, and upon the complementary sets of attitudes that heads and teachers have towards one another:

> On the part of the head these attitudes combine to mean 'paternalism' (Coulson 1976:285) and include influencing teachers to adopt his own aims and methods, filtering information from outside the school and protecting teachers from parents. . .On the part of the class teachers, the

characteristic set is 'acquiescence in subordination to the head's dominance'
...These attitudes preserve a kind of mutual autonomy in preferred
professional activities. Heads are in charge of what they like to call 'their'
school, and teachers in charge of 'their' class.

(Campbell 1985:154–5)

For another, the classroom is a microcosm of the school in terms of power
relations:

Where children must attend school the relationships between pupils and
teachers must involve an element of power. Waller (1932) dramatically
called teaching 'institutionalised domination and subordination'.

(King 1983:15)

Teachers, being dominant in their own spheres of influence and accepting the
dependence of the pupils upon them in turn, accept the head's right to exercise
power over them as teachers.

The third thing suggested by the discussion of identity is that the power
structures of primary schools and classrooms and the occupational assumptions of
teachers provide a fertile bed for the persistence of domination. Organizational
structures and professional identities combine and reinforce each other. The agent
is a product of both structure and his/her occupational selves. As Hodgkinson
(1983:80) says, organizations are identity sites. The seeds of Ron's domination in
the school were sown in the classrooms where he worked as a teacher. On becoming a head it is the scale of the individual's domination which expands — an
increase from classroom to school.

Moreover, it should not be a surprise that Ron, in regarding himself as the
pre-eminent figure in the school, resembled a pattern of headship identified by
others up to twenty years before the case study. (Donaldson 1970; Cook and
Mack 1972; Coulson 1976). The recruitment of heads is an inherently conservative
process, biased towards role reproduction and the continuity of institutional structures rather than the creation of new roles and structures. As Wolcott (1973)
argues, the selection of principals ensures continuity in power relations (p. 194).
Aspiring candidates tacitly demonstrate they accept the authority system of the
school and can live with the hierarchy (p. 196). So it was with Ron since his spell
as acting deputy enabled him, amongst other things, to demonstrate that he was
willing to maintain the authority structure of the school. Ron might have been a
pioneer in respect of developing his school, but he also preserved the organizational status quo. While he wished to develop the curricula of the schools he led,
he also worked within a set of parameters which ensured that prevailing power
relations would remain undisturbed.

Expressed another way, the interactionist perspective of headship provided
by the case study does not show a picture of pure voluntarism. Rather, it suggests
that the school's organization created a framework of interactions which produced
and reproduced a set of power relations amongst the adults and adults and pupils
(Tyler 1988:225). As Tyler demonstrates, the formal organization of the school
enters into interaction in two ways: as an instrument of division and domination;
and as an apparatus of surveillance, scheduling and recording which serves the
interests of administrative authority (pp. 120–1). Much the same argument is advanced by Bates (1983:8–9; 24–6; 32–3) when he says management is a technology

of control. In short, the school as an organization is a powerful instrument of social control (Tyler 1988:226). Teachers' and headteachers' professional identities are situated in hierarchical structures. Power *over* is sedimented into the occupational identities of teachers and heads, thereby making domination a norm for those in positions of responsibility in the organization.

It seems to me that these arguments extend and develop the conclusions drawn from the case study in Chapter 4. Given that the discussion has been stimulated by conclusions drawn from a single case; there is a lack of previous work concerning primary heads' professional identities; the discussion has sometimes moved from the particular case of Ron to a more general theory of primary headteachers; and that no empirical data exist by which to gauge the proportion of primary heads who are dominating leaders, it is only safe to answer the question, 'What conditions allow heads to dominate?' with an hypothesis. It is: *Domination in primary schools occurs as a result of both organizational structure and occupational identities. A primary headteacher approaches the role and discharges his/her responsibilities with a sense of situational self wherein domination is an integral part of his/her professional identity. This professional identity includes both being a head and a teacher and, because the two are consistent and complementary in terms of power, domination is learned and exercised as a teacher as well as when a head.*

There are four riders to add to this hypothesis. First, I am aware that the discussion of professional identity is possibly too neat. I have emphasized points of congruence between the self-as-teacher and the self-as-head and so may have underplayed possible tensions between the two. Second, the hypothesis will not apply to all primary heads. In addition to my intentions about generalization, set out in Chapter 2, I need to make it clear that just as some teachers do not regard their work as a vocation, so some heads will see headship as 'just a job'. In my experience, a number of heads (albeit relatively few) are not motivated by their educational beliefs, nor propelled by a wish to see their aims and teaching practice emulated by staff colleagues. Some heads do not regard the job as all-consuming and do not invest as much of their selves as Ron appeared to do. For some the job is not an identity in the way it was for Ron and, I believe, certain other heads.

Third, in using Nias' (1989a) work as a reference point it needs to be emphasized that the ideas she developed about teachers were derived from a sample of mid-life teachers. Insofar as Ron was a mid-life headteacher it seems fair to assume parallels. However, the point I wish to make is that younger teachers may not entirely match Nias' picture and younger heads may not always resemble Ron. Younger heads may differ in terms of their occupational concepts. Indeed, there may be generational differences since we are all, more or less, products of our past circumstances and experiences as well as our present contexts. I would, for example, anticipate there being some differences between Ron and a head trained in the late 1970s and appointed to headship in 1990. During the career span of this younger head he or she will have matured as a teacher while encountering rather different professional experiences and ideas to Ron. Hence, some of this young head's norms are likely to vary from an older head's outlook. Nevertheless, in terms of my argument here, what will be of critical importance is the extent to which, if any, a younger head differs in regard that domination is sedimented into his/her professional identity. In truth, we do not know whether there is change or continuity in this respect, although my inclination is to anticipate little change in terms of power relations, as I argued in Chapter 4.

Fourth, much of the foregoing is but an initial discussion. I have roamed selectively over three large literatures, power, identity and leadership to reach this hypothesis. Clearly there is a need for further research and analysis.

Summary

In this chapter I have taken the conclusion that Ron was dominant in his school and that domination was part of his professional identity; I have explored it by addressing two questions. The first question was whether an individual's domination of a group is morally acceptable. I argued that domination should be rejected because it negates participative democracy and establishes a morally unacceptable distribution of power in schools.

The second question considered the conditions which allow heads to dominate. I argued that schools as organizations generally reflect a bureaucratic belief in authority and the exercise of power over others. However, recognizing that a structuralist argument was not sufficient to explain why Ron would adopt a bureaucratic rationale, I examined his sense of professional identity. Here I argued that his occupational identity was composed of two selves; teacher and head. While these are different, they are not disconnected and overlap. Indeed, they embody a complementary understanding of power as power over. I also speculated that the roots of domination stretch back into the classrooms where teachers control and subordinate pupils. Following on from the discussions of power and identity I combined the two arguments and proposed the hypothesis set out above.

At the start of this chapter I noted a third question which arises from the conclusions drawn from the case study: are there alternative ways of conceptualizing school leadership which avoid domination? Although others (Coulson 1976, 1986; Winkley 1983; Alexander 1984; Lloyd 1985; Southworth 1987, 1988a) have examined primary school leadership and have been critical of the head's power, they have not suggested detailed alternatives. Nor have these writers examined the concept of domination, rather they have simply recognized its existence. Moreover, the interrelationship between domination and identity has not been recognized or explored. Given that dominating heads create a morally indefensible authority structure in their schools, it is now necessary to consider alternatives to such a model of school leadership.

Chapter 6

School Management and Leadership Theory

In the previous chapter I argued that domination is morally unacceptable in a democratic society. In this chapter I shall search for an alternative approach to school leadership which is socially just and is not preoccupied with control and subordination. Moreover, in rethinking school leadership, I will keep in mind the idea that headship is an identity within which domination is long established, as it is rooted in class teaching.

The search for an alternative approach to headship is developed in four sections. I begin by returning to the bureaucratic rationale which underpins domination. I do so in order to examine the assumptions of the theory movement, that is the educational management theories which sustain bureaucracy and *power over*. In the second section I consider four other theoretical perspectives which are antagonistic to the theory movement. I shall review these four perspectives not only to see which offers the most forceful critique of the theory movement, but also to seek the one which provides a platform for reconceptualizing school leadership. I shall argue that the fourth perspective, critical theory, offers the strongest counter view to the assumptions of the theory movement and a basis for rethinking headship.

While the theory movement has been under attack for some years it continues to influence the way school leadership is conceptualized. I substantiate this claim in the third section by examining school effectiveness research and its prescriptions for school leadership. In the fourth section I consider the critical theorists' ideas for reconceptualizing leadership, drawing substantially on the work of Foster and his ideas concerning critical, transformative leadership. I shall argue that while providing an attractive alternative, Foster's work is overly optimistic since there are practical problems to overcome. Also, Foster fails to regard headship as an identity, hence he underestimates the nature of the personal change individuals will need to make. To become a critical leader necessitates not a shift in role, but a switch in professional identity.

Educational Management Theory

In this section I shall briefly review educational management theory. I shall draw upon work undertaken in Britain, North America and Australia. In Britain the term management is used while elsewhere administration is preferred. I shall use the two interchangeably.

they work with their headteachers. Moreover, studies of deputy heads' partnership with their heads can reflect headteachers' conceptions of headship. Deputy headship in primary schools is a rich seam which awaits investigation.

Second, given that the work of a headteacher is in several ways context specific, there is much to examine in terms of the situational variables which influence the work of headteachers. In particular, there is more to learn about the effects of school size upon the work of heads. Also, there is scope for studies to investigate headteacher succession, the differences created by organizational cultures and the effects of a school's location upon heads' task priorities.

Third, there is a need for research to be undertaken into micropolitics in primary schools. To date no such studies have been published. Furthermore, there is a need to consider whether a conflict perspective accounts for all the micropolitical activity in a school or whether open interactions account for some, or all that occurs.

Fourth, the idea of headteacher maturation warrants close examination. At present the idea of phases in headship is notional. It is unclear whether headteacher development occurs as a result of time in post, experience of different schools and/or life circumstances. Nor is it known how professional development opportunities influence headteacher development. There is much to investigate here.

Fifth, given the male bias in school management theorizing and research, there is an urgent need for studies to be conducted into women headteachers. A feminist conceptualization of headship needs to be developed. Moreover, virtually all the issues so far discovered about primary heads, for example, power, domination and notions of effective leadership, need to be re-examined in the light of women headteachers' views and experience.

There is then, no shortage of research possibilities. In this sense, the study suggests that the more closely one looks at a research topic, the more there is to investigate. However, what we also need are more personal accounts from headteachers themselves. What does it *feel* like to be a headteacher? What are the dilemmas they face? What do they think is an effective and ethical headteacher? In a sense, I have looked into headship from the outside, we now need some insiders to tell their stories to the outsiders.

Finally, I should note that in setting out some of my discoveries about headship, my explorations have been 'not so much a matter of covering ground as of digging beneath the surface' (Geertz 1988:43). I can claim only to have dug a little beneath the surface of primary headship, but I have learned much from this excavation.

References

ABERCROMBIE, M.L.J. (1969) *The Anatomy of Judgement*, London: Hutchinson.

ACHILLES, C. (1987) 'A vision of better schools', in GREENFIELD, W. (Ed.) *Instructional Leadership: Concepts, Issues and Controversies*, New York: Allyn and Bacon, pp. 17–37.

ACKER, S. (1987) 'Primary school teaching as an occupation' in DELAMONT, S. (Ed.) *The Primary School Teacher*, Lewes: Falmer Press, pp. 83–99.

ACKER, S. (1988) 'Managing the drama: The headteacher's work in an urban primary school', Paper presented at the Conference on Histories and Ethnographies of Teachers at Work, Oxford: University of Bristol mimeo.

ACKER, S. (Ed.) (1989) *Teachers, Gender and Careers*, London: Falmer.

ADELMAN, C. (1985) 'Who are you? some problems of ethnographer culture shock', in BURGESS, R.G. (Ed.) *Field Study Methods in the Study of Education*, Lewes: Falmer Press, pp. 51–78.

AGAR, M.H. (1986) *Speaking of Ethnography*, Newbury Park, CA: Sage.

ALEXANDER, R. (1984) *Primary Teaching*, London: Holt, Rinehart and Winston.

ALEXANDER, R., ROSE, J. and WOODHEAD, C. (1992) *Curriculum Organisation and Classroom Practice: A Discussion Paper*, London: DES.

ANGUS, L. (1989) 'New leadership and the possibility of educational reform', in SMYTH, J. (Ed.) *Critical Perspectives on Educational Leadership*, London: Falmer Press, pp. 63–92.

ANGUS, L. and RIVZI, F. (1989) 'Power and the politics of participation', *Journal of Educational Administration and Foundations*, 4, (1), pp. 6–23.

ARNOT, M. and WEINER, G. (Ed.) (1987) *Gender and the Politics of Schooling*, London: Unwin and Hyman.

ASPINWALL, K. (1986) 'Teacher biography: The in-service potential', *Cambridge Journal of Education*, 16, (3), pp. 210–15.

AUSTIN, G. and REYNOLDS, D. (1990) 'Managing for improved school effectiveness: An international survey', *School Organisation* 10, (2 and 3), pp. 167–78.

BACHARACH, P. and BARATZ, M. (1962) 'Two faces of power', *American Political Science Review*, 56, pp. 947–52.

BACHARACH, S.B. and LAWLER, E. (1980) *Power and Politics in Organizations*, San Francisco, CA: Jossey-Bass.

BALDRIDGE, J.V., CURTIS, D.V., ECKER, G. and RILEY, G.L. (1978) *Policy-making and Effective Leadership*, San Francisco, CA: Jossey-Bass.

BALL, D.W. (1972) 'Self and identity in the context of deviance: The case of criminal abortion', in SCOTT, R. and DOUGLAS, J. (Eds) *Theoretical Perspectives on Deviance*, New York: Basic Books, pp. 158–86.

BALL, S.J. (1987) *The Micropolitics of the School*, London: Methuen.

BALL, S.J. (1991) 'Power, conflict, micropolitics and all that!', in WALFORD, G. (Ed.) *Doing Educational Research*, London: Routledge, pp. 166–92.

BALL, S.J. and GOODSON, I. (1985) *Teachers' Lives and Careers*, London: Falmer Press.

BALL, S.J. and BOWE, R. (1990) 'The micropolitics of radical change: Budgets, management and control in British schools', Paper presented at AERA, Boston, MA: King's College, London mimeo.

BARNETT, B., CAFFARELLA, R., DARESH, J., KING, R., NICHOLSON, T. and WHITAKER, K. (1992) 'A new slant on leadership preparation', in *Educational Leadership*, **49**, (5), pp. 72–5.

BARON, G. (1980) 'Research in educational administration in Britain', in BUSH, T. *et al.* (Eds) *Approaches to School Management*, London: Harper and Row, pp. 3–25.

BARTLETT, T. (1991) 'Rationality and the management of curriculum change', *Educational Management and Administration*, **19**, (1), pp. 20–9.

BATES, R.J. (1982) 'Towards a critical practice of educational administration', *Commonwealth Council for Education Administration*, 27 Sept., pp. 1–15.

BATES, R.J. (1983) *Educational Administration and the Management of Knowledge*, Geelong: Deakin University Press.

BATES, R.J. (1986) *The Management of Knowledge and Culture*, Geelong: Deakin University Press.

BATES, R.J. (1988) 'Is there a new paradigm in educational administration?' Paper presented at AERA, New Orleans, LA: Deakin University mimeo.

BATES, R.J. (1989) 'Leadership and the rationalization of society', in SMYTH, J. (Ed.) *Critical Perspectives on Educational Leadership*, Lewes: Falmer Press, pp. 131–56.

BEARE, H., CALDWELL, B.J., MILLIKAN, R.H. (1989) *Creating an Excellent School*, London: Routledge.

BECKER, H.S. (1958) 'Problems of inference and proof in participant observation', in McCORMICK, R., BYNNER, J., CLIFT, P., JAMES, M. and MORROW BROWN, C. (Eds) (1982) *Calling Education to Account*, London: Heinemann/Open University Press, pp. 247–60.

BELL, L. (1988) *Management Skills in Primary School*, London: Routledge.

BENNIS, W. (1959) 'Leadership theory and administrative behaviour: the problem of authority', *Administrative Science Quarterly*, **4**, pp. 251–69.

BENNIS, W. (1984) 'Transformative power and leadership', in SERGIOVANNI, T.J. and CORBALLY, J.E. (Eds) *Leadership and Organizational Culture*, Chicago, IL: University of Illinois Press, pp. 64–71.

BENNIS, W. and NANUS, B. (1985) *Leaders: The Strategies for Taking Charge*, New York: Harper and Row.

BERGER, J. (1960) *Permanent Red: Essays in Seeing*, London: Writers and Readers.

BERGER, J. (1972) *Ways of Seeing*, London: Penguin.

BERGER. J. (1982) *Another Way of Telling*, London: Readers and Writers.

BLACKMORE, J. (1989) 'Educational leadership: A feminist critique and reconstruction', in SMYTH, J. (Ed.) *Critical Perspectives on Educational Leadership*, London: Falmer Press, pp. 93–129.

BLASE, J. (1987) 'Dimensions of ineffective school leadership: The teachers' perspective', *Journal of Educational Administration*, **24**, pp. 193–213.

BLASE, J. (1989) 'The micropolitics of the school: The everyday political orientation of teachers', *Educational Administration Quarterly*, **25**, (4), pp. 377–407.

BLASE, J. (1991) 'The micropolitics of leadership: Teachers' perspectives on open and effective principals', Paper presented to Annual Meeting of AERA, Chicago, IL: University of Georgia mimeo.

BLUMBERG, A. and GREENFIELD, W. (1986) *The Effective Principal: Perspectives on School Leadership*, Newton, MA: Allyn and Bacon, 2nd ed.

BOLAM, R., McMAHON, A., POCKLINGTON, K. and WEINDLING, D. (1993) 'Effective management in schools: A report for the Department of Education via the school management task force professional working party, London: HMSO.

BOLSTER, S.J. (1989) 'Vision: Communicating it to the staff', Paper presented at AERA, San Francisco, CA: Arizona Dept. of Education mimeo.

BONNETT, M. (1991) 'Developing children's thinking. . .and the national curriculum', *Cambridge Journal of Education*, **21**, (3), pp. 277–92.

BOTTERY, M.P. (1988) 'The hidden curriculum of primary management', in COSTELLO, P.J.M. *Primary Education into the 1990s*, Hull: Aspects of Education, 38, University of Hull, pp. 100–16.

BOTTERY, M. (1992) *The Ethics of Educational Management*, London: Cassell.

BOYD-BARRETT, O. (1981) *School Management: The Wider Context*, Block 2, E323, Management and the School, Milton Keynes: Open University Press.

BOYDELL, D. (1990) '. . .The gerbil on the wheel': Conversations with primary headteachers about the implications of ERA', *Education 3–13*, **18**, (2), pp. 20–4.

BRADLEY, H. (1991) *Staff Development*, London: Falmer Press.

BRANDES, D. and GINNIS, P. (1990) *The Student-Centred School*, Oxford: Blackwell.

BREDESON, P. (1991) 'Letting go of outlived professional identities: A study of role transition for principals in restructured schools', paper presented at AERA Conference, Chicago, IL: Pennsylvannia State University mimeo.

BURDIN, J.L. (Ed.) (1989) *School Leadership: A Contemporary Reader*, Newbury Park, CA: Sage.

BURGESS, R.G. (Ed.) (1984) *The Research Process in Educational Settings: Ten Case Studies*, Lewes: Falmer Press.

BURGESS, R.G. (Ed.) (1985) *Field Methods In the Study of Education*, Lewes: Falmer Press.

BURGESS, H. (1989) 'A sort of career: Women in primary schools', in SKELTON, C. (Ed.) *Whatever Happens to Little Women? Gender and Primary Schooling*, Milton Keynes: Open University Press, pp. 79–91.

BURLINGAME, M. (1987) 'Images of leadership in effective schools literature', in GREENFIELD, W. (Ed.) *Instructional Leadership: Concepts, Issues and Controversies*, Boston, MA: Allyn and Bacon, pp. 3–16.

BURNS, J.M. (1978) *Leadership*, New York: Harper and Row.

BURRELL, G. (1988) 'Modernism, post modernism and organizational analysis 2: The contribution of Michael Foucault' *Organizational Studies*, **9**, (2), pp. 221–35.

BUSH, T. (1981) *Key Roles in School Management*, Part 3 in Policy-making, organization and leadership in schools, Block 4, E323, Management and the School, Milton Keynes: Open University.

BUSH, T, (1986) *Theories of Educational Management*, London: Harper and Row.

BUSH, T., GLATTER, R., GOODEY, J. and RICHES, C. (Eds) (1980) *Approaches to School Management*, London: Harper and Row.

CAMPBELL, J. (1985) *Developing the Primary School Curriculum*, London: Holt, Rinehart and Winston.

CAPPER, G.A. (1991) 'The limitations of critical theory in educational administration: What does it mean for non-dominant groups?' paper presented at AERA, Chicago, IL: University of Wisconsin-Madison mimeo.

CARR, W. and KEMMIS, S. (1983) *Becoming Critical: Knowing Through Action Research*, Geelong: Deakin University.

CENTRAL ADVISORY COUNCIL FOR EDUCATION (England) (1967) *Children and their Primary Schools*, (Plowden Report), London: HMSO.

CHAPMAN, J.D. (1984) *A Descriptive Profile of Australian School Principals*, Canberra: Commonwealth Schools Commission.

CLARK and MELOY (1990) 'Recanting bureaucracy: A democratic structure for leadership in schools', in LIEBERMAN, A. (Ed.) *Schools as Collaborative Cultures: Creating the Future Now*, London: Falmer Press, pp. 3–23.

CLEGG, S.R. (1989) *Frameworks of Power*, London: Sage Books.

CLERKIN, C. (1985) 'What do primary school heads actually do all day?', *School Organization*, **5**, (4), pp. 287–300.

CLIFFORD, J. (1970) *From Puzzles to Portraits*, London: Oxford University Press.

CODD, J. (1989) 'Educational leadership as reflective action', in SMYTH, J. (Ed.) *Critical Perspectives on Educational Leadership*, London: Falmer Press, pp. 157–78.

COHEN, A. (1976) 'The elasticity of evil: Changes in the social definition of deviance', in HAMMERSLEY M. and WOODS, P. (Eds) *The Process of Schooling*, London: Routledge and Kegan Paul.

COHEN, I.J. (1989) *Structuration Theory: Anthony Giddens and the Constitution of Social Life*, London: Macmillan.

CONNELL, R.W. (1985) *Teachers' Work*, Sydney: Allen and Unwin.

CONWAY, J.A. (1978) 'Power and participatory decision-making in selected English schools', in BUSH, T. *et al.* (1980) *Approaches to School Management*, London: Harper and Row, pp. 210–30.

COOK, A. and MACK, M. (1972) 'The headteacher's role' *British Primary Schools Today*, **2**, pp. 283–353.

COULSON, A.A. (1974) 'The deputy head in the primary school: Role conceptions of heads and deputy heads', unpublished MEd thesis, University of Hull.

COULSON, A.A. (1976) 'The role of the primary head', in BUSH, T. *et al.* (Eds) (1980) *Approaches to School Management*, London: Harper and Row, pp. 274–92.

COULSON, A.A. (1978) 'Power and decision-making in the primary school', in RICHARDS, C. (Ed.) *The Study of Primary Education: A Source Book*, Volume **3**, Lewes: Falmer Press, pp. 77–82.

COULSON, A.A. (1986) *The Managerial Work of Primary School Headteachers*, Sheffield Papers in Education Management, No. 48, Sheffield City Polytechnic.

COULSON, A.A. (1988a) 'Primary school headship: A review of research', paper presented at BEMAS Conference, Cardiff, April 1988; reprinted in SARAN, R. and TRAFFORD, V. (Eds) (1990) *Research in Education Management and Policy: Retrospect and prospect*, Lewes: Falmer Press, pp. 101–07.

COULSON, A.A. (1988b) 'An approach to headship development through personal and professional growth', in CLARKSON, M. (Ed.) *Emerging Issues in Primary Education*, Lewes: Falmer Press, pp. 253–76.

CRAIG, I. (Ed.) (1987) *Primary School Management in Action*, London: Longman.

CRAIG-WILSON, L. (1978) *School Leadership Today*, Boston, MA: Allyn and Bacon.

CROMER PUBLICATIONS (1992) *The Head's Legal Guide*, New Malden, Essex: Cromer Publications.

DAHL, R.A. (1957) 'The concept of power', *Behavioural Science*, **2**, pp. 201–5.

DARESH, J. and PLAYKO, M. (1989) 'In search of critical skills for beginning principals', paper presented to Annual meeting of University Council for Educational Administration, Phoenix, AR.

DAVIES, L. (1987) 'The role of the primary school head', *Educational Management and Administration*, **15**, pp. 43–7.

DAY, C., JOHNSTON, D. and WHITAKER, P. (1985) *Managing Primary Schools: A Professional Development Approach*, London: Harper and Row.

DEAN, J. (1987) *Managing the Primary School*, London: Croom-Helm.

DEAL, T. and KENNEDY, A. (1982) *Corporate Cultures*, Reading, MA: Addison-Wesley.

DEAL, T. and KENNEDY, A. (1983) 'Culture and school performance', *Educational Leadership*, **40**, (5), pp. 14–15.

DE BEVOISE, W. (1984) 'Synthesis of research on the principal as instructional leader', *Educational Leadership*, **41**, (5), pp. 14–20.

DELAMONT, S. (1987) 'The primary teacher 1945–1990: Myths and realities', in DELAMONT, S. (Ed.) *The Primary School Teacher*, Lewes: Falmer Press, pp. 3–17.

DELAMONT, S. (1992) *Fieldwork in Educational Settings*, London: Falmer Press.

DENZIN, N.K. (1989) *Interpretive Biography*, Newbury Park, CA: Sage.

DES (1959) *Primary Education*, London: HMSO.

DES (1977) *Ten Good Schools: A Secondary School Enquiry by HMI*, London: HMSO.

DES (Welsh Office) (1985) *Leadership in Primary Schools*, HMI (Wales) Occasional paper, Cardiff: DES/Welsh Office.

DES (1987) *Primary Schools: Some Aspects of Good Practice*, London: HMSO.

DES (1989) *Primary Education*, London: HMSO.

DES (1990) *The Teaching and Learning of Reading in Primary Schools*: A report by HMI, London: DES ref. 10/91/NS.

DES (1991) *Mentor Scheme for New Headteachers*, London: DES.

DES (1992) *Statistics of Schools in England: 1991*, London: DES.

DEWEY, J. (1975) *Philosophy of Education: Problems of Men*, Totowa, USA: Littefield Adams.

DONALDSON, P.R. (1970) 'Role expectations of primary school headteachers', Diploma in Child Development dissertation, University of London.

DUIGNAN, P. (1988) 'Reflective management: The key to quality leadership', *International Journal of Education Management*, **2**, (2), pp. 3–12.

DUIGNAN, P. and MACPHERSON, R.J. (1987) 'The educative leadership project', *Educational Management and Administration*, **15**, pp. 49–62.

DUKE, D. (1986) 'Understanding what it means to be a teacher', *Educational Leadership*, **44**, (2), pp. 27–32.

EDWARDS, G. (1989) 'Primary headship — A widening role', *Management in Education*, **3**, (4), pp. 30–2.

EISENSTEIN, H. (1987) 'Patriarchy and the universal oppression of woman: Feminist debates', in ARNOT, M. and WEINER, G. (Eds) *Gender and the Politics of Schooling*, London: Unwin and Hyman, pp. 35–49.

EISNER, E.W. (1979) *The Educational Imagination*, New York: Macmillan.

ELLIOTT, J. (1981a) 'How do parents judge schools?', in ELLIOTT, J., BRIDGES, D., EBBUTT, D., GIBSON, R. and NIAS, J. (Eds) *School Accountability*, London: Grant McIntyre, pp. 40–57.

ELLIOTT, J. (1981b) 'School accountability to governors', in ELLIOTT, J. *et al. School Accountability*, pp. 163–77.

EVERS, C.W. and Lakomski, G. (1991) *Knowing Educational Administration*, Oxford: Pergamon Press.

EVERHART, R.B. (1977) 'Between stranger and friend: Some consequences of "long term", fieldwork in schools', *American Educational Research Journal*, **14**, (1), pp. 1–15.

EVETTS, J. (1990) *Women in Primary Teaching: Career Contexts and Strategies*, London: Unwin Hyman.

FAY, B. (1975) *Social Theory and Political Practice*, London: Allen and Unwin.

FAY, B. (1977) 'How people change themselves: The relationship between critical theory and I to audience', in BALL, T. (Ed.) *Political Theory and Praxis: New Perspectives*, Minneapolis, MN: University of Minnesota Press.

FIELDER, F. (1967) *A Theory of Leadership Effectiveness*, New York: McGraw-Hill.

FIRESTONE, W. and WILSON, B. (1989) 'Using bureaucratic and cultural linkages to improve instruction: The principal's contribution', in BURDIN, J. (Ed.) *School Leadership*, Newbury Park, CA.: Sage, pp. 275–96.

FOSTER, W. (1986) *Paradigms and Promises: New Approaches to Educational Administration*, New York: Prometheus Books.

FOSTER, W. (1989) 'Towards a critical practice of leadership', in SMYTH, J. (Ed.) op. cit. pp. 39–62.

FOSTER, W. (1990) 'Educational leadership and the struggle for mind', paper presented at AERA, Boston, MA: University of San Diego mimeo.

FOSTER, W. (1991) 'Moral theory, transformation and leadership in school settings', paper presented at AERA, Chicago, IL: University of San Diego mimeo.

FULLAN, M. (1991) *The New Meaning of Change*, London: Cassell (2nd ed.)

FULLAN, M. and HARGREAVES, A. (1991) *What's Worth Fighting For? Working Together for Your School*, Ontario, Canada: Ontario Public School Teachers' Federation.

GEERTZ, C. (1973) 'Thick description: Toward an interpretive theory of culture', in GEERTZ, C. (Ed.) *The Interpretation of Culture*, New York: Basic Books.

GEERTZ, C. (1983) *Local Knowledge*, New York: Basic Books.

GEERTZ, C. (1988) *Works and Lives: The Anthropologist as Author*, Cambridge: Polity Press.

GETZELS, J.W. and GUBA, E.C. (1957) Social behaviour and the administrative process', *School Review*, **55**, pp. 423–41.

GIBSON, R. (1981) 'Structures of accountability', in ELLIOTT, J., BRIDGES, D., EBBUTT, D., GIBSON, R. and NIAS, J. (Eds) *School Accountability*, London: Grant McIntyre, pp. 189–210.

GIDDENS, A. (1976) *New Rules of Sociological Method*, London: Hutchinson.

GIDDENS, A. (1977) *Studies in Social and Political Theory*, London: Hutchinson.

GIDDENS, A. (1979) *Central Problems in Social Theory*, London: Macmillan.

GIDDENS, A. (1982) 'A reply to my critics', *Theory, Culture and Society*, **1**, (2), pp. 107–13.

GIDDENS, A. (1984) *The Constitution of Society*, Cambridge: Polity Press.

GIDDENS, A. (1987) *Social Theory and Modern Sociology*, Cambridge: Polity Press.

GLASER, B. and STRAUSS, A. (1967) *The Discovery of Grounded Theory*, Chicago, Ill: Aldine.

GLATTER, R. (1990) 'Charting a path forward', *Management in Education*, **4**, (2), pp. 34–7.

GOODLAD, J. (1984) *A Place Called School: Prospects for the Future*, New York: McGraw-Hill.

GOODSON, I. (1980) 'Life histories and the study of schooling', *Interchange*, **11**, (4).

GOODSON, I. (1991) 'Sponsoring the teacher's voice: Teachers' lives and teacher development', *Cambridge Journal of Education*, **21**, (1), pp. 35–45.

GOODSON, I. and WALKER, R. (Eds) (1991) *Biography, Identity and Schooling*, London: Falmer Press.

GRANT, R. (1989) 'Women teachers' career pathways: Towards an alternative model of career', in ACKER, S. (Ed.) *Teachers, Gender and Career*, London: Falmer Press, pp. 35–50.

GRAY, H. (1981) 'School effectiveness research: Key issues', *Educational Research*, **24**, (1), pp. 23–9.

GRAY, H. (1987) 'Gender considerations in school management: Masculine and feminine leadership styles', *School Organization*, **7**, (3), pp. 297–302.

GREENFIELD, T.B. (1975) 'Theory about organization; A new perspective for schools', in HUGHES, M.G. (Ed.), *Administering Education: International Challenge*, London: Athlone Press, and reprinted in BUSH, T. *et al.* (Eds) (1980) *Approaches to School Management*, Milton Keynes: Open University Press, pp. 154–71.

GREENFIELD, T.B. (1978) 'Reflections on organization theory and the truths of irreconcilable realities', *Educational Administration Quarterly*, **14**, (2), pp. 1–23.

GREENFIELD, T.B. (1980) 'The man who comes back through the door in the wall: Discovering truth, discovering self, discovering organisations', *Educational Administration Quarterly*, **16**, (3), pp. 26–59.

GREENFIELD, T.B. (1986) 'The decline and fall of science in educational administration', *Interchange*, **17**, (2), pp. 57–80.

GREENFIELD, W. (1987a) *Instructional Leadership: Concepts, Issues and Controversies*, Boston, MA: Allyn and Bacon.

GREENFIELD, W. (1987b) 'Moral imagination and interpersonal competence: Antecedents to instructional leadership', in GREENFIELD, W. (Ed.) *Instructional Leadership: Concepts, Issues and Controversies*, Newton, MA: Allyn and Bacon, pp. 56–73.

GREENFIELD, W. (1991) 'Rationale and methods to articulate ethics and adminstrator training', paper presented at AERA, Chicago.

GRIFFIN-BEALE, C. (Ed.) (1979) *Christian Schiller: In His Own Words*, London: A. and C. Black/National Association for Primary Education.

GROB, L. (1984) 'Leadership: The socratic model', in KELLERMAN, B. (Ed.) *Leadership: Multi-disciplinary Perspectives*, Englewood Cliffs, NJ: Prentice Hall, pp. 135–52.

GRONN, P. (1988) 'Talk as the work: The accomplishment of school administration', in WESTOBY, A. (Ed.) *Culture and Power in Educational Organizations*, Milton Keynes: Open University Press, pp. 289–314.

HALES, C.P. (1986) 'What do managers do? A critical review', *Journal of Management Studies*, **23**, (1), pp. 88–115.

HALL, V., MACKAY, H. and MORGAN, C. (1986) *Headteachers At Work*, Milton Keynes: Open University Press.

HALLINGER, P. and MURPHY, J. (1987) 'Assessing and developing principal instructional leadership', *Educational Leadership*, **45**, September, pp. 54–61.

HALPIN, A. (1966) *Theory and Research in Administration*, New York: Macmillan.

HAMMERSLEY, M. (1992) *What's Wrong With Ethnography?*, London: Routledge.

HAMMERSLEY, M. and ATKINSON, P. (1983) *Ethnography: Principles in Practice*, London: Routledge.

HANDY, C. (1981) *Understanding Organizations*, London: Penguin, 2nd. ed.

HANDY, C. (1989) *The Age of Unreason*, London: Hutchinson.

HANSON, M. (1977) 'Beyond the bureaucratic model: A study of power and autonomy in educational decision-making', *Interchange*, **7**, (2), pp. 27–38.

HARGREAVES, A. (1990) 'Individualism and individuality: Reinterpreting the teacher culture', paper presented at the symposium on 'Tensions in Teachers' Culture, Career and Context', at AERA, Boston, MA.

HARGREAVES, A. (1991) 'Restructuring restructuring: Postmodernity and the prospects for educational change', paper from The Ontario Institute for Studies in Education, mimeo.

HARGREAVES, D.H. (1967) *Social Relations in a Secondary School*, London: Routledge and Kegan Paul.

HARGREAVES, D.H. (1974) 'Do we need headteachers?', *Education 3–13*, **2**, (1), pp. 24–7.

HARGREAVES, D.H. (1978), 'What teaching does to teachers', *New Society*, 9 March, pp. 540–2.

HARGREAVES, D. and HOPKINS, D. (1991) *The Empowered School*, London: Cassell.

HARLING, P. (1981) 'School decision-making and the primary headteacher', *Education 3–13*, **8**, (2), pp. 44–8.

HARVEY, C.W. (1986) 'How primary heads spend their time', *Educational Management and Administration*, **14**, pp. 60–8.

HELLAWELL, D. (1991) 'The changing role of the head in the primary school in England', *School Organization*, **11**, (3), pp. 321–37.

HEMPHILL, J. and COONS, A. (1954) *Leader Behaviour Description*, Columbus, Ohio: Personnel Research Board, Ohio State University.

HILL, T. (1989) *Managing the Primary School*, London: Fulton.

HODGKINSON, C. (1983) *The Philosophy of Leadership*, Oxford: Blackwell.

HOLLY, P. and SOUTHWORTH, G. (1989) *The Developing School*, London: Falmer Press.

HOLTOM, V. (1988) 'Primary school headteachers' conceptions of their professional responsibility in England and France: Change and the implications', unpublished MPhil thesis, University of Bristol.

HOPKINS, D. (1990) 'The international school improvement project (ISIP) and effective schooling: Towards a synthesis', *School Organization*, **10**, (2 and 3), pp. 179–94.

HOPKINS, D., BOLLINGTON, R. and HEWETT, D. (1989) 'Growing up with qualitative research and evaluation', *Evaluation and Research in Education*, **3**, (2), pp. 61–80.

HOYLE, E. (1969) 'Organizational theory and educational administration', in BARON, G. and TAYLOR, W. (Eds) *Educational Administration and the Social Sciences*, London: Athlone Press pp. 36–59.

HOYLE, E. (1981) 'The process of management', in *Management and the School*, E323, Block 3, Milton Keynes: Open University Press, pp. 6–51.

HOYLE, E. (1986) *The Politics of School Management*, London: Hodder and Stoughton.

HUBERMAN, M. (1988) 'Teacher careers and school improvement', *Journal of Curriculum Studies*, **20**, (2), pp. 119–32.

HUBERMAN, M. (1990) 'The social context of instruction in schools', paper presented at AERA, Boston MA.

HUGHES, M. (1976) 'The professional-as-administrator: The case of the secondary school head', in PETERS, R.S. (Ed.) *The Role of the Head*, London: Routledge and Kegan Paul, pp. 50–62.

HUGHES, M. (1985) 'Leadership in professionally staffed organisations,' in HUGHES, M. *et al.* (Eds) (1985) *Managing Education: The System and the Institution*, London: Holt, Rinehart and Winston, pp. 262–90.

HULTMAN, G. (1989) 'The state of the art of school administration: A review of facts and theory', *Scandinavian Journal of Educational Research*, **33**, (2), pp. 123–62.

INGLIS, F. (1989) 'Managerialism and morality: The corporate and the republican school', in CARR, W. (Ed.) *Quality in Teaching*, London: Falmer Press, pp. 35–54.

ILEA (1985) *Improving Primary Schools*, London: ILEA.

JACKSON, P.W. (1968) *Life in Classrooms*, New York: Holt, Rinehart and Winston.

JACKSON, P.W. (1989) 'Report on the moral life of classrooms', paper presented at Annual Meeting AERA, San Francisco, CA: University of Chicago mimeo.

JANIS, I.L. (1972) *Victims of Group Think*, Boston, MA: Houghton Miflin.

JENKINS, H. (1991) *Getting It Right: A Handbook for Successful School Leadership*, Oxford: Blackwell.

JOHNSTON, J. (1986) 'Gender differences in teachers' preferences for primary school leadership', *Educational Management and Administration*, **14**, pp. 219–26.

JONES, M.-L. (1990) 'The attitudes of men and women primary school teachers to promotion and education management', *Educational Management and Administration*, **18**, (3), pp. 11–16.

KATZ, D. (1960) 'The functional approach to the study of attitude change', *Public Opinion Quarterly*, **24**, pp. 163–204.

KELSALL, R.K. and KELSALL, H.M. (1969) *The School-Teacher in England and the United States*, London: Pergamon.

KENT, G. (1989) *The Modern Primary School Headteacher*, London: Kogan Page.

KING, R. (1983) *The Sociology of School Organization*, London: Methuen.

KEMTZ, J.T. and WILLOWER, D.J. (1982) 'Elementary school principals' work behaviour, *Educational Administration Quarterly*, **19**, (4), pp. 62–78.

KOTTKAMP, R.B. (1990) 'The administrative platform as a means of reflection', paper presented to AERA, Boston, MA.

LACEY, C. (1977) *The Socialization of Teachers*, London; Methuen.

LAWS, J. and DENNISON, W.F. (1990) 'Researching the role of the primary school head. A limited base for promoting managerial self-development', *Educational Studies*, **16**, (3), pp. 269–80.

LEITHWOOD, K. and JENTZI, D. (1990) 'Transformational leadership: How principals can help reform school cultures', paper presented at the Annual Meeting of the Canadian Association for Curriculum Studies, Victoria, OISE Centre for Leadership Development mimeo.

LEITHWOOD, K. and MONTGOMERY, D. (1986) *Improving Principal Effectiveness: The Principal Profile*, Toronto: The Ontario Institute for Studies in Education (OISE) Press.

LEWIN, K. (1944) 'The dynamics of group action', *Educational Leadership*, **1**, pp. 194–208.

LEWIN, K., LIPPITT, R. and WHITE, R.K. (1939) 'Patterns of aggressive behaviour in experimentally created Social Climates' in *Journal of Social Psychology*, **10**, pp. 271–99.

LIEBERMAN, A. and MILLER, L. (1984) *Teachers: Their World and their Work*, Alexandria, VA: Association for Supervision and Curriculum Development.

LINCOLN, Y. and GUBA, E. (1985) *Naturalistic Inquiry*, Newbury Park, CA: Sage.

LITTLE, J.W. (1989) 'The persistence of privacy: Autonomy and initiative in teachers' professional relations', paper presented at AERA symposium on Teachers' Work and Teacher Culture, San Francisco, CA.

LLOYD, K. (1981) 'Primary school headship types: A study of the primary head's leadership role perceptions', unpublished MEd dissertation, University of Birmingham.

LLOYD, K. (1985) 'Management and leadership in the primary school', in HUGHES, M. *et al.* (Eds) 1985, *Managing Education: The System and the Institution*, London: Holt, Rinehart and Winston, pp. 291–307.

LOFLAND, J. (1971) *Analyzing Social Settings: A Guide to Qualitative Observation and Analysis*, Belmont, CA: Wadsworth.

LORTIE, D. (1969) 'The balance of control and autonomy in elementary school teaching', in ETZIONI, A. (Ed.) *The Semi-Professions and the Organization*, New York: Free Press.

LORTIE, D. (1975) *School Teacher: A Sociological Study*, Chicago, IL: Chicago University Press.

LORTIE, D. (1990) 'Experience and the elementary principal: Some hypotheses', paper presented at the AERA, Boston, MA: University of Chicago mimeo.

LUKES, S. (1974) *Power: A Radical View*, London: Macmillan.

LURIE, A. (1988) *The Truth About Lorin Jones*, London: Penguin.

LYMAN, S.M. and SCOTT, M.B. (1975) *The Drama of Social Reality*, New York: Oxford University Press.

MACINTYRE, A. (1981) *After Virtue*, London: Duckworth, 2nd ed., 1985.

MCLAUGHLIN, M. and YEE, S. (1988) 'School as a place to have a career', in LIEBERMAN, A. (Ed.) *Building a Professional Culture in Schools*, New York: Teachers College Press pp. 23–44.

MACLURE, M. and STRONACH, I. (1989) 'Seeing through the self: contemporary biography and some implications for educational research', paper presented to AERA, San Francisco, CARE School of Education, University of East Anglia mimeo.

MANASSE, A.L. (1985) 'Improving conditions for principal effectiveness: Policy implications of research', *The Elementary School Journal*, **85**, (3), pp. 439–63.

MARRIS, P. (1975) *Loss and Change*, London: Routledge and Kegan Paul.

MEZIROW, J. (1981) 'A critical theory of adult learning and education', *Adult Education*: **32**, (1), pp. 13–24.

MINTZBERG, H. (1973) *The Nature of Managerial Work*, New York: Harper and Row.

MISKEL, C. and COSGROVE, D. (1985) 'Leadership succession in school settings', *Review of Educational Research*, **55**, (1), pp. 87–105.

MORGAN, C., HALL, V. and MACKAY, M. (1983) *The Selection of Secondary School Headteachers*, Milton Keynes: Open University Press.

MORGAN, G. (1986) *Images of Organization*, London: Sage.

MORTIMORE, P. and MORTIMORE, J. (1991) *The Primary Head: Roles, Responsibilities and Reflections*, London: Paul Chapman.

MORTIMORE, P., SAMMONS, P., STOLL, L., LEWIS, D. and ECOB, R. (1988) *School Matters*, Wells: Open Books.

MUELLER, K. and KENDALL, M.A. (1989) 'Capturing leadership in action: *Portraiture as a collaborative tool*', paper presented at AERA, San Francisco, CA.

MUSE, I. and WALLACE, M. (1988) 'Effective primary headship: Looking to the future', *Education 3–13*, **16**, (3), pp. 22–6.

MYER, J., (1987) 'The first year of primary headship', report for Cambridgeshire LEA, Cambridgeshire CC mimeo.

NIAS, J. (1980) 'Leadership styles and job satisfaction in primary schools', in BUSH, T. *et al.* (Eds) *Management and the School*, Milton Keynes: Open University Press, pp. 255–73.

NIAS, J. (1987a) 'Learning from difference: A collegial approach to change', in SMYTH, W.J. (Ed.) *Educating Teachers: Changing the Nature of Pedagogical Knowledge*, Lewes: Falmer Press, pp. 137–52.

NIAS, J. (1987b) 'One finger, one thumb: A case study of the deputy head's part in the leadership of a nursery/infant school', in SOUTHWORTH, G. (Ed.) *Readings in Primary School Management*, Lewes, Falmer, pp. 30–53.

NIAS, J. (1987c) *Seeing Anew: Teachers' Theories of Action*, Geelong, Deakin University Press.

NIAS, J. (1989a) *Primary Teachers Talking*, London: Routledge.

NIAS, J. (1989b) 'Teaching and the self', in HOLLY, M.L. and McLOUGHLIN, C. (Eds) *Perspectives on Teacher Professional Development*, London: Falmer, pp. 155–71.

NIAS, J. (1989c) 'Subjectively speaking: English primary teachers' careers', *International Journal of Educational Research*, **13**, (4), pp. 391–402.

NIAS, J., SOUTHWORTH, G. and CAMPBELL, P. (1992) *Whole School Curriculum Development in Primary Schools*, London: Falmer Press.

NIAS, J., SOUTHWORTH, G. and YEOMANS, R. (1989) *Staff Relationships in the Primary School*, London: Cassell.

NIGHTINGALE, D. (1990) *Local Management of Schools at Work in Primary Schools*, London: Falmer Press.

NORQUAY, N. (1990) 'Life history research: Memory, schooling and social difference', *Cambridge Journal of Education*, **20**, (3), pp. 291–300.

OPEN UNIVERSITY (1981) *Key Roles in School Management*, in Management and the School, E323, Block 4, Part 3, Policy-making, organization and leadership in schools, Milton Keynes: Open University Press, pp. 51–88.

OPEN UNIVERSITY (1988) *Managing Schools*, E325, Block 2: Leadership and Decision-making in Schools, Milton Keynes: Open University Press.

ORNSTEIN, R.E. (1975) *The Psychology of Consciousness*, London: Pelican Books.

OSBORN, M. (1985) 'Profiles of a typical French and English primary teacher: Teachers' conceptions of their professional responsibility project', Bristol University mimeo.

PAISEY, A. and PAISEY, A. (1987) *Effective Management in Primary Schools*, Oxford: Blackwell.

PARSONS, T. (1967) *Sociological Theory and Modern Society*, New York: The Free Press.

PASCALE, R.T. and ATHOS, A.G. (1983) *The Art of Japanese Management*, London: Simon and Schuster.

PEACOCK, J.L. (1986) *The Anthropological Lens: Harsh Light, Soft Focus*, Cambridge: Cambridge University Press.

PETERS, T. and AUSTIN, N. (1985) *A Passion for Excellence: The Leadership Difference*, London: Collins.

PETERS, T. and WATERMAN, R. (1982) *In Search of Excellence: Lessons from America's Best Run Companies*, New York: Harper and Row.

POLLARD, A. (1985) *The Social World of the Primary School*, London: Cassell.

POLLARD, A. (1987) 'Primary teachers and their colleagues', in DELAMONT, S. (Ed.) *The Primary School Teacher*, Lewes: Falmer Press, pp. 100–19.

PURKEY, S. and SMITH, M. (1983) 'Effective schools: A review, *The Elementary School Journal*, **83**, (4), pp. 426–52.

RABINOW, P. (1977) *Reflections on Fieldwork in Morocco*, London: Quantum Books/ University of California Press.

RADNOR, H.A. (1990) 'Complexities and compromises: The new ERA at Parkview School', paper presented at AERA, Boston, MA: University of Exeter mimeo.

REAY, E. and DENNISON, W.F. (1990), 'Deputy headship in primary schools: Is it a real job?, *Education 3–13*, **18**, (1), pp. 41–6.

REID, K., HOPKINS, D. and HOLLY, P. (1987) *Towards The Effective School*, Oxford: Blackwell.

REYNOLDS, D. (1982) 'School effectiveness research: A review of the literature', *School Organization and Management Abstracts*, **1**, (1), pp. 5–14.

RICH, R. (1933) *The Training of Teachers in England and Wales in the Nineteenth Century*, Cambridge: Cambridge University Press.

RICHARDSON, L. (1990) *Writing Strategies: Reaching Diverse Audiences*, Newbury Park, CA: Sage.

RICHES, C. (1990) 'Gender and school management', in SARAN, R. and TRAFFORD, V. (Eds) *Research in Educational Management and Policy*, London: Falmer Press, pp. 142–8.

RIFFEL, J.A. (1986) 'The study of educational administration: A developmental point of view', *Journal of Educational Administration*, **24**, (2), pp. 152–72.

RIVZI, F. (1989) 'Bureaucratic rationality and the promise of democratic schooling', in CARR, W. (Ed.) (1989) *Quality in Teaching: Arguments for a Reflective Profession*, London: Falmer Press, pp. 55–75.

RIVZI, F. (1990) 'Efficiency, utopia and making democratic hopes practical', paper presented at AERA, Boston, MA: Deakin University mimeo.

ROCK, P. (1979) *The Making of Symbolic Interactionism*, London: Macmillan.

ROKEACH, M. (1960) *The Open and Closed Mind*, New York: Basic Books.

ROKEACH, M. (1964) *The Three Christs of Ypsilanti: A Psychological Study*, New York: Knopf.

ROKEACH, M. (1968) *Beliefs, Attitudes and Values*, San Francisco, CA: Jossey-Bass.

ROSENHOLTZ, S. (1985) 'Effective schools: Interpreting the evidence', *American Journal of Education*, **93**, (3), pp. 352–86.

RUTTER, M., MAUGHAN, B., MORTIMORE, P. and OUSTEN, J. (1979) *Fifteen Thousand Hours: Secondary Schools and their Effects on Children*, London: Open Books.

SANJEK, R. (1990) 'On ethnographic validity', in SANJEK, R. (Ed.) *Fieldnotes: The Making of Anthropology*, London: Cornell University Press, pp. 385–418.

SARASON, S. (1982) revised edition, *The Culture of the School and the Problem of Change*, Boston, MA: Allyn and Bacon.

SARASON, S. (1990) *The Predictable Failure of Educational Reform*, San Francisco, CA: Jossey-Bass.

SCHATZMAN, L. and STRAUSS, A.L. (1973) *Field Research; Strategies for a Natural Sociology*, Englewood Cliffs, NJ, Prentice Hall.

SCHEFFLER, I. (1985) *Of Human Potential*, London: Routledge and Kegan Paul.

SCHEIN, E.H. (1985) *Organizational Culture and Leadership*, San Francisco, CA: Jossey-Bass.

SCHLESINGER, R. (1978) *Robert Kennedy and His Times*, London: Futura.

SCHON, D. (1971) *Beyond the Stable State*, New York: Norton.

SCHON, D. (1986) *Educating the Reflective Practitioner*, San Francisco, CA: Jossey-Bass.

SCHOOL MANAGEMENT TASK FORCE DES (1990) *Developing School Management*, London: HMSO.

SCOTTISH EDUCATION DEPARTMENT (1990) *Effective Primary Schools: A Report by HM Inspectors of Schools*, Edinburgh: HMSO.

SEDGWICK, F. (1989) *Here Comes the Assembly Man: A Year in the Life of a School*, London: Falmer Press.

SERGIOVANNI, T. (1984) 'Leadership and excellence in schooling', *Educational Leadership*, **41**, (5), pp. 4–13.

SERGIOVANNI, T. and CORBALLY, J. (Eds) (1984) *Leadership and Organizational Culture*, Chicago, IL: University of Illinois Press.

SERGIOVANNI, T.J. and ELLIOTT, D.L. (1975) *Educational and Organizational Leadership in Elementary Schools*, Englewood Cliffs, NJ: Prentice Hall.

SEYMOUR-SMITH, C. (1986) *Dictionary of Anthropology*, London: Macmillan.

SHAKESHAFT, C. (1989) *Women in Educational Administration*, Newbury Park, CA: Sage, (updated edition).

SHAKESHAFT, C. (1991) 'A cup half full: A gender critique of the knowledge base in educational administration', paper presented at AERA, Chicago, IL, Hofstra University mimeo.

SHEIVE, L.T. and SCHOENHEIT, M.B. (Ed.) (1987) *Leadership: Examining the Elusive*, Alexandria, VA: Association for Supervision and Curriculum Development.

SHIPMAN, M. (1990) *In Search of Learning: A New Approach to School Management*, Oxford: Blackwell.

SIKES, P., MEASOR, L. and WOODS, P. (1985) *Teacher Careers: Crises and Continuities*, Lewes: Falmer.

SIMON, H. (1982) 'Conversation piece: The practice of interviewing in case study research', in MCCORMICK R., BYNNER, J., CLIFT, P., JONES, M. and MORROW BROWN, C. (Eds) *Calling Education to Account*, London: Heinemann/Open University Press, pp. 239–46.

SKRTIC, T. (1985) 'Doing naturalistic research into educational organizations', in LINCOLN, Y.S. (Ed.) *Organizational Theory and Inquiry*, Beverley Hills, CA: Sage, pp. 185–220.

SMIRCICH, L. (1983) 'Concepts of culture and organizational analysis', *Administrative Science Quarterly*, **28**, pp. 339–58.

SMITH, J. (Ed.) *Critical Perspectives on Educational Leadership*, London: Falmer Press.

SMITH, L.M. (1979) 'An evolving logic of participant observation: Educational ethnography and other case studies', in SHULMAN, L. (Ed.) *Review of Research in Education*, Chicago, IL: Peacock Press, pp. 62–73.

SMITH, L.M. (1990) 'The experience of biography: Coming to know Nora Barlow', paper presented at AERA, Boston, MA.

SMITH, L.M., KLEINE, P.F., PRUNTY, J.P. and DWYER, D.C. (1986) *Educational Innovators: Then and Now*, Lewes: Falmer Press.

SOUTHWORTH, G.W. (1985) 'Primary heads' reflections on training', *Education*, **165**, (25), p. 560.

SOUTHWORTH, G.W. (1987) 'Primary school headteachers and collegiality', in SOUTHWORTH, G.W. (Ed.) *Readings in Primary School Management*, Lewes: Falmer Press, pp. 61–75.

Southworth, G.W. (1988a) 'Looking at leadership: English primary school head-teachers at work', *Education 3–13*, **16**, (2), pp. 53–6.

SOUTHWORTH, G.W. (1988b) *Management Roles and Responsibilities: the Primary School*, Part 2, Block 2: Leadership and Decision-making in schools, E325 Managing Schools, Milton Keynes: Open University Press, pp. 31–70.

SOUTHWORTH, G.W. (1989) 'Pied pipers and a distant drummer: A case study of a year at Orchard Community Junior School', Cambridge Institute of Education mimeo.

SOUTHWORTH, G.W. (1990a) 'Leadership, headship and effective primary schools,' *School Organization* **10**, (1), pp. 3–16.

SOUTHWORTH, G.W. (Ed.) (1990b) *The Study of Primary Education: A Source Book*, Volume **3**; School Organization and Management, London: Falmer Press, editor's preface to 'Teachers and Teaching', pp. 68–73.

SOUTHWORTH, G.W. (1994) 'Headteachers and deputy heads: Partners and cultural leaders', in SOUTHWORTH, G.W. (Ed.) *Readings in Primary School Development*, London: Falmer Press, pp. 29–47.

SPENDER, D. (1981) 'Education: The patriarchal paradigm and the response to feminism', in ARNOT, M. and WEINER, G. (Eds) (1987) *Gender and the Politics of Schooling*, London: Unwin and Hyman, pp. 143–54.

SPRADLEY, J.P. (1980) *Participant Observation*, London: Holt, Rinehart and Winston.

STENHOUSE, L. (1978) 'Case study and case records: Towards a contemporary history of education', *British Educational Research Journal*, **4**, (2), pp. 21–39.

STENHOUSE, L. (1982) 'A note on case study and educational practice', in BURGESS, R.G. (Ed.) (1985) *Field Methods in the Study of Education*, Lewes: Falmer Press, pp. 263–71.

STONE, C. (1989) 'All that remains is ambivalence: A headteacher's reflections', *Education 3–13*, **17**, (3), pp. 4–9.

STRAUSS, A.L. (1987) *Qualitative Analysis for Social Scientists*, Cambridge: Cambridge University Press.

STYAN, D. (1990) 'School management: The way forward for the service', *NUT Education Review*, **4**, (2), pp. 17–20.

TYLER, W. (1988) *School Organization: A Sociological Perspective*, London: Croom Helm.

VERNON, M.D. (1962) *The Psychology of Perception*, London: Penguin.

VIALL, P. (1984) 'The purposing of high-performing systems', in SERGIOVANNI, T. and CORBALLY, J. (Eds) *Leadership and Organizational Culture*, Chicago, IL: University of Illinois Press, pp. 85–104.

WALKER, R. (1986) 'The conduct of educational case studies: ethics, theory and procedures', in HAMMERSLEY, M. (Ed.) *Controversies in Classroom Research*, Open University Press, pp. 187–219.

WALKER, B. (1991) 'Tight ship to tight flotilla: The first century of scholarship in educational administration', paper presented at AERA Chicago, IL: Monash University mimeo.

WALLACE, M. (1988) 'Towards a collegiate approach to curriculum management in primary and middle schools', *School Organization*, **8**, (1), pp. 25–34.

WALLER, W. (1932) *Sociology of Teaching*, New York: Russell and Russell.

WATERS, D. (1979) *Management and Headship in the Primary School*, London: Heinemann.

WATKINS, P. (1983) 'Scientific management and critical theory in educational administration', in BATES, R. (Ed.) *Educational Administration and the Management of Knowledge*, Geelong: Deakin University Press, pp. 119–35.

WATKINS, P. (1989) 'Leadership, power and symbols in educational administration', in SMYTH, J. (Ed.) (1989) *Critical Perspectives on Educational Leadership*, London: Falmer Press, pp. 9–37.

WEBB, R. (1994) 'The changing nature of teachers' roles and responsibilities in primary schools', Report Commissioned by the Association of Teachers and Lecturers, London: ATL.

WEBER, M. (1947) *The Theory of Social and Economic Organization*, New York: Free Press.

WEINDLING, D. (1989) 'The process of school improvement: Some practical messages from research', *School Organization*, **9**, (1), pp. 53–64.

WEINDLING, D. and EARLEY, P. (1987) *Secondary Headship: The First Years*, Windsor: NFER-Nelson.

WESTOBY, A. (Ed.) (1988) *Culture and Power in Educational Organizations*, Milton Keynes: Open University Press.

WHITAKER, P. (1983) *The Primary Head*, London: Heinemann.

WHITAKER, P. (1986) 'A humanistic approach to teacher in-service education', *Self and Society*, **4**, (6), pp. 276–81.

WHITE, P. (1983) *Beyond Domination*, London: Routledge and Kegan Paul.

WINKLEY, D. (1983) 'An analytical view of primary school leadership', *School Organization*, **3**, (1), pp. 15–26.

WOLCOTT, H. (1973) *The Man in the Principal's Office: An Ethnography*, Prospect Heights, IL: Waveland Press.

WOLCOTT, H. (1975) 'Criteria for an ethnographic approach to research in schools', *Human Organization*, **34**, (2), pp. 111–27.

WOLCOTT, H. (1990) *Writing Up Qualitative Research*, Newbury Park, CA: Sage.

WOODS, P. (1981) 'Strategies, commitment and identity: Making and breaking the teachers role', in BARTON, L. and WALKER, S. (Eds) *Schools, Teachers and Teaching*, Lewes: Falmer, pp. 283–302.

WOODS, P. (1984) 'Teachers, self and curriculum', in GOODSON, I. and BALL, S. (Eds) *Defining the Curriculum: Histories and Ethnographies of School Subjects*, Lewes: Falmer Press, pp. 239–61.

WOODS, P. (1985a) 'Ethnography and theory construction in educational research', in BURGESS, R.G. (1985) *Field Methods in the Study of Education*, Lewes: Falmer Press, pp. 54–78.

WOODS, P. (1985b) 'Conversations with teachers: Some aspects of the life-history methods', *British Educational Journal*, **11**, (1), pp. 13–26.

WOODS, P. (1986) *Inside Schools: Ethnography in Educational Research*, London: Routledge.

WOODS, P. (1987) 'Managing the primary teachers role', in DELAMONT, S. (Ed.) *The Primary School Teacher*, Lewes: Falmer Press, pp. 120–43.

WOODS, P. (1991) 'The struggle for self: Teacher development through grounded life history', paper presented at Conference on Educational Development: The Contribution of Research on Teachers' Thinking and Action, University of Surrey, Open University mimeo.

YIN, R. (1989) *Case Study Research: Design and Methods*, Newbury Park, CA: Sage, revised edition.

YEOMANS, R. (1987) 'Checking and adjusting the lens: Case study clearance', *Cambridge Journal of Education*, **17** (2), pp. 89–90.

YUKL, G. (1975) 'Towards a behavioural theory of leadership', in HOUGHTON, V. *et al. The Management of Organizations and Individuals*, London: Ward Lock.

Source: DES 1989, School Teachers' Pay and Conditions Document, London, HMSO

PART VIII — Conditions of employment of head teachers

Overriding requirements

27. A head teacher shall carry out his professional duties in accordance with and subject to —

    (1) the provisions of the Education Acts 1944 to 1988;

    (2) any orders and regulations having effect thereunder;

    (3) the articles of government of the school of which he is head teacher, to the extent to which their content is prescribed by statute;

    (4) where the school is a voluntary school or a grant-maintained school which was formerly a voluntary school, any trust deed applying in relation thereto;

    (5) any scheme of local management approved or imposed by the Secretary of State under section 34 of the Education Reform Act 1988 (**a**);

    and, to the extent to which they are not inconsistent with these conditions —

    (a) provisions of the articles of government the content of which is not so prescribed;

    (b) in the case of a school which has a delegated budget;

        (i) any rules, regulations or policies laid down by the governing body under their powers

as derived from any of the sources specified in sub-paragraphs (1) to (5) and (a)
above; and

(ii)   any rules, regulations or policies laid down
by his employers with respect to matters
for which the governing body is not so
responsible;

(c)   in any other case, any rules, regulations or policies laid down by his employers; and

(d)   the terms of his appointment.

General functions

28.   Subject to paragraph 27 above, the head teacher shall be
responsible for the internal organisation, management and
control of the school.

Consultation   29.   In carrying out his duties the head teacher shall consult,
where this is appropriate, with the authority, the govern-
ing body, the staff of the school and the parents of its
pupils.

Professional duties

30.   The professional duties of a head teacher shall include —

School aims   (1)   formulating the overall aims and objectives of the
school and policies for their implementation;

Appointment
of staff   (2)   participating in the selection and appointment of the
teaching and non-teaching staff of the school;

Management
of staff   (3)   (a)   deploying and managing all teaching and non-
teaching staff of the school and allocating par-
ticular duties to them (including such duties of
the head teacher as may properly be delegated
to the deputy head teacher or other members of
the staff) in a manner consistent with their conditions of employment, maintaining a reasonable
balance for each teacher between work carried
out in school and work carried out elsewhere;

(b)   ensuring that the duty of providing cover for
absent teachers is shared equitably among all

teachers in the school (including the head teacher), taking account of their teaching and other duties;

Liaison with staff unions and associations

(4) maintaining relationships with organisations representing teachers and other persons on the staff of the school;

Curriculum

(5) (a) determining, organising and implementing an appropriate curriculum for the school, having regard to the needs, experience, interests, aptitudes and stage of development of the pupils and the resources available to the school; and his duty under sections 1(1) and 10(1)(b) and (2) of the Education Reform Act 1988 (**a**);

(b) securing that all pupils in attendance at the school take part in daily collective worship in pursuance of his duty under section 10(1)(a) of the Education Reform Act 1988;

Review

(6) keeping under review the work and organisation of the school;

Standards of teaching and learning

(7) evaluating the standards of teaching and learning in the school, and ensuring that proper standards of professional performance are established and maintained;

Appraisal, training and development of staff

(8) (a) supervising and participating in any arrangements within an agreed national framework for the appraisal of the performance of teachers who teach in the school;

(b) ensuring that all staff in the school have access to advice and training appropriate to their needs, in accordance with the policies of the maintaining authority or, in the case of a grant-maintained school, of the governing body, for the development of staff;

Management information

(9) providing information about the work and performance of the staff employed at the school where this is relevant to their future employment;

Pupil progress

(10) ensuring that the progress of the pupils of the school is monitored and recorded;

Pastoral care

(11) determining and ensuring the implementation of a policy for the pastoral care of the pupils;

Discipline	(12)	determining, in accordance with any written statement of general principles provided for him by the governing body, measures to be taken with a view to promoting, among the pupils, self-discipline and proper regard for authority, encouraging good behaviour on the part of the pupils, securing that the standard of behaviour of the pupils is acceptable and otherwise regulating the conduct of the pupils; making such measures generally known within the school, and ensuring that they are implemented;
	(13)	ensuring the maintenance of good order and discipline at all times during the school day (including the midday break) when pupils are present on the school premises and whenever the pupils are engaged in authorised school activities, whether on the school premises or elsewhere;
Relations with parents	(14)	making arrangements for parents to be given regular information about the school curriculum, the progress of their children and other matters affecting the school, so as to promote common understanding of its aims;
Relations with other bodies	(15)	promoting effective relationships with persons and bodies outside the school;
Relations with governing body	(16)	advising and assisting the governing body of the school in the exercise of its functions, including (without prejudice to any rights he may have as a governor of the school) attending meetings of the governing body and making such reports to it in connection with the discharge of his functions as it may properly require either on a regular basis or from time to time;
Relations with authority	(17)	(except in the case of grant-maintained schools) providing for liaison and co-operation with the officers of the maintaining authority; making such reports to the authority in connection with the discharge of his functions as it may properly require, either on a regular basis or from time to time;
Relations with other educational establishments	(18)	maintaining liaison with other schools and further education establishments with which the school has a relationship;
Resources	(19)	allocating, controlling and accounting for those financial and material resources of the school which are under the control of the head teacher;

Premises	(20)	making arrangements, if so required by the maintaining authority or the governing body of a grant-maintained school (as appropriate), for the security and effective-supervision of the school buildings and their contents and of the school grounds; and ensuring (if so required) that any lack of maintenance is promptly reported to the maintaining authority or, if appropriate, the governing body;

Appraisal of head teacher (21) (a) participating in any arrangements within an agreed national framework for the appraisal of his performance as head teacher;

(b) participating in the identification of areas in which he would benefit from further training and undergoing such training;

Absence (22) arranging for a deputy head teacher or other suitable person to assume responsibility for the discharge of his functions as head teacher at any time when he is absent from the school;

Teaching (23) participating, to such extent as may be appropriate having regard to his other duties, in the teaching of pupils at the school, including the provision of cover for absent teachers.

Daily break 31. A head teacher shall be entitled to a break of reasonable length in the course of each school day, and shall arrange for a suitable person to assume responsibility for the discharge of his functions as head teacher during that break.

Appendix 2

Characteristics Associated with Effective Headteachers

What Does an Effective Primary Headteacher Appear to Look Like?

This list is not in any order of priority. Nor is it necessarily exhaustive, rather it is my interpretation of and selection from a number of references. Principally this list is derived from: ILEA (1985); Coulson (1986, 1988a); DES (1987); Mortimore *et al.* (1988); Southworth (1988a, b); Nias *et al.* (1989a). An effective head:

- emphasizes the centrality of teaching and learning, via his/her teaching commitment, persistent interest in the children's work and development, through attention to teachers' plans, practice, reflections and evaluations.
- ensures that there are explicit curriculum aims, guidelines and pupil record-keeping systems and that all of these are utilized by teachers and other staff in order to establish some consistency, continuity and coherence.
- acts as an exemplar. Regularly teaches, leads assemblies, works long and hard for the school.
- ensures that the teachers have some non-contact time.
- sets high expectations for self, children and staff.
- encourage and develops others to take on positions of responsibility and leadership.
- involves the deputy head in policy decision-making; head and deputy operate as partners.
- involves teachers (and sometimes others) in curriculum planning and school organization; generally (but not necessarily always) adopts a consultative approach to decision-making.
- is conscious of the school's and individual teacher's needs with regard to teacher attendance on in-service training courses; is aware of own professional development needs.
- is considerate towards staff; offers psychological support, takes an interest in staff as people, is willing (on occasions) to help reconcile, make allowance for personal/professional role conflicts (health problems, domestic crises, clash of evening commitments).
- constantly enquires into many aspects of the school as an organization; tours the school before, during and after school, visits staff in the classroom and work places, perceives the school from different perspectives, observes and listens, manages 'by wandering about'.

- develops and sustains a whole school perspective insofar as there is a shared and agreed vision of effective practice which is adopted by and becomes the staff's collective mission.
- nurtures and maintains a school culture which is inclusive of the school's staff and which facilitates professional and social collaboration.
- is personally tolerant of ambiguity.
- ensures that the school has an explicit and understood development plan; has a sense of direction.
- involves parents and governors in the work and life of the school; is an effective communicator of the school's successes and challenges, presents a positive image of the school, staff and children.

Source: Southworth, G.W. (1990a).

Appendix 3

Ethical Code

Ethical Code

Definitions

Participants — those whose activities are being studied by the research team or whose views are solicited by them.

Researcher — any member of the project research team or other person delegated to conduct research on their authority.

1. Participants have a right to control the researcher's access to direct observation of situations.
2. Participants have a right to control the use to which accounts and recordings of situations are put.
3. The researcher has a responsibility to help participants anticipate the reactions of others to accounts of situations upon release.
4. Participants have a right to control the researcher's use of their interview material.
5. The researcher has a responsibility to ensure that participants understand the context in which s/he proposes to use their interview.
6. The researcher has a responsibility to help participants anticipate the reactions of others to interview material upon release.
7. The researcher has a responsibility to ensure that participants have an opportunity to produce responses to case studies, and a responsibility to include these responses in any final draft.
8. The researcher has a responsibility to help participants to anticipate the reactions of others to the case studies upon release.

Index